APPLIED RESEARCH AND EVALUATION METHODS IN RECREATION

Diane C. Blankenship, EdD

Frostburg State University

Human Kinetics

Library of Congress Cataloging-in-Publication Data

Blankenship, Diane
   Applied research and evaluation methods in recreation / Diane Blankenship.
      p. cm.
   Includes bibliographical references and index.
   ISBN-13: 978-0-7360-7719-4 (hardcover)
   ISBN-10: 0-7360-7719-7 (hardcover)
   1. Recreation--Research. 2. Recreation--Evaluation. I. Title.
   GV14.5.B53 2010
   790'.072--dc22

                                                    2009028331

ISBN-10: 0-7360-7719-7 (print)
ISBN-13: 978-0-7360-7719-4 (print)

The Web addresses cited in this text were current as of September 2009, unless otherwise noted.

Acquisitions Editor: Gayle Kassing, PhD; **Developmental Editor:** Jacqueline Eaton Blakley; **Assistant Editors:** Lauren B. Morenz, Anne Rumery, and Elizabeth Evans; **Copyeditor:** Patrick Connolly; **Indexer:** Bobbi Swanson; **Permission Manager:** Dalene Reeder; **Graphic Designer:** Bob Reuther; **Graphic Artist:** Kathleen Boudreau-Fuoss; **Cover Designer:** Keith Blomberg; **Photographer (cover):** © Human Kinetics/Tom Roberts; **Photographer (interior):** pp. x, 26, 34, 42, 70, 80, 96, 135 © Human Kinetics; p. 10 © Alaska Stock; p. 52 © Jeff Greenberg/agefotostock; p. 56 iStockphoto/Edwin Verin; p. 73 Ben Moon/Aurora Photos; p. 110 Yellow Dog Productions/The Image Bank/Getty Images; p. 128 Corey Rich/Aurora Photos; p. 144 Associated Press/George Widman; and p. 166 Associated Press/Al Golub; **Photo Asset Manager:** Laura Fitch; **Visual Production Assistant:** Joyce Brumfield; **Photo Production Manager:** Jason Allen; **Art Manager:** Kelly Hendren; **Associate Art Manager:** Alan L. Wilborn; **Illustrator:** Tammy Page; **Printer:** Sheridan Books

Printed in the United States of America   10 9 8 7 6 5 4 3 2 1

The paper in this book is certified under a sustainable forestry program.

Human Kinetics
Web site: www.HumanKinetics.com

United States: Human Kinetics
P.O. Box 5076, Champaign, IL 61825-5076
800-747-4457
e-mail: humank@hkusa.com

Canada: Human Kinetics
475 Devonshire Road Unit 100,
Windsor, ON N8Y 2L5
800-465-7301 (in Canada only)
e-mail: info@hkcanada.com

Europe: Human Kinetics
107 Bradford Road, Stanningley,
Leeds LS28 6AT, United Kingdom
+44 (0) 113 255 5665
e-mail: hk@hkeurope.com

Australia: Human Kinetics
57A Price Avenue, Lower Mitcham,
South Australia 5062
08 8372 0999
e-mail: info@hkaustralia.com

New Zealand: Human Kinetics
P.O. Box 80
Torrens Park, South Australia 5062
0800 222 062
e-mail: info@hknewzealand.com

CONTENTS

CONTINUED ▶

As a recreation professional, you could find yourself working for a public park and recreation agency, within the adventure recreation area, as a recreation therapist, within a park, or in the travel and tourism section. Each of these jobs is unique, and the expectations are different within each job. However, one common denominator can be found within each area of the industry: research and evaluation. These terms strike fear in the hearts and minds of students and young professionals. But with the right resources to assist you, you can avoid the anxiety attacks that often strike during the research and evaluation process.

When you work in the world of parks and recreation, you need to have the skills, competencies, and confidence to face the demands of research and evaluation. Increasingly strained budgets often require recreation agencies to justify their existence in terms of cost and benefit. Agencies must be able to show how financial investment in their operations results in benefits to the community. These benefits may relate to quality of life, residents' health, tourism, and property values. They may also address community concerns about at-risk behaviors of residents.

Furthermore, some of the agencies you might work for will be involved with the CAPRA accreditation process, which has significant standards linked to research and evaluation. In other words, to help your agency gain or maintain this accreditation, you will be required to conduct meaningful research that not only benefits your agency, but also meets specific standards and guidelines established by the National Parks and Recreation Association CAPRA accreditation.

This textbook, along with the online student resource, presents the research and evaluation process in a friendly and nonthreatening manner. For many people, just hearing the word *research* may be off-putting, and this can be especially true for people with active careers in parks and recreation. The word conjures images of boring desk work, tedious math, and mind-numbing busywork.

But the process of research and evaluation in the real world of parks and recreation is very much like investigative work. The steps of the research process are similar to those needed when detectives investigate crimes, including searching for evidence, finding clues, and doing methodical work. The researcher methodically puts together the pieces—the type of research, the research question, the research plan, the data, and the results. Shazam! The mystery is solved, and the researcher discovers the answer to the research question. As a researcher, you become the investigator digging for information to solve a mystery. This is an exhilarating experience that is challenging and fun!

As you move through this book, you need to put yourself in the mind-set of an investigator trying to solve a mystery. This is what you will face when you perform research as a professional in the field of parks and recreation. While working in this field, you may be asked to investigate local gang activity, the needs of the seniors in the community, current national trends in activity, or the effectiveness of existing programs. Each situation represents a mystery that must be investigated to identify the answer to the mystery.

Content Overview

In this book, you will discover all the steps involved in the research and evaluation process. Each step in the process represents a piece of information that is needed to solve the mystery. Chapter 1 provides an overview about the importance of research and evaluation in the field of recreation. It also provides your first experience in participating in a research project. Chapter 2 provides more in-depth information about the options for research and evaluation. The information in this chapter and chapter 1 provides you, the investigator, with the foundational knowledge that you need in order to move through the research process, or the investigation. Chapter 3 helps you focus the research efforts or area of investigation by developing the research problem, the purpose of the study, and the research questions. This keeps you on track and focuses your efforts on the area of the investigation. Chapter 4 walks you through the process of gathering existing facts, research, and information related to the topic that is being investigated. Every investigator should be thoroughly knowledgeable about the existing information related to the investigation or research topic. The review of literature builds your knowledge on the topic and provides you with valuable information that can guide your efforts in investigating a topic.

At this point in the text, you should understand the research or investigative process, and you should be capable of defining the area and focus of the investigation. In addition, you will have gathered relevant information related to the topic area. It is then time to more narrowly focus the scope and purpose of the study or investigation.

Chapter 5 helps you further define the scope of the study by identifying the specific variables of the study. A variable is a specific trait, element, or item that is being studied. This is not unlike an investigator identifying specific people to talk with to gather relevant information for the investigation. In addition, chapter 5 helps you determine if a hypothesis is appropriate to use in the study, just as an investigator hypothesizes about who committed the crime. A hypothesis is an educated guess that predicts the outcome of the study. This step provides more focus to the investigative efforts and keeps the research study manageable. In all investigations and research, you must ensure that all actions and efforts are ethical. The investigator or researcher does not want to do anything in the course of the investigation that might result in legal action. Standard guidelines must be followed by all researchers to ensure that the study is conducted in an ethical manner. These guidelines are reviewed and explained in chapter 6.

As you move further through this text, the information becomes more specific and assists you in planning the "nuts and bolts" of the study. As an investigator or researcher, you will at times need to gather information from people. The process and options that can be used for identifying people (or subjects) to involve in the study are reviewed in chapter 7. A multitude of options may be used, and you must select the best option for your study. The process of selecting individuals to participate in your research study is referred to as sampling. This is a critical process that will help ensure that you gather the necessary information to answer the research question or solve the mystery. As an investigator, you also need to specifically identify what data are needed, when and where to collect the data, who will collect the data, and how to analyze the data. Chapter 8 walks you through

the process for making these important decisions.

As an investigator working on a mystery or a researcher conducting a study, you now must decide specifically what tools will be used to gather the information that is needed to solve the mystery or answer the research question. Should you interview the subjects? Observe the subjects? Give them a survey? Which is the best method for obtaining the necessary information? Chapter 9 assists you in making this decision. This chapter reviews a variety of data collection tools that are commonly used in the field. In addition, the chapter reviews the advantages and disadvantages of each data collection tool so that you can make an educated decision.

The next chapter, chapter 10, shifts the focus from the nuts and bolts of the investigation process to an evaluation of the internal validity of that process. This chapter covers the ways that the investigation process might affect the truthfulness of the results or conclusions of the investigation. You must review the threats to the internal validity of the study to ensure that the previous decisions made during the study will provide accurate and truthful data as well as valid conclusions. If this is not done, an investigator could accuse the wrong person of a crime. In other words, the research could lead to false conclusions. The information presented in this chapter helps you avoid reaching false conclusions in a study. Chapter 11 reviews how a researcher can analyze the data that were gathered during the investigation. The analysis of the data provides the researcher with conclusions to solve the mystery or answer the research question. Many options are available for summarizing and analyzing data.

Once the research project has been completed, the researcher needs to generate some sort of report to communicate the process and conclusion of the study. Chapter 12 provides guidelines on how to prepare a report for supervisors and other individuals. The research or investigation process should be documented so that the reviewer of the report understands what was done, how the data were gathered and analyzed, and the conclusions of the study. The report is the final step in a research project.

By now, you have surely concluded that research is an investigation. Research can be challenging, and it demands organizational skills to work through the process from beginning to end. These demands can be viewed with a spirit of fun as they present a stimulating challenge to you as part of your job.

Unique Features

This text and ancillary package are built to be *useful* above all. The text is tailored to the specific needs of students preparing for careers in parks and recreation. Each chapter builds on the previous chapter (instead of presenting independent concepts and omitting how they are all interrelated). Real-world examples highlight the research and evaluation process throughout.

Each chapter closes with several learning aids that apply the principles covered in the chapter:

- Exercises use varying formats (multiple choice and fill in the blank, for example) to practice applying chapter principles in parks and recreation scenarios. In addition, the exercises include analysis of two scholarly articles (one quantitative and one qualitative) throughout the entire course.
- A case study can be used for assessment of students' comprehension of the chapter or as a discussion scenario in class or a discussion thread online.
- "For the Investigator" links the content of the chapter to a project that can be used throughout the semester and can serve as the foundation for a research paper.

These learning aids can all be downloaded (in Microsoft Word format) from the online student resource, which can be accessed using the key code in this book.

In addition to the online student resource, this textbook offers online resources for instructors who are teaching courses that use the textbook. The extras for this course can easily be loaded on Blackboard or similar online instructional packages. These extras include the following:

- PowerPoint slides for each chapter
- Test bank questions
- Exercises for each chapter
- Suggestions for the instructor for each chapter
- Case study linked to the professional perspective for each chapter that presents a real world problem or issue to analyze
- Scholarly articles with analysis for each chapter
- A sample survey study with data for analysis for each chapter (For the Investigator)
- Guide for a syllabus and paper

The focus of the ancillary package is to provide multiple opportunities for students to practice, discuss, and apply the concepts of the text (instead of providing a passive stand-and-deliver course).

Taken together, this textbook and online resource package make the basics of research and evaluation accessible, useful, and maybe even a little fun. Most important, they will prepare students to be more effective leaders in their careers within parks and recreation.

ACKNOWLEDGMENTS

I want to extend special thanks to the following people:

Ronnie, Robert, and CC Williams gave me a kick in the pants to start this journey. The students at the Frostburg State University recreation and parks management program suffered through many ideas and versions of this book and continued to ask, "How's it going?" Gayle and Jackie at Human Kinetics guided me through this journey. My family (June, Roger, Calvin, and Brice) offered me their shoulders to cry on and faith that the job would get done.

What an accomplishment for someone who nearly failed freshman composition! Anything is possible once the goal is set.

CHAPTER 1

• OBJECTIVES •

After completing this chapter, you will be able to

- summarize how conducting research and evaluation is similar to conducting an investigation,
- identify three reasons why evaluation and research are important within the park and recreation industry,
- identify two CAPRA issues related to evaluation and research, and
- describe two benefits of conducting research and evaluation.

Investigative Overview

You have just been hired into a new position at the local parks and recreation department, and you are eager to begin work and to do what you love, which is programming. During orientation for your new position, you discover that the director expects programmers to conduct regular evaluation and research studies of all programs and events. The agency you are working for is a CAPRA (Commission for Accreditation of Park and Recreation Agencies) accredited agency. All staff members are involved in the process of ensuring that the standards are met related to research and evaluation. You vaguely remember your research methods class in college, and you begin to feel very uneasy about this requirement.

People enter the field of recreation for many reasons other than to conduct research and evaluation. Although the very words **research** and **evaluation** strike fear in the hearts of many students and professionals, becoming comfortable with the research and evaluation process is a critical professional competency within the recreation industry today. In the current environment of budgetary shortfalls and financial competition, parks and recreation agencies are expected to run their facilities as a business, which means conducting business as efficiently and effectively as possible. To secure the future of the agency, research and evaluation are critical elements within business-based operations. This book will help you become comfortable with research and evaluation, and it will also help you build your skills as a researcher.

Doing research and evaluation is a lot like being a detective: You must work methodically to find clues, chase down leads, evaluate evidence, and use all the information you have gathered to solve a mystery. It's an exhilarating experience that is challenging and fun! Adopting the mind-set of an investigator will help you make the most of learning and practicing research and evaluation.

Foundational Knowledge for Researchers

To become comfortable with research and evaluation, you first need to understand the following:

- The mission and purpose of parks and recreation
- The need for research and evaluation
- How research and evaluation assist an organization
- The expectations for evaluation and research within the industry related to professional certification and agency accreditation

Mission and Purpose of Recreation Agencies

In the United States, the field of recreation and parks has deep roots grounded within societal needs, community needs, and individual needs (see figure 1.1). As you probably remember, the original needs of the community emerged during the Industrial Revolution. With the population shifting from rural areas to urban centers, children needed a safe place to play and socialize. The scope of facilities and services expanded from that point to include providing public parks, public recreation facilities, and instructional classes. The focus of this expansion was to (1) provide places for people to play, (2) offer programs that were educational and considered "wholesome" for the participant, and (3) provide recreational opportunities for individuals, families, and seniors within local communities.

Every park and recreation agency is challenged by—and exists to address—social concerns that become the needs within the community. For example, many American communities are concerned about gang activity, risk-taking behavior of youth, single-parent households, drug and alcohol abuse, and the growing need for sport fields and other public open spaces. Obesity is a primary example of a social concern that park and recreation programs are well positioned to address. This epidemic is prevalent in children, teenagers, and adults within the United States. Researchers predict that many members of the current generation of children will die before their parents because of factors related to obesity (high cholesterol, high blood pressure, diabetes, and a lack of exercise). The National Recreation and Park Association has partnered with other organizations to provide initiatives that address obesity factors, such as Hearts N' Parks, Step Up to Health, and Teens Outside. Each initiative is a community mobilization model that is designed to assist local communities in planning, marketing, and promoting healthy lifestyles related to diet and exercise. In addition, park and recreation agencies provide a wide variety of health and fitness programs, such as swimming lessons, open swim, aerobic classes, sport skill classes, movement classes for preschoolers, weight rooms for working out, and the simple reminder to get outside and play an hour a day. Healthy lifestyles go beyond physical fitness to emotional and psychological wellness. Park and recreation agencies also provide a wide variety of art classes, dance lessons, and concerts.

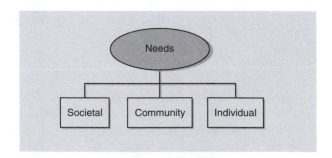

Figure 1.1 Mission of parks and recreation.

All these kinds of programs and services work toward a healthier community.

Parks and recreation departments provide a wide variety of programs and services to their local communities. But are these programs accomplishing what they are intended to do for the individual, the organization, or the community?

The Need for Research and Evaluation

Every park and recreation agency needs to answer a number of questions about its programs, services, and operations which are noted in figure 1.2. These questions include the following:

- Is the agency meeting the objectives of the programs?
- Is the agency meeting the needs of the customer?
- Is the agency financially stable?

These are only a small sample of the questions that a park and recreation agency needs to answer. How does a park and recreation agency go about answering these questions? The best way is to use the process of research and evaluation. Let's explore these three questions further in order to gain an understanding of the importance of evaluation and research in providing the answers.

Is the Agency Meeting the Objectives of the Programs? All programs provided by park and recreation agencies have a purpose or an objective related to the outcomes for the participants. For example, the objective of a beginning swimming class is to have the participants move through water adjustment skills and learn a basic stroke on their front and back. For the organization, the objective for swimming classes is to have more people learn to swim. This can help reduce the number of rescues or deaths at the organization's aquatic facilities. In addition, the programs should cover costs associated with the programs and generate revenues for the agency. The agency must always consider the cost and revenues generated from the programs. For the community, the objective of swimming classes could be to have a variety of opportunities available for family members to learn to swim and to enjoy the aquatic facilities year-round. Many park and recreation agencies have indoor facilities, outdoor facilities, or both. Swimming is also a physical activity that people can enjoy throughout their lifetime, either in formal classes or individually. Park and recreation agencies must work to gather the information they need to determine

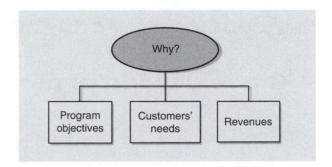

Figure 1.2 Reasons to conduct research and evaluation.

if the objectives of the program are being met and whether these are class objectives, agency objectives, or objectives for the community. The research and evaluation process is the primary method for gathering this information and making this assessment. This process gives recreation professionals specific information and evidence to support or negate the notion that their agencies are achieving their objectives. Without research and evaluation, professionals might have only a vague sense of whether objectives are being met, or they may have no idea at all.

Is the Agency Meeting the Needs of the Customer? What are the customer needs and expectations in relation to recreational activities? For swimming classes, the needs of the customers are generally to have a safe environment for the class and to have the class conducted by a qualified instructor. The needs of the participants' parents are to have their children learn to swim in a safe environment so that the children can be safer at pools, lakes, and beaches during the summer. The swimming classes provide one way to meet these needs. Additionally, customers have expectations about their experience or their children's experience in the program. These expectations may be associated with the registration process, how to get to the facility, cleanliness of the locker rooms, cleanliness of the facility, and the quality of the instructor. The agency must gather information to determine if the needs and expectations of the customers are being met during the program.

Is the Agency Financially Stable? Historically, park and recreation departments received a majority of their funding for operations from local taxes. The agency was considered a type of social service that needed tax-based funding for the annual operations. This perception regarding park and recreation agencies has shifted from a social service model to a business-based model.

■ The real world of parks and recreation

Creating recreation programs for a target market without doing research on the wants and needs of that market is a shotgun approach to hitting your mark. This approach does not give you much chance of a bull's-eye. Without proper insight from surveys, anecdotal evidence, and research, programmers are just guessing about what services and programs to offer their clientele. This haphazard methodology is likely to waste time, energy, and money. It will not serve the public well in their desired outcomes for their leisure experience. Before implementing any recreational program, take a look at the big picture affecting your community.

As an outdoor recreation programmer for the Department of the Army, I had to understand the missing pieces, challenges, target market needs, demographics, and outside sources affecting users or statistics. Once I knew the SWOT (strengths, weaknesses, opportunities, and trends) of the members of my target market, I better understood what programs to create to meet their challenges and needs. I started with the needs first, then I used a benefits-based programming approach to plan something that would fill that need (instead of trying to fit a new square program into the round hole of the target market).

I have used suggestion cards and needs assessment surveys to identify a want or need for scuba classes. After contracting a scuba instructor and arranging a course to be held one night per week for six weeks (plus open-water classes), we marketed the course, and nobody registered. Further investigation found that those who wanted the course (military service members) could not commit to six consecutive weeks and did not have the transportation to get to the pool or open-water sessions. After researching alternative schedules for the course and arranging for transportation to the site, we marketed the course again, and the scuba classes were filled. The classes were scheduled for just two full weekends, reading materials could be reviewed at the participant's leisure before class, and the participants could arrange their open-water session during their individual vacations over the next few months. It took research to discover the reasons why the first attempt at a program that was needed had failed. To be successful, I needed to keep researching until I found the root cause of the failure, and then I rearranged the program to fit the needs of my participants.

Why was research important in this case?

Research is a critical link in deciding what programs to offer and determining what programs will provide a solution to community challenges. Recreation departments should use benefits-based programming and should identify the essential links to improving the economy and individual or community-based challenges. Otherwise, recreation departments run the risk of losing funding and credibility in the eyes of the decision makers and those who hold the purse strings. The success of the recreation agency depends on successful programs, and the motivation to participate is dependent on a need being met. Motivation comes from needs. To find those needs, recreation professionals must do research and evaluation.

Today, park and recreation agencies are expected to operate as a business. This has resulted in departments receiving very little tax-based funding for operations and has increased the need to generate revenues from programs and services. The agency gathers financial information on a regular basis to determine if the agency is generating sufficient funds to meet the financial needs of the organization. These research activities provide valuable information to assist the managers in making decisions related to the future operations of the agency. The information gained through research and evaluation helps managers decide which programs and services need to be revised, which ones should be added, and which ones should be phased out to ensure that the agency is financially stable. The decision on whether to add or phase out a program cannot be properly made unless the managers have current information about new community needs or needs within the community that no longer exist. The best method for gathering this information is through research and evaluation.

For agencies to answer these fundamental questions concerning their programs, services, and financial operations, research and evaluation have become a necessary activity. Historically, park and recreation agencies did not regularly evaluate program outcomes for the participants. In the past, evaluation efforts centered on the agency's need to know "the numbers"—the number of participants, the hours of the programs, the revenues generated by the programs, and the expenses associated with the programs. This type of evaluation misses the essence and purpose of the park and recreation agency (i.e., meeting the program objectives for the participants and meeting the needs of the customers and community). Evaluating and researching participant outcomes, needs, and expectations are critically important to the future of every park and recreation agency. Agencies that regularly conduct evaluation and research projects gain many benefits that help to sustain the operation of the agency.

Benefits of Conducting Research and Evaluation

Research and evaluation projects provide evidence that can be used to document the achievements of the agency (see figure 1.3). The information gathered can provide documentation of the skills being taught through instructional programs, the perceived value of the programs and services, and the level of customer satisfaction with the programs and services. This information is generally compiled into an annual report to present to policy makers, recreation councils, mayors, city councils, or any other entities considered to be decision makers regarding the operations of the park and recreation agency. In the past, park and recreation agencies did not gather this type of evidence to justify the operations of the agency. The justification for continuing operations revolved around statements such as "We are meeting the needs of the community" without the necessary supporting documentation. Research and evaluation provide the necessary information to back up claims of meeting the needs of the community. This is one benefit of conducting research and evaluation within parks and recreation agencies.

In addition, the information gathered from research and evaluation provides the necessary evidence to justify the future investment of tax dollars or other revenue sources into the agency. The amount of tax dollars available for public agencies—such as park and recreation agencies, police departments, and fire departments—is limited at best. Not all agencies or projects requiring financial support can be funded. The evidence gathered through research and evaluation projects provides information that can be used to educate the decision makers about the value and worth of the organization. This can allow the recreation agency to compete for the available funds. The investment of tax dollars in the recreation department can be viewed as an investment that will help meet the needs of the community and will enhance the quality of life within the community. In this time of limited funding and intense competition for tax dollars, agencies have no choice but to evaluate the worth and value of their operations. Without this type of focused effort to gather meaningful information to educate the public and decision makers, the future of park and recreation agencies is uncertain.

Research and Evaluation

- Provide evidence of achievements
- Serve as justification of operations or expansions
- Educate the community leaders
- Provide foundation for decisions

Figure 1.3   Benefits of research and evaluation.

CAPRA Issues Related to Research and Evaluation

The need for research and evaluation goes beyond the local community. The National Recreation and Park Association conducts a national accreditation program for park and recreation agencies. This program is called the **CAPRA (Commission for Accreditation of Park and Recreation Agencies) accreditation**. Evaluation and research are an important component in every park and recreation agency in light of the CAPRA standards. The CAPRA accreditation process has very extensive standards that specifically require evaluation analysis of the components within the organization, including goals and objectives, financial records, need index, service management and evaluation. The standards related to evaluation require a comprehensive evaluation plan to evaluate the operations of the organization. The evaluation plan uses the steps of the scientific method of inquiry (see chapter 2), but for different outcomes.

The purpose of the evaluation is to gather information about the operation of the agency. This information is then used to help managers make decisions regarding programs, services, personnel, marketing, and the future direction of the agency. The evaluation process also examines the efficiency and effectiveness of the agency's operation: Is the agency doing what it should be doing? Can the agency do it better? Is it being done as cost efficiently as possible? In the evaluation process, the performance of the organization is documented so that the managers can determine what features are outstanding and what things need to be changed in the future.

Within the CAPRA standards, one standard specifies that the agency should conduct experimental and demonstration projects, such as action recreation, exploratory investigations, or operational studies. These research efforts focus on a better technique in conducting programs or techniques used within the operation of the agency. It also could involve an operational change or a new program that is being introduced on a small scale to determine the effect of the program. For example, many golf courses struggle with the problem of wildlife, such as geese, being on the course. This serves as an example of an action research project needed within the agency. The agency decides to experiment with new techniques to discourage geese from staying at the golf course (and to get the geese to move to a more appropriate wildlife area). The agency tries using noise makers to scare the geese away instead of holding a drive hunt to eliminate the birds that continue to reside at the facility. This new operational procedure proves to be successful in deterring the geese from residing at the golf course. The research projects focus on a particular problem or need within the agency. These projects encourage agencies to research and solve their own internal issues. The goal of the research effort is to enhance the operations of the agency and better serve the customer.

Another standard within the CAPRA program specifies that the agency should have a staff member within the organization who manages the evaluation analysis for the agency. This ensures that the agency has resources internally to conduct research projects or manage a contact with an external agency for the service. In addition, the agency should have an in-house process for training employees on how to plan and conduct research and evaluation. This also enables employees to plan and conduct research and evaluation projects within their area of responsibility. The final evaluation standard focuses on quality assurance in the area of customer service, programs and facilities with an emphasis on total quality management. By doing this, the agency can identify how to improve quality through decision making and employee efforts to meet or exceed the expectations of the customers. The focus on research and evaluation within the CAPRA standards should reinforce the importance of professionals being comfortable with planning and conducting research projects within their agency. Figure 1.4 shows the CAPRA standards related to research and evaluation that have been touched on within this chapter.

■ *TEST YOUR SKILLS WITH EXERCISE 1.1.*

Benefits of Research and Evaluation for the Professional

Another point to consider related to research and evaluation is the professional certification program within the park and recreation industry. To become a **certified park and recreation professional,** one must take a national certification exam that covers a broad range of topics. Several of the topic areas on the exam address issues related to research and evaluation. These topics include evaluating a participant's experience, evaluating whether a program has met the program goals and objectives, doing needs assessment, and evaluating marketing effectiveness. Certification of park

6.3   Program Evaluation
[Program shall be evaluated regularly and systematically based on stated program objectives]

10.1   Evaluation Analysis
[There shall be a process for evaluation to assess the outcomes of park and recreation programs, services areas and facilities, completed annually at a minimum and linked to the agency's planning process.]

10.1.1 Position responsibility for evaluation
[There should be a specific personnel within the agency responsible for managing the evaluation analysis.]

10.2   Experimental and demonstration projects
[There should be at least one experimental or demonstration project or involvement in some aspect of research as related to any part of park and recreation operations, each year.]

10.3   Staff Training for evaluation of programs, services, areas, facilities.
[There should be ongoing training opportunities for all personnel for the agency involved in evaluation of programs, services, areas and/or facilities.]

10.4   Quality assurance.
[The agency should monitor and evaluate the quality of its programs, services, areas and facilities for the user's perspective.]

Figure 1.4   CAPRA standards related to research and evaluation.
Reprinted from NRPA.

and recreation professionals is one way to assure the public that the professionals in the field have the foundational knowledge needed to provide effective services to their constituents.

This book covers foundational knowledge related to the research and evaluation process, the components of studies, planning considerations for research and evaluation projects, and the various methods that can be used for those projects. In addition, the content of this text integrates relevant information related to the CAPRA standards and professional certification criteria. The book provides all the information that young professionals and seasoned veterans need in order to become comfortable with conducting research and evaluation projects.

■ *TEST YOUR SKILLS WITH EXERCISE 1.2.*

Conclusion

The investigative skills needed to solve a mystery are now a necessary requirement within park and recreation agencies. Professionals must integrate these activities into their annual plan at all levels of the organization. The results of these efforts provide valuable information to justify the operations of the agency and to document how the agency positively influences the quality of life within the community. More important, evaluation and research projects are a required activity for accredited agencies and those agencies seeking accreditation. Conducting research and evaluation is now an expected activity for those working within park and recreation agencies.

EXERCISES

■ Exercise 1.1: CAPRA Accreditation

Go to the National Recreation and Park Association Web site (www.nrpa.org) and find the following information.

1. What is CAPRA accreditation?
2. How many agencies are CAPRA accredited?
3. What is a certified park and recreation professional (CPRP)?
4. When can you become certified and what do you need to do?
5. What does the research indicate is the benefit of the initiative?

■ Exercise 1.2: Article Review

Read the two research articles provided to you in class. Then answer the following questions.

1. What is the purpose of the study?

   Article 1:

   Article 2:
2. How is each topic important to the park and recreation industry?

   Article 1:

   Article 2:

CASE STUDY

You have overheard many stay-at-home moms state that they need some sort of group exercise class and a way to connect and communicate with each other. You program a morning aerobics class, but nobody shows up. Similarly, you know there is a need for senior programming, so you create educational and social events that are held in the evenings in your center. These events have very low turnout. What do you think are the issues in each of these scenarios? What may be the missing links in your research or implementation that could make the programs successful?

FOR THE INVESTIGATOR

One of the best ways to begin the research class is with the end. What does that mean? As a class, complete the Health and Leisure Survey (which can be downloaded from the online student resource) and summarize the data. This gives you a taste of what research encompasses, and it provides you with a study to work with throughout this course.

Why do this? Research is a terrifying topic for most students. You need to discover that research is a process that requires (1) the creativity required in program planning; (2) the ability to think, analyze, and work a plan that is required in leadership; and (3) the foundational knowledge learned in the introduction classes. In other words, research pulls together the skills you have been developing through course work and personal experiences, and it applies these things to a new topic area. If you enjoy exploring new places that you have never been before (e.g., hiking a new trail, skiing a new mountain, or visiting a new beach), you will enjoy research. Exploring a new place is similar to investigating a mystery—you try to find out what type of people live there, what the culture is, what you can do there, and what is unique about the area. Research is an expedition into new territory or uncharted waters, which is fun, engaging, and exhilarating.

CHAPTER 2

• OBJECTIVES •

After completing this chapter, you will be able to

- describe six key characteristics of the scientific method of inquiry,

- identify six key characteristics of evaluation research,

- compare and contrast the scientific method of inquiry and evaluation research,

- summarize the steps used in the scientific research process,

- identify the characteristics of quantitative studies, and

- identify the characteristics of qualitative studies.

The Research and Evaluation Process

The park and recreation director calls a meeting of the staff and announces that the agency will begin the process of becoming a CAPRA accredited agency. The room is filled with silence and looks of confusion. The director then begins to explain the accreditation process, which begins with a self-study to determine how well the operation of the agency meets the CAPRA standards. The staff is then divided into teams. Each team is assigned a number of standards to investigate. For each standard, the teams will assemble the necessary documentation to demonstrate that the standard is being met within the operations of the agency. The teams that discover a standard that the agency is not meeting must then develop the procedures and documents needed to meet the standard. You find yourself on the team that has been assigned to pull together all the documentation for the evaluation standards. The group begins to examine the standards and realizes that the agency's operation lacks many of the evaluation and research activities that the standards require. The group's next step is to try to determine what research and evaluation are, what steps are involved in each, and how they are similar and different.

The group discovers that the research and evaluation processes involve a number of decisions that must be made before a project begins. These decisions enable the researcher to conduct a research project or study in the most efficient and effective manner using the available resources. The research process focuses on gathering information that can answer a research question. The group realizes that they must first understand the differences and similarities between research and evaluation. In learning about research and evaluation projects, the group discovers that the scientific method of inquiry serves as the foundation for all studies.

This chapter provides you with the foundational knowledge that you need in order to understand the scientific method of inquiry, evaluation research, and the process used in both methods for conducting a research study. This knowledge helps you determine what type of study you need to conduct for your investigation of a particular area of interest. The second part of this chapter reviews quantitative and qualitative research methods. Each method provides valuable information that enables the investigator to solve the mystery.

Elements of the Scientific Method of Inquiry

The **scientific method of inquiry** is one of the options available to you as a researcher who needs to investigate a topic. When using this method, you explore a topic from a broad perspective and produce results that can apply to groups beyond your agency. To fully understand the scientific method of research, you must examine the key features of the process:

- Focus
- Purpose
- Content
- Time frame
- Discipline
- Method

Table 2.1 provides the key elements of the scientific method of inquiry and an example that will be reviewed in the following sections.

Focus

The first element to review in the scientific method of inquiry is the **focus** of the study, which frames the intent of the study. In this method, the focus is always based on a theory. A **theory** is a statement that explains an event or an occurrence of something. In the area of health and fitness, various theories are used to predict success in personal fitness and health. The theory serves as a foundation that explains a relationship between variables within a phenomenon or event. A **variable** is a characteristic or element used within the theory. For example, a variable can be weight, age, self-confidence, or any other characteristic defined in the theory.

In the scientific method of inquiry, the theory serves as the foundation that defines the area of a study. This could include testing an existing theory in a new setting, within a different organization, or with a new group of people. As previously mentioned, one current national concern within the United States is the obesity epidemic in children. The Centers for Disease Control and Prevention (CDC) has reported that there is a lack of regular physical activity among children in the United States. This is leading to a nation of obese children with high blood pressure, diabetes, and the potential to be the first generation of children

• TABLE 2.1 •
Key Elements of the Scientific Method of Inquiry

Elements	Defined	Example
Focus	Theory	Walking 10,000 steps a day will improve a person's physical health.
Purpose	Broadly focused on applying the theory	Apply the theory to children ages 10 to 12 years old.
Content	Isolated from real world; variables are manipulated, and environment is controlled.	Conduct a walking class for children to reach 10,000 steps three times a week. Researcher controls when, where, and how long the children walk.
Time frame	Long time frame	Conduct the study over 6 months during the program.
Discipline	Single discipline	Study is based on the health field.
Method	Limited number of variables studied	Focus is to assess the effect on weight, percentage of body fat and muscle mass, and blood pressure.

Based on C. Cutler Riddick and R.V. Russell, 1999, *Evaluative research in recreation, parks, and sport settings: Search for useful information* (Champaign, IL: Sagamore Publishing), 18.

who will die before their parents. The theory that the park and recreation agency wants to test is the following: "Walking 10,000 steps three days a week will improve the physical health of individuals." The variables being studied are cholesterol, weight, and percentage of body fat. These variables define the "physical health" of an individual. The focus of this scientific method of inquiry is to test this theory within the park and recreation agency.

Purpose

The focus of the study helps the researcher specify the **purpose** of the study. In other words, the focus and purpose of the study are directly related to each other. The purpose of the study used in the example (see table 2.1) is to test the theory that walking 10,000 steps a day improves a person's health by applying the theory to 10- to 12-year-old children at the park and recreation agency. The programmers at the park and recreation agency want to determine if the theory is true for 10- to 12-year-old children. The manner in which this theory will be tested is through a focused program series where the programmer can control (1) the program content; (2) the measurement of cholesterol, weight, and body fat density; and (3) the components of the walking program. The variables of this study are the walking program, weight, cholesterol, and percentage of body fat. Information will be gathered on these variables only and no others. Once the purpose is defined, the next element to examine is the content of the study.

Content

The **content** of the study is guided by the focus and purpose of the study. In the case of the walking program, the content is the content of the program itself. This focuses the study on the key variables. The content of the program will consist of the following: At the first meeting, the participants will be weighed, measured for body fat density, and tested to determine their cholesterol level. The youth will be given pedometers to measure the number of steps they take. This will ensure that each individual walks 10,000 steps during the class time. The walking class will be held on Mondays, Wednesdays, and Fridays. If the theory is true, at the conclusion of the study, the participants should have lowered their weight, their percentage of body fat, and their cholesterol. The content of the study more specifically defines the purpose of the study; for example, the content

identifies whom to study and how they should be studied.

Time Frame

Once the content of the study is determined, the researcher must determine how long the study will be conducted, or the **time frame.** The time frame of the study is directly influenced by the content of the study. For the sample study, the walking program will be conducted over six months. This length of time is necessary to determine if the theory is true. If this study was conducted for only six weeks, the researchers would find it difficult to determine the effects of walking 10,000 steps three days a week. This study focuses on the health-related benefits of regular physical activity; therefore, a longer period of time is needed to accurately measure the effects of the walking program and to test the theory.

Discipline and Method

The last two elements of the scientific method of inquiry are the **discipline** and the **method** used within the study. These final features help further define and narrow the efforts within the study. Within the scientific method of inquiry, the study is focused on a single discipline. Disciplines commonly used within the field of parks and recreation include leisure, psychology, sociology, outdoor resources management, and health. In the walking program study, the health discipline is the focus of the study and the theory being investigated in the study. The variables being measured in relation to the theory are all contained within the health discipline. The limited number of variables being examined is a key characteristic of the scientific method of inquiry. When using the scientific method of inquiry, researchers will use some method of gathering information related to the variables during the duration of the study. The method used in the study is selected from options that produce accurate data and are recognized as acceptable methods within the research community. This is done to determine the effects of the program on the variables of interest. In this case, the variables being measured are weight, percentage of body fat, and cholesterol. These are being measured to determine if the theory being tested is true for children ages 10 to 12 years who walk 10,000 steps three days a week for six months. The researcher has a variety of research methods to choose from that can provide the necessary data to test the theory. In the example, the method used in the study focuses on using a systematic process to gather numeric data on the variables being measured.

To better understand the method used to gather data, let's return to the content of the program. The researchers will gather data on four variables in this study. A variable is something (e.g., a concept, behavior, or other items) that the researcher wants to measure in the study. In the sample study, the variables are as follows:

- Number of days the participant walked 10,000 steps over six months
- Beginning and ending weight
- Beginning and ending percentage of body fat
- Beginning and ending cholesterol level

The measurements of the variables provide numbers, or what researchers refer to as **data,** for analysis. If the theory is true—that walking 10,000 steps a day will improve personal health—then what would the researcher anticipate that the results would be for this study? The programmer predicts that the participants should have lost weight, decreased their percentage of body fat, and lowered their blood cholesterol. The data collected on these three variables at the beginning of the study will be compared to the data collected on the same variables at the conclusion of the study. If the differences between the beginning and ending numbers are significant, then the programmer can conclude that the theory is true.

As you have probably concluded, the six key features of the scientific method of inquiry are all interrelated. Each element influences the other elements of the study. In addition, these relationships assist the researcher in planning studies that take a theory and test the theory within a park and recreation setting. Now that you understand the key characteristics of the scientific method of inquiry, it is time to review the same key characteristics in evaluation research. This will enable you to understand the differences between the two processes.

■ *TEST YOUR SKILLS WITH EXERCISE 2.1.*

Elements of the Evaluation Research Process

Evaluation research provides an avenue for recreation professionals to examine specific programs, services, or operational elements within the agency. This type of focused research enables the agency to assess the outcomes of programs and services, the efficiency and effectiveness of the agency's operations, and whether the agency is achieving its mission within the community. The results from evaluation studies are also a powerful tool that can be used to educate the decision makers and the community about the value and worth of the agency. Information is power, and without the proper information, the agency becomes powerless in communicating its value, worth, and contributions to the community. To fully understand the process of evaluation research, one must examine the key components of focus, purpose, content, time frame, discipline, and method. These features are the same features discussed for the scientific method of inquiry, but they are also important in understanding evaluation. Table 2.2 provides a summary of each of the six key components as they relate to evaluation research, along with an example to fully explain each feature. The first component to review is the focus of the study.

Focus

The focus of an evaluation study is the agency's programs, services, or operations. Evaluation studies are narrowly focused on something within the agency or within the operations of the agency. For example, a park and recreation agency wants to evaluate the outcomes of its swimming lesson program. Each swimming level has very specific objectives that are directly related to the skills taught within that swimming level. The focus of the study is to assess the outcomes for the participants within the swimming lesson program and to assess each individual's self-confidence with his or her swimming skills. For example, the programmer might ask, "What skills are the participants learning within each swimming level as defined by the Red Cross swimming curriculum?" This question defines the focus of the evaluation study, which is the outcome for the swimming lesson students. Simply stated, the researcher wants to find out what skills the students have learned during their swimming lessons and how confident the participants are with their skills.

Purpose

In evaluation research, the focus helps define the scope and purpose of the study. In other words, the focus and purpose of the study are related to each other. This is the same relationship as in the scientific method of inquiry, but the intent is more limited in scope. In the example in table

● TABLE 2.2 ●

Key Elements of Evaluation Research

Elements	Defined	Example
Focus	Agency operations	Evaluate swim lesson program in terms of participants' skills and self-confidence.
Purpose	Narrowly focused on operational issues or program issues	Review skills learned at each swimming level and the percentage of students who complete all skills on the level. Also assess students' self-confidence.
Content	Conducted in the real world	Determine the swimming lesson outcomes through skills sheets and discussions. The experience is not controlled or manipulated.
Time frame	Short time frame	Conduct the study for 6 weeks.
Discipline	Multiple disciplines	Study is based on the psychology and health fields.
Method	Can be a limited number of variables or a larger scope	Review records of all swimming classes and interview parents and/or children.

Based on C. Cutler Riddick and R.V. Russell, 1999, *Evaluative research in recreation, parks, and sport settings: Search for useful information* (Champaign, IL: Sagamore Publishing), 18.

2.2, the focus of the evaluation study is to evaluate the swimming lesson program in two ways: skills learned and self-confidence. The purpose of the evaluation is to comprehensively review the skills sheets for all swimming classes to determine what skills are being learned at each level. By doing this, the programmer can determine what percentage of students at each level of swimming are prepared to move to the next higher level. The programmer also wants to assess the students' self-confidence in their swimming skills. Swimming lessons involve a natural progression from beginning to intermediate to advanced skill levels. The programmer believes that as a student's skills progress, so does the student's self-confidence with swimming. The students must demonstrate all the skills at their current level before they can move up to the next swimming level. This type of program evaluation allows the programmer to evaluate the outcomes of the swimming lessons and to document those outcomes. The data can also be used to educate decision makers about the contributions that the programs are making to the community.

Content

The focus and purpose of the study help define the content of the evaluation research. The content of evaluation research narrows the study further to identify what data will be gathered in relation to the focus and purpose of the study. This ensures that the researcher is examining what needs to be examined during the research study. It also further narrows the researcher's efforts to focus on the program or service that is being evaluated. In the example in table 2.2, the content of the evaluation study is the swimming lesson outcomes. The skills learned are documented on the Red Cross skills sheet for each individual in the class, and the self-confidence can be assessed through a discussion with the students. The content of evaluation studies is always based in the real world, as in the example. The researcher does not control the environment and does not manipulate variables during the course of the study, but rather allows events to occur naturally. In evaluation studies, researchers generally gather data or information at the conclusion of an experience, not at the beginning or during the experience. This is the case with the evaluation of the swimming class. The classes are conducted by the instructors without any influence from the researcher and students in the class. At the conclusion of the classes, the researcher then gathers the necessary information from each instructor.

Time Frame

The content of the study also defines the time frame of the evaluation. Every program or service within parks and recreation has a defined beginning point and ending point. Programs and services can be provided over various time frames, such as a 1-day seminar; a 6-, 8-, or 10-week session; a 1-week full-day program (as with day camps); or services provided over a 9- to 10-month period (as with park operations). The time frames for programs and services are defined by the type of program or the season of the program. For example, day camps occur 5 days a week for the entire day, while instructional classes, such as swimming, are provided 1 day a week for 6 or more weeks. In contrast, parks are generally open to the public either seasonally or year-round. This time frame is very different from day camps and instructional classes. In the example in table 2.2, the swimming lessons are conducted over a 6-week period. This time frame is relatively short within the scope of research, but this is unavoidable because of the class schedule. The time frame for evaluations of programs is always defined by the program schedule. Each park and recreation department has schedules of classes that are conducted for a defined number of weeks.

Discipline and Method

The parks and recreation industry uses many disciplines within its operations, such as psychology, sociology, and health. These disciplines are not used in isolation from each other; rather, they are mixed together through the programs and services provided to the community. Because evaluation research examines something within the agency, multiple disciplines are used within the evaluation study to accurately review programs, services, or events. In the swimming lesson example, all three disciplines could be examined. The programmer could evaluate the individual's self-confidence, the importance of the group, and the skills learned. In the example, the programmer decided that the evaluation of the swimming lessons will focus on the disciplines of health and psychology.

The method refers to the process that the researcher uses to gather data. The method used in evaluation research is generally selected from options that are commonly used within research and evaluation. The options are recognized by researchers as preferred methods for gathering the data needed for the study. In the example, the method that the programmer will use to gather the data needed for the evaluation is by reviewing the skill sheet for each class and by holding discussions with the participants. This will provide the programmer with the information needed to determine what skills are being learned at each

level, the number of students who are prepared to move to the next swimming level, and the participants' level of confidence with their swimming skills. The method used in evaluation studies is influenced by the focus, purpose, and content of the evaluation. The evaluation could be focused very broadly or very narrowly. In the example, the scope of the study is very narrow and centered on the objectives of the swimming classes.

Now that you have reviewed the key features of evaluation research and the scientific method of inquiry, it is time to compare the two methods in order to fully understand when to use each method.

■ TEST YOUR SKILLS WITH EXERCISE 2.2.

Comparing the Scientific Method of Inquiry and Evaluation Research

The scientific method of inquiry and evaluation studies both provide valuable information to an agency. The challenge facing a recreation professional at the beginning of a research project is to decide which method to use. To make this decision, a recreation professional needs to compare the components of the two methods. Table 2.3 provides information to help in this comparison.

To choose between the two research methods, the researcher must think about what needs to be researched and the desired outcomes of the study. If the researcher wants to test a theory within the programs of the agency, purposely manipulate variables, and conduct the study over an extended length of time, then the researcher will use the scientific method of inquiry. If the researcher wants to focus on an aspect of the agency's operations as it occurs in the real world (without manipulating variables), then the researcher will use the evaluation method. These two methods are both used in research studies but for distinctly different purposes. Understanding the foundational differences between the two is the first step in developing the necessary knowledge to become comfortable in conducting research and evaluation projects. To better understand the two research methods, you must move beyond the six elements of each and examine the eight steps of the research process. These steps are completed within all research projects—regardless of which research method is used—in order to help ensure that the study produces credible results and conclusions.

● *TABLE 2.3* ●

Comparing Key Elements of the Scientific Method of Inquiry and Evaluation Research

Element	Scientific method of inquiry	Evaluation
Focus	Theory	Agency operations
Purpose	Broadly focused on applying the theory	Narrowly focused on the problem
Content	Isolated from the real world	Conducted in the real world
Time frame	Long	Short
Discipline	Single	Multiple
Method	Limited number of variables based on the theory	Limited or broad number of variables

Steps of the Research Process

Scientific research involves a systematic process that focuses on being objective and gathering a multitude of information for analysis so that the researcher can come to a conclusion. This process is used in all research and evaluation projects, regardless of the research method (scientific method of inquiry, evaluation research, or action research). The process focuses on testing hunches or ideas in a park and recreation setting through a systematic process. In this process, the study is documented in such a way that another individual can conduct the same study again. This is referred to as **replicating** the study. Any research done without documenting the study so that others can review the process and results is not an investigation using the scientific research process. The scientific research process is a multiple-step process where the steps are interlinked with the other steps in the process. If changes are made in one step of the process, the researcher must review all the other steps to ensure that the changes are reflected throughout the process. Parks and recreation professionals are often involved in conducting research or evaluation projects within the agency. These professionals need to understand the eight steps of the research process as they apply to conducting a study. Table 2.4 lists the steps of the research process and provides an example of each step for a sample research study.

Step 1: Identify the Problem

The first step in the process is to identify a problem or develop a research question. The research problem may be something the agency identifies as a problem, some knowledge or information that

is needed by the agency, or the desire to identify a recreation trend nationally. In the example in table 2.4, the problem that the agency has identified is childhood obesity, which is a local problem and concern within the community. This serves as the focus of the study.

Step 2: Review the Literature

Now that the problem has been identified, the researcher must learn more about the topic under investigation. To do this, the researcher must review the literature related to the research problem. This step provides foundational knowledge about the problem area. The review of literature also educates the researcher about what studies have been conducted in the past, how these studies were conducted, and the conclusions in the problem area. In the obesity study, the review of literature enables the programmer to discover horrifying statistics related to the long-term effects of childhood obesity in terms of health issues, death rates, and projected medical costs. In addition, the programmer finds several articles and information from the Centers for Disease Control and Prevention that describe the benefits of walking 10,000 steps a day. The information discovered during this step helps the programmer fully understand the magnitude of the problem, recognize the future consequences of obesity, and identify a strategy to combat obesity (i.e., walking).

Step 3: Clarify the Problem

Many times the initial problem identified in the first step of the process is too large or broad in scope. In step 3 of the process, the researcher clarifies the problem and narrows the scope of the study. This can only be done after the literature

• TABLE 2.4 •

Research Steps Within the Scientific Method of Inquiry

Step	Example
1. Identify the problem or question.	Childhood obesity
2. Review the literature.	Look for similar studies that have been conducted.
3. Clarify the problem—specifically identify the purpose of the study.	The purpose of the study is to determine if walking 10,000 steps a day for three days a week improves a person's health.
4. Clearly define terms and concepts.	This is done so that the readers understand exactly what each term means.
5. Define the population.	Children who are 10 to 12 years old
6. Develop the instrumentation plan.	Data will be collected on the variables at the beginning of the program and at the conclusion of the study.
7. Collect data.	Collect the data on the specified variables at the first and last session of the program.
8. Analyze the data.	Compare data gathered from each participant. The first measurements are compared to the second measurements to see if there is a difference. Report the results and the differences if there are any.

Based on J.R. Fraenkel and N. E. Wallen, 2003, *How to design and evaluate research in education*, 5th ed. (New York: McGraw-Hill Companies), 19, 20.

has been reviewed. The knowledge gained through the review of literature guides the researcher in clarifying and narrowing the research project. In the example, the programmer has identified childhood obesity as the problem and the purpose of the study. This topic is very broad and could be studied based on genetics, family environment, diet, exercise, self-confidence, leisure activities, or health issues. All of these areas cannot be investigated in a single study; therefore, the problem and purpose of the study must be more clearly defined. The programmer has decided that the purpose of the study is to determine if walking 10,000 steps a day for three days a week will improve the individual's health. This purpose is more narrowly focused and researchable than the original problem.

Step 4: Clearly Define Terms and Concepts

Terms and concepts are words or phrases used in the purpose statement of the study or the description of the study. These items need to be specifically defined as they apply to the study. Terms or concepts often have different definitions depending on who is reading the study. To minimize confusion about what the terms and phrases mean, the researcher must specifically define them for the study. In the obesity study, the concept of "individual's health" can be defined in hundreds of ways, such as physical, mental, emotional, or spiritual health. For this study, the individual's health is defined as physical health. The concept of physical health may also be defined and measured in many ways. In this case, the programmer decides to more narrowly define "individual health" to refer to the areas of weight, percentage of body fat, and cholesterol. By defining the terms or concepts more narrowly, the scope of the study is more manageable for the programmer, making it easier to collect the necessary data for the study. This also makes the concepts more understandable to the reader.

Step 5: Define the Population

Research projects can focus on a specific group of people, facilities, park development, employee evaluations, programs, financial status, marketing efforts, or the integration of technology into the operations. For example, if a researcher wants to examine a specific group of people in the community, the study could examine a specific age group, males or females, people living in a specific geographic area, or a specific ethnic group. Literally thousands of options are available to the researcher to specifically identify the group to study. The research problem and the purpose of the study assist the researcher in identifying the group to involve in the study. In research terms, the group to involve in the study is always called the population. Defining the population assists the researcher in several ways. First, it narrows the scope of the study from a very large population to one that is manageable. Second, the population identifies the group that the researcher's efforts will be focused on within the study. This helps ensure that the researcher stays on the right path during the study. Finally, by defining the population, the researcher identifies the group that the results will apply to at the conclusion of the study. In the example in table 2.4, the programmer has identified the population of the study as children ages 10 to 12 years. This narrower population makes the study more manageable in terms of time and resources.

Step 6: Develop the Instrumentation Plan

The plan for the study is referred to as the instrumentation plan. The instrumentation plan serves as the road map for the entire study, specifying who will participate in the study; how, when, and where data will be collected; and the content of the program. This plan is composed of numerous decisions and considerations that are addressed in chapter 8 of this text. In the obesity study, the researcher has decided to have the children participate in a walking program for six months. The group of participants is called the sample, which is a smaller group selected from the population specified for the study. The study cannot possibly include every 10- to 12-year-old child in the community, so a smaller group is used to represent the population. The researcher develops the plan for the walking program, indicating what data will be collected, when and how the data will be collected, who will collect the data, and how the data will be analyzed. The instrumentation plan specifies all the steps that must be completed for the study. This ensures that the programmer has carefully thought through all these decisions and that she provides a step-by-step plan to be followed in the study.

Step 7: Collect Data

Once the instrumentation plan is completed, the actual study begins with the collection of data. The collection of data is a critical step in providing the information needed to answer the research question. Every study includes the collection of some type of data—whether it is from the literature or from subjects—to answer the research question. Data can be collected in the form of words on a survey, with a questionnaire, through observations, or from the literature. In the obesity study, the programmers will be collecting data on the defined variables: weight, percentage of body fat, cholesterol levels, and the number of days the person walked a total of 10,000 steps during the class.

The researcher collects these data at the first session and at the last session of the program. These two sets of data are necessary to determine the effect of the walking program on weight, body fat, and cholesterol level. Once the data are collected on the variables, the researcher is ready to move to the final step of the process, which is the data analysis.

Step 8: Analyze the Data

All the time, effort, and resources dedicated to steps 1 through 7 of the research process culminate in this final step. The researcher finally has data to analyze so that the research question can be answered. In the instrumentation plan, the researcher specified how the data will be analyzed. The researcher now analyzes the data according to the plan. The results of this analysis are then reviewed and summarized in a manner directly related to the research questions. In the obesity study, the researcher compares the measurements of weight, percentage of body fat, and cholesterol that were taken at the first meeting of the subjects to the measurements of the same variables at the final program session. These two sets of data will be analyzed to determine if there was a difference between the first measurement and the second measurement for each individual in the program. Then, the data will be analyzed to determine if the differences are statistically significant. If the differences are statistically significant, the study validates the theory that was the focus of the study. The results of the study also provide valuable information about one strategy to combat childhood obesity in the community.

As you have probably concluded, conducting studies using the eight steps of the scientific research process requires you to dedicate time and effort to the planning process. You cannot conduct a study using the scientific research process when time is limited or the study is done at the last minute. Researchers who do this conduct studies that result in either false conclusions or conclusions that are not of any value to the organization.

Quantitative and Qualitative Study Designs

Now that you understand the key components of the scientific method of inquiry and evaluation research, as well as the steps of the research process, let's review the two major categories of study design: **quantitative design** and **qualitative design.** Each design has a specific purpose, focus, and intent in relation to research. The purpose of the study will guide you in choosing the type of design to use for the research project. The first option is the quantitative study design.

■ *TEST YOUR SKILLS WITH EXERCISE 2.3.*

Quantitative Design

In quantitative studies, the research project is approached in a focused manner. The focus is on measuring the defined variables of the study. In the swimming class example, the programmer is measuring the skills learned during the class. The data are gathered in the form of numbers—the number of individuals who could perform a specific skill. This information is gathered from the skills checklist for each class. The number of people to gather data from or about is generally selected in a specific manner. The individuals included in the study are referred to as **subjects.** The subjects are selected from a larger group that they are a member of. In this case, the subjects are members of the swimming lesson group. For this study, it would be pointless to select subjects from any other class except the swimming lesson groups. The study procedures within quantitative studies are very rigid and are specified before the study begins. The procedures identify every step of the study in a sequential manner. For the sample study, the first step is to gather the enrollment for every swimming class, the second step is to identify the instructors for each class, the third step is to gather blank skills sheets for each swimming lesson, and so on through the entire process. The procedures are a predetermined plan that must be completed step by step during the course of the study.

Within the study plan, one of the later steps specified is how to analyze the data and report the results. Because the data are numbers, the data are analyzed using some type of statistical analysis. The statistical analysis used in the study provides the information needed to formulate conclusions; this information is also reported as the results of the study. The results are generally reported as a summary of the statistical analysis. In other words, the numbers tell the story.

In quantitative studies, the focus is on predetermined variables and is very narrow; in addition, this method relies solely on numeric data and statistical analysis to yield the results of the study. Quantitative studies are very useful when the researcher wants to measure specific variables within a program, an experience, or some element of the operations of the agency. If a researcher wants to examine an experience as a whole, the qualitative research method should be used.

Qualitative Design

In the qualitative study design, the research project is approached in a different manner. The goal of a qualitative study is to understand the entire experience, not just a limited number of variables. Qualitative studies can examine a person, a group of people, historical documents, or the development of a societal trend (e.g., snowboarding). In the case of the swimming lessons, the entire experience encompasses registration, parking, the locker room, the pool facility, the equipment, the instructor, the confidence of the child, and the parents' satisfaction with the lessons. This goes far beyond performing swimming skills. The data gathered are generally in the form of words obtained from an interview or observation notes, not numeric information. To evaluate the swimming lessons, the researcher would choose a limited number of parents and children to interview about their experience during the swimming lessons.

In qualitative studies, the researcher purposely selects a limited number of individuals to gather information from to analyze. The people who are selected to be involved in the study are selected because they have information or knowledge that the researcher needs for the study. In qualitative studies, researchers know where to begin and what type of conclusion is needed, but the middle is very vague. Because of this, the study design is a basic outline that is flexible so the researcher can make changes when needed to gather the information necessary for the study. Because the data can be from observations or interviews, the information is analyzed in a different manner. A process is used to code the information; the data are broken down into different pieces and then put back together in a different way to come to conclusions.

For the study of the swimming lessons, the researcher chooses 10 parents and 10 children from the beginning lessons to interview about

PROFESSIONAL PERSPECTIVES

■ The real world of parks and recreation

As a recreation therapist at a training center for people with mental retardation, I used the scientific method of inquiry on a daily basis. For example, one resident had very abusive behavior toward himself and others. Every day, he would hit people and throw himself on the ground, landing on his knees and elbows. This was very painful to watch, and it was disturbing to staff who were helpless in stopping him from this type of behavior. The team decided to develop a behavior modification program to address these inappropriate behaviors. The program was the most severe behavior modification program that I had to run at this facility. The plan came from studying literature, failures of previous attempts at changing this behavior, and the injuries that were occurring to staff as a result of working with this particular resident. The behavior modification program was called a sensory deprivation program. When the resident acted out, we gave him two verbal warnings, and if the behavior did not stop, we ran the program.

This program required four or five staff members to drag the resident into a soundproof room and tie him into restraints connected to the chair at his legs, arms, and chest. Then the staff placed a blindfold on him, closed the door, and watched him. If he calmed down for a specific period of time, he was released; otherwise, he remained there for 15 minutes and then was released. Data were gathered about his behavior every day to determine if the behavior modification program was effective in decreasing the frequency of his self-abusive behavior and aggressive behavior toward others.

Why was research important in this case?

The resident had very violent behavior, and this created a dangerous situation for the resident and those who work with him 24 hours a day in the residential setting. The scientific method of inquiry provided baseline data, a behavior modification program, and data to analyze to determine if the behavior was decreasing. Without this process, who knows what would have happened to the resident and staff.

their experience. These interviews provide a large amount of information to analyze. The researcher takes all the information and begins to break it apart based on common statements or themes, such as statements about the faculty. The common statements or information within each theme is then put together and reexamined. Then the researcher can come to conclusions about the swimming lesson experience based on this analysis. These results are presented in a narrative form instead of a numeric form. The narration summarizes the conclusions from the study.

The qualitative research design provides a means to examine an experience holistically instead of examining a limited number of pieces or variables (as with the quantitative design). Each design method serves different purposes, and both methods are necessary within the park and recreation industry. Table 2.5 provides a summary of the key elements and can be used to compare quantitative and qualitative research designs. Either design can be used in the scientific method of inquiry or an evaluation study. The researcher must make the decision about which design to use based on the intent of the study. If the researcher wants to test a theory with a limited number of variables, then a quantitative design should be used in the study. If the researcher wants to evaluate a person's experience as a whole, then a qualitative design should be used in the study. These decisions are part of the foundation for every research project and will guide the research planning and implementation process. Researchers must think through these decisions carefully instead of charging ahead without dedicating time to this first step. The time dedicated at the beginning of the research process will help ensure that the results are of value to the agency.

• TABLE 2.5 •
Key Elements of Quantitative and Qualitative Designs

	Quantitative methodologies	Qualitative methodologies
Focus	Variables	The experience as a whole
Data	Collected as numbers or numerical scores	Collected as narrative description, words, or observations
Selection of people involved in the study	Purposely selected group of people to study based on the group they represent	Limited number of subjects involved in the study based on their knowledge
Study procedures	Rigid design procedures	Less rigid design procedures
Data analysis	Statistically analyzed	Coding of narration, not statistics
Summary of results	Preference for statistical summary of results	Preference for narrative summary of results

■ *TEST YOUR SKILL WITH EXERCISES 2.4 AND 2.5.*

Conclusion

This chapter covered the fundamental decisions related to conducting a research and evaluation study. The major features of the study, such as the focus and purpose, will guide the researcher in deciding which of the two research methods to use (scientific method of inquiry or evaluation research). Each method has distinctly different purposes and outcomes. Once this decision has been made, the next critical decision is whether to use qualitative or quantitative techniques or a blended method that uses both techniques. By using a blended method, the researcher can focus on specific variables during the quantitative portion of the study and focus on more in-depth information during the qualitative portion. The results of a study using both techniques provide much richer data than either of the techniques could provide alone. This decision is also influenced by the research focus and purpose. Does the researcher want to study specific variables in a theory or explore an experience holistically? Does the researcher want to use a combination of both quantitative and qualitative techniques within the study? The lesson to learn from this chapter is that any study can be explored through any of these options. The scientific method and the evaluation method can use quantitative techniques, qualitative techniques, or a combination of both. These decisions are what make research exciting and fun!

EXERCISES

■ Exercise 2.1: Scientific Method of Inquiry

Read the following problem and then complete the information for a research study to address the problem:

The problem at XYZ University is the total absence of any type of outdoor recreation programs, services, and outings. The surrounding area near campus has a multitude of opportunities for fishing, kayaking, canoeing, hiking, backpacking, skiing, snowshoeing, and bike riding. The administration sees this as a problem, but it does not know what activities, services, and outings the students desire.

1. Research question
2. What to look for in the literature
3. Purpose fo the study
4. Terms to define in the problem or question
5. Population of the study
6. Instrumentation process
7. How will data be collected?
8. How will data be analyzed?

■ Exercise 2.2: Evaluation

Review the CAPRA standards in figure 2.1 and identify five specific evaluations that can be conducted within a park and recreation agency. Think of a public parks and recreation agency that has a multitude of classes such as swimming, water aerobics, indoor sport leagues, spinning classes, yoga classes, gymnastics, soccer, and other sport clinics for children.

6.3   Program Evaluation
[Program shall be evaluated regularly and systematically based on stated program objectives]

10.1   Evaluation Analysis
[There shall be a process for evaluation to assess the outcomes of park and recreation programs, services areas and facilities, completed annually at a minimum and linked to the agency's planning process.]

10.1.1 Position responsibility for evaluation
[There should be a specific personnel within the agency responsible for managing the evaluation analysis.]

10.2   Experimental and demonstration projects
[There should be at least one experimental or demonstration project or involvement in some aspect of research as related to any part of park and recreation operations, each year.]

10.3   Staff Training for evaluation of programs, services, areas, facilities.
[There should be ongoing training opportunities for all personnel for the agency involved in evaluation of programs, services, areas and/or facilities.]

10.4   Quality assurance.
[The agency should monitor and evaluate the quality of its programs, services, areas and facilities for the user's perspective.]

Figure 2.1   CAPRA standards.
Reprinted from NRPA.

1.

2.

3.

4.

5.

■ Exercise 2.3: Scientific Method of Inquiry and Evaluation

Read the following description of an evaluation topic for a park and recreation department. Then complete the information for the evaluation.

The park and recreation agency, like most across the nation, has a large summer day camp program that generates the largest amount of revenues for the agency of any single program group. The director realizes that the day camp program has not been evaluated in the past. He is very interested in what the parents and children like and dislike about the day camp.

1. Research question
2. What to look for in the literature
3. Purpose of the study
4. Terms to define in the problem or question
5. Population of the study
6. Instrumentation process
7. How will data be collected?
8. How will data be analyzed?

■ Exercise 2.4: Quantitative Versus Qualitative Research

For each of the following problems, identify a quantitative study and a qualitative study that will investigate the problem. Almost every problem can be investigated either in a quantitative or qualitative process.

1. Problem: The rate of childhood obesity is increasing at an alarming rate within the community.

    Quantitative study:

    Qualitative study:

2. Problem: An evaluation of the adult fitness classes (spinning, aerobics, water aerobics, and yoga) needs to be conducted.

    Quantitative study:

    Qualitative study:

3. Problem: At a local park, visitors are leaving an increased amount of trash at the park for employees to pick up. This is not within the scope of the Leave No Trace principles that the park tries to use in the educational program provided by the staff.

    Quantitative study:

    Qualitative study:

■ Exercise 2.5: Research Review

Review the research articles used in exercise 1.2 and complete the following.

1. Article:
    a. Did the study use evaluation research or the scientific method of inquiry?
    b. What was the purpose of the study?

    c. What was the time frame of the study?

    d. What discipline or disciplines were used in the study?

    e. What method was used in the study?

2. Article:

    a. Did the study use evaluation research or the scientific method of inquiry?

    b. What was the purpose of the study?

    c. What was the time frame of the study?

    d. What discipline or disciplines were used in the study?

    e. What method was used in the study?

CASE STUDY

You are the director of a day camp in your local community, and you have noticed that there is a high frequency of children acting out. What could you do using the scientific method of inquiry to address, study, and correct this problem?

FOR THE INVESTIGATOR

Let's revisit the Health and Leisure Survey that you previously completed and begin to take a closer look at it based on the subject matter in chapter 2. You can now begin to analyze the use of such an instrument. Review the survey and answer the following questions.

1. Identify the focus, purpose, content, time frame, discipline, and method for a study using the Health and Leisure Survey.

2. What type of study would this survey be used within (either the scientific method of inquiry or evaluation research)? Justify your answer.

3. Would the study be a quantitative or qualitative study? Explain your decision.

CHAPTER 3

• OBJECTIVES •

After completing this chapter, you will be able to

- describe the characteristics of a research problem and research questions,
- explain the relationship between the research problem, research questions, and research study design,
- describe the various types of research designs that can be used for a quantitative or qualitative study,
- select a research design based on the research problem or research questions.

The Research Problem

Your supervisor has asked you to evaluate the existing preschool Wiggles and Giggles classes. These are movement and music classes that require a parent to participate in the class with each child. The class is very popular with the children and parents, but you discover that the classes have never been evaluated. You realize that you are now starting at ground zero and have to develop the evaluation plan for these classes. You remember that the evaluation process is composed of multiple steps and involves multiple decisions that must be made throughout the process. The first critical decision is deciding whether to conduct a research or evaluation project. Your assignment is to conduct an evaluation study of the Wiggles and Giggles class. With that in mind, you must decide what to evaluate about these classes. You go back and review your material on research methods, and you realize that the research problem helps define what to evaluate.

One of the first steps in the research process is to identify the problem to examine. This problem guides the researcher's focus and efforts throughout the entire research process. Throughout the process, the researcher is trying to come to some conclusion to resolve the problem. Many young professionals tend to make mistakes in identifying the research problem—for example, having a problem that is too large, too small, or insignificant to the organization. Certain criteria should be used when working to specifically identify a research problem. This step in the process seems to be very simple, but it is more complicated than it appears. Researchers must approach this step very carefully to help ensure that the time and effort dedicated to the research are used efficiently and effectively.

Defining the Research Problem

The **research problem** is usually generated out of a need within an agency or some issue or concern within the community. In the case of the Wiggles and Giggles classes, the problem is the absence of an evaluation process for these classes. This is a researchable problem for a recreation programmer. The focus of the evaluation research is to develop the evaluation plan and then evaluate the Wiggles and Giggles classes provided by the park and recreation agency.

When identifying a research problem, the researcher must make sure that the problem meets three criteria:

1. The problem can be researched. This criterion is straightforward but very important in order to ensure that the resources of the agency are used properly in research and evaluation. To ensure that a problem can be researched, you first need to determine that there is information that can be gathered in a timely and cost-efficient manner. Second, you must verify that you can gain access to the information that is needed to answer the question. If you can do both, then the problem is researchable; if not, then you need to identify another problem that does meet this criteria. For example, if you wanted to research the problem of gang activity in your community and why youth join gangs, you would discover that this is not a researchable question for a variety of reasons. First, the information that is needed would be difficult and dangerous to obtain. Second, the cost associated with gathering the information would far exceed what your agency could afford in manpower cost and time. On the other hand, the problem regarding the need for the Wiggles and Giggles classes to be evaluated is a researchable issue. Information can be gathered from the parents in a timely and cost-efficient manner. Also, the scope of the problem is manageable for the agency and not too large for the available resources.

2. The problem requires an answer that goes beyond a simple yes or no. If the programmer asks whether the participants of the Wiggles and Giggles class had a good time, this is a yes or no question and is not a good research problem. Creating an evaluation for the classes goes beyond a yes or no question that is researchable. This second criterion for a research problem can be met for the evaluation of the Wiggles and Giggles classes. The problem "An evaluation plan and process do not exist for the Wiggles and Giggles class" goes beyond a simple yes or no answer.

3. The researcher can gather information that can be used for some type of analysis of the problem. The Wiggles and Giggles research problem meets this criterion because several elements of the classes can provide data to be evaluated. The data that can be collected include the following:
   - Data on the instructors' performance in conducting the classes
   - Skills the children perform at the beginning and at the conclusion of the classes
   - Data documenting that the objectives for the class were met through the class content
   - Verbal feedback from parents about what they liked the best and least about the class

   These four sources of data can provide the researcher with a wealth of information for evaluating the Wiggles and Giggles class.

These three criteria may appear to be common sense, but they are often overlooked. The most common mistake made at this stage is defining the problem either too narrowly or too broadly. For example, someone may state, "Our problem is that we do not know what the needs are within our community." This is too broad in scope and should be refined to a smaller focus, such as focusing on the recreational needs of preteens in the local community. This narrows the scope to a specific age group and geographic location. On the flip side, a problem can be too narrowly focused—for example, "The bluebird boxes need to be repaired." This problem does not demand research; rather, it requires a maintenance and repair plan for the birdhouses. The research problem provides the focus and purpose of the research project and helps define the proper scope of the study.

Purpose of the Study

After the problem has been identified, the next step in the planning phase of a study is to write a **purpose statement** for the study. The purpose statement is one sentence that states what the study is investigating. If you review journal articles, you will always find a purpose statement for the study being described. This statement allows the reader to quickly identify the research topic for the study. To write a purpose statement, you simply begin with this: "The purpose of this study is to . . ." Then you complete the sentence. In the example of evaluating the Wiggles and Giggles class, the purpose statement is as follows: "The purpose of this study is to evaluate the Wiggles and Giggles classes." The reader of this statement knows that the study is an evaluation study and that a specific kind of class is being evaluated. The purpose statement alone does not provide the reader with enough information about the intent of the study. The next item that must be developed is the research questions for the study.

Research Questions

The **research questions** more clearly define the scope and focus of the study. These questions also indicate whether a quantitative study or qualitative study is being conducted. A study will often include a series of research questions that the study will address. During the study, conclusions will be formulated to specifically answer each individual question. In the case of evaluating the Wiggles and Giggles classes, the programmer is interested in several pieces of information: (1) how the content of the class has achieved the class objectives, (2) how satisfied the adults are with the content of the class, (3) how satisfied the adults are with the instructor's performance in conducting the class, and (4) what suggestions the adults have for improving the class experience. Each of these pieces of information can be turned into a research question to help focus the purpose and intent of the study. Figure 3.1 provides a summary of the research problem, the purpose, and the related research questions for the study of the Wiggles and Giggles classes.

As with the research problem, each research question needs to meet three criteria:

1. The question should be researchable, meaning that information can be collected to answer the question. The four questions listed in figure 3.1 meet this criterion because data can be gathered to answer each of them.
2. The question should be of importance to the agency conducting the research. The research efforts must provide valuable information that the agency needs and is lacking at that time. The research questions for the sample study

Problem: An evaluation plan and process do not exist for the Wiggles and Giggles class.

Purpose: The purpose of this study is to evaluate the Wiggles and Giggles classes.

Research questions:

1. How has the content of the class achieved the class objectives?
2. What is the satisfaction level of the adults with the class?
3. What is the satisfaction level of the adults with the instructor's performance in conducting the class?
4. What recommendations do the adults have to improve the class?

Figure 3.1   Summary of the Wiggles and Giggles evaluation.

also meet this criterion because the agency does not have an evaluation process or plan for the Wiggles and Giggles class.

3. The question should be brief and understandable. The words or phrases used in the research question must be selected carefully to ensure that the intent of the study is understandable. Researchers often need to define words or phrases at this stage so that the reader clearly understands the definition of each one within the scope of the study.

In the example of evaluating the Wiggles and Giggles classes, the researcher must clearly define what is meant by *satisfaction level*. This phrase means different things to different people. The researcher must define what variables will be used to determine satisfaction and how they will be measured. Satisfaction can be measured using many different variables, such as satisfaction with the helpfulness of the staff at the facility, the registration process, the cleanliness of the facility, the overall experience, the instructor, or the class content. In the example, the researcher is interested in the participants' satisfaction with the content of the class and the class instructor. The researcher will develop a series of questions related to each of these two variables. The adults will be asked to indicate their level of satisfaction on a five-point **Likert scale.** A Likert scale is used to measure an individual's attitudes about something. In this case, it is used to measure attitudes about the content of the class and the instructor. Figure 3.2 provides an example of an evaluation question that uses the Likert scale to measure the participant's attitude about the instructor.

The research problem, research questions, and purpose of the study are all logically interlinked. These elements work together to define the intention of the study. They also narrow the focus of the study to something that is manageable in scope but represents the agency's need for specific information. In the example in figure 3.1, the scope of the study is to develop and conduct an evaluation of the Wiggles and Giggles classes.

The next decision that needs to be made is what type of research design to use for the evaluation study—either a qualitative design or a quantitative design. The answer lies within the research questions. Each of these design categories includes several designs that the researcher can select for a study.

Quantitative Research Designs

Researchers have a wide variety of research designs to choose from when planning a study. To determine what type of research design to use in the study, the researcher must revisit the research questions. The research questions help to guide this decision. If the researcher decides that a quantitative design is the best option for the study, the researcher can choose from the following quantitative research designs: (1) experimental design, (2) correlation design, or (3) survey design.

Experimental Design

The **experimental design** is often used for studies in which the research question examines a cause-and-effect relationship—that is, if A is done, then B will occur (A and B represent variables that are the focus of the study). Variables can be abstract concepts such as enjoyment, satisfaction, or self-confidence. Variables can also be more concrete elements, such as time, weight, blood pressure, or a score on an exam. The researcher defines the variables to examine in the experimental study. The research question states two variables that are the focus of the study. Experimental

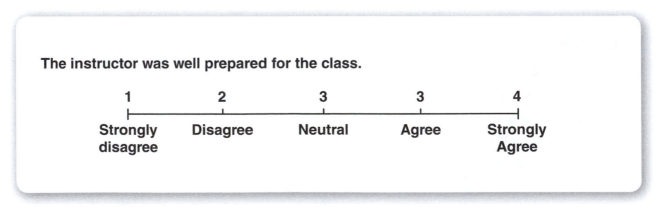

The instructor was well prepared for the class.

1	2	3	3	4
Strongly disagree	Disagree	Neutral	Agree	Strongly Agree

Figure 3.2   Sample evaluation scale.

research designs are the only designs in which the researcher purposely manipulates one variable (A) to measure the effects on the other variable (B). This manipulation of the variable allows the researcher to determine if there is a cause-and-effect relationship.

An example of an experimental study is an outdoor school that is trying to determine which type of paddle is the best to use when teaching beginning kayaking. The school decides to test the two primary options for paddles—a single-blade paddle that is used most often in canoeing and the traditional double-blade paddle used in kayaking. The school takes all the beginner kayakers and divides them into two groups. One group is taught using the single-blade paddle, while the second group is taught using the double-blade paddle. Both groups receive the same instruction and curriculum for kayaking during the weeklong class. At the end of the class, the students from both groups are tested on their kayaking skills. The results of the groups are compared in order to determine which group performed the beginning kayaking skills better. At the end of the week, the school instructors concluded that the group using the single-blade paddle consistently performed the basic kayaking skills better than the group using the double-blade paddle. Therefore, the instructors concluded that students learn the beginning kayaking skills better with the single-blade paddle. The A variable in this example is the type of paddle, and the B variable is the performance of beginning kayaking skills. Figure 3.3 provides a diagram of the experimental design for the kayaking study.

In the experimental research design, one variable (variable A) is manipulated, and this variable is often referred to as the **treatment variable.** The effect of the treatment on variable B is then measured. In the case of kayaking instruction, the treatment was the type of paddle used, and the effect was measured by assessing the skill performance of the groups.

Another commonly used experimental design is to use an experimental group that receives the treatment and a control group that does not receive the treatment. This is a common experimental design in the medical community. For example, a pharmaceutical company wants to test a new medication for allergies. Two groups are used in the experiment; the experimental group receives the new medication, and the control group receives a sugar pill. At the end of the experiment, both groups are assessed for symptoms in order to determine if the new medicine was effective in controlling the allergy symptoms. The differences between the groups are measured and evaluated to determine if they are significant.

The experimental design is the only design that requires the researchers to control the environment and purposely manipulate a variable. This type of structure can be difficult to implement in the public setting of parks and recreation. This design is more commonly used in residential therapeutic settings, such as training centers for people with mental retardation or psychiatric hospitals. If the researcher discovers that this type of design is not possible to use or is not appropriate for the focus of the study, the researcher should consider one of the other options available.

The experimental design is not an appropriate design for evaluating the Wiggles and Giggles class. First, this design is used in the scientific method of inquiry, not in evaluation. In the evaluation study of the Wiggles and Giggles classes, variables are not manipulated to determine a cause-and-effect relationship. Instead, the variables occur in the real world (in this case, within the class). Since the experimental design is not appropriate for the Wiggles and Giggles study, let's move on to review the second quantitative option, which is the correlation research design.

VARIABLE A	**VARIABLE B**
Type of paddle	**Performance of beginning kayaking skills**
Group A Single-blade paddle	Kayaking skills performance
Group B Double-blade paddle	Kayaking skills performance

Figure 3.3 Diagram of experimental design for study on teaching kayaking skills.

Correlation Design

Researchers use the **correlation research design** when they want to study the strength of the relationship between two variables as they occur in a natural setting. This design is similar to the experimental design in that both designs examine two variables; however, in the correlation design, there is no manipulation of the variables. In addition, the correlation design examines the relationship between the two variables in the natural environment. This design is much easier to use in a public setting (such as a park and recreation setting) because a controlled environment is not needed when conducting a correlation study.

An example of a correlation study is examining the relationship between time spent studying and the student's grade on an exam for an Introduction to Recreation class. The researcher gathers data on the time spent studying and the grade received on the exam. The data are then analyzed to determine if there is a statistically significant relationship. The data analysis results in a number between −1.0 and +1.0, which is called the **correlation coefficient.** The closer the correlation coefficient is to either −1.0 or +1.0, the stronger the relationship. In the study of time spent studying and exam score, the correlation coefficient for this relationship was +0.92. This number indicates a strong relationship between time spent studying and exam score. Figure 3.4 is a graph showing the relationship between the grade on the exam and the time spent studying for all the students in the class (each person's information is represented by a dot or point on the chart).

The plus (+) or minus (−) sign indicates whether the relationship is a positive correlation or a negative correlation. A **positive correlation** means that as one variable increases, so does the other variable. In the example, the correlation coefficient is +0.92; this means that as the time spent studying increases, the exam grade increases. A **negative correlation** means that as one variable increases, the other variable decreases. An example of a negative correlation is the time spent studying and the number of days spent drinking. In this case, the negative correlation would be that as the time spent studying increases, the number of days spent drinking decreases. A correlation coefficient of 0 means that there is no relationship between the variables. Ideally, researchers would want a correlation coefficient to be 0.90 (plus or minus) or better to determine a strong relationship. However, researchers' opinions vary regarding the lowest correlation coefficient that can be considered a significantly strong relationship. Literature recommends that a correlation coefficient of 0.80 or above should be considered a strong relationship; any value below that point indicates that no relationship exists between the variables.

The correlation study design is a useful design when the researchers want to examine the relationship between two variables. This type of research can be conducted within the "real world" without controlling the environment. This design can be used in the areas of land management, program management, or customer service. Within the field of parks and recreation, the possibilities for using the correlation design are virtually endless as long as the researchers can identify two variables to examine. Correlation studies also provide valuable information for agencies that need to document the outcomes of programs and events.

In the example of evaluating the Wiggles and Giggles class, a correlation study design is not an appropriate choice. The evaluation is not examining the strength of the relationship between two variables. Rather, the evaluation is being done to identify satisfaction levels, to examine whether program objectives are being achieved, and to seek recommendations on how to improve the class. Because a correlation design is not appropriate for the evaluation study, let's review a third option for a quantitative study—a survey design.

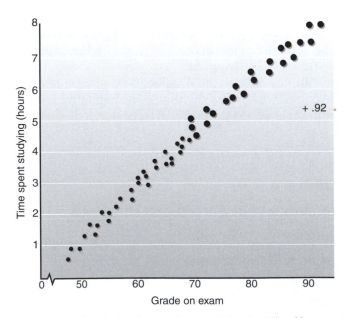

Figure 3.4 Graph showing a typical correlational relationship.

Survey Design

In many cases, researchers do not want to examine relationships within a study. Instead, they want to gather information about preferences, demographic characteristics, opinions, or attitudes. To gather this type of information, the experimental design and the correlation design are not appropriate. These designs will not provide the data needed to answer a research question seeking this type of information. The purpose of **survey** research is to gather data that will describe the group being examined in order to better understand their characteristics, attitudes, preferences, or beliefs.

Conducting a needs assessment is an example of how the survey research design can be used within parks and recreation. The purpose of a needs assessment is to gather information from the community about preferences, likes, and dislikes related to the agency's recreation programs. For example, a needs assessment conducted within one community identified a large need for an arts center within the community. This center should provide rehearsal and class space for dance and provide studio space for artists. It also should serve as the community center for visual and performing art classes for adults and children. If the park and recreation director did not have a needs assessment conducted, the director would have had to guess what was needed in the community. The results from the needs assessment identified the needs of the community and provided the information necessary for the future planning and development within the agency.

In the case of evaluating the Wiggles and Giggles class, the survey design is the most appropriate method for determining the satisfaction level of the adults (i.e., satisfaction with the class content and instructors) and whether they thought the objectives of the class were met. In this example, the programmer is measuring the adults' beliefs and attitudes about their experience in the class. The survey provides the data needed to answer the research questions related to the level of satisfaction with the course content and instructors. It also gathers numerical data that can be analyzed to answer these specific research questions.

To answer the research question regarding what suggestions the adults have for improving the class, one simple question can be asked at the end of the survey: "What suggestions do you have to improve the Wiggles and Giggles class?" This type of question allows the adults to write any thoughts they have on how the class could be improved in the future. The survey method of research is the best method for answering the four research questions listed in figure 3.1 for the Wiggles and Giggles class evaluation.

Survey research is one of the most frequently used designs for research and evaluation within the field of parks and recreation, particularly for the evaluation of programs. The survey, correlation, and experimental designs all have distinctly different purposes in research and evaluation. The research question will determine which type of design is appropriate for the study. In addition, these three designs all provide quantitative or numeric data for analysis to help the researcher answer the research question. But what if the researcher needs something beyond numbers to answer the research question? In this case, the researcher must review research designs that provide qualitative data.

Qualitative Research Designs

As previously mentioned, the use of quantitative research designs is not appropriate for all research projects. For many studies, the researchers want to examine the experience as a whole, not just a limited number of variables. In these cases, a qualitative design is needed. Qualitative research designs provide data that have a different focus and purpose than the data from quantitative designs. The experimental, correlation, and survey designs all focus on gathering data on two or more specific variables noted in the research question. In qualitative designs, the focus is entirely different and much broader than two or more variables. Qualitative research designs focus on the entire experience, occurrence, or phenomenon, not on specific variables. The researcher gathers data in the form of observations, interviews, artifacts, and notes from the field. Three qualitative designs may be used by researchers depending on the purpose of the study and the research question. The three options are (1) ethnographic design, (2) historical design, and (3) case study design.

Ethnographic Design

In the **ethnographic research design,** the purpose of the research is to record the everyday life practices and daily occurrences of an individual, group, or culture. The researcher can live with the subjects or follow their daily routine for an extended period of time. The researcher wants to understand what it is like to be part of the group being studied. An example of how this study design could be used is studying the culture of white-water river guides. This particular occupation has its own culture, which is a lifestyle that involves values, dress, language, attitudes, and norms. To fully understand this subculture, the researcher must spend time within the culture and must document the cultural components. The researcher could live and work side by side with the guides (working as a river guide himself), or the researcher could spend a season among the guides observing them on a daily basis.

This type of study design could also be used to better understand the gang culture. Law enforcement agencies, recreation agencies, and other social service agencies are constantly trying to understand the gang culture. These agencies want to learn how to break the cycle of young people joining local gangs and continuing the lifestyle. To understand the gang culture, the researcher must study it from the inside and learn about the daily lifestyle from the gang members themselves. Once the culture is understood, agencies can better plan interventions to try to stop young people from choosing that lifestyle.

When using the ethnographic research design, the researcher is focused on gathering data holistically about what is being studied (e.g., gang culture or white-water rafting guides) in order to fully understand the subculture. This requires the researcher to gather data about every aspect of the daily lives of the people, not just one or two variables. This comprehensive data collection provides very rich data that can be analyzed to formulate conclusions and to answer the research questions for the study.

Historical Design

In some qualitative studies, the researcher wants to gather data related to other elements beyond what is occurring in today's society. Researchers often want to understand where we came from in a particular area in order to better understand where we are today in relation to our culture. The purpose of the **historical research design** is to investigate and record the development of a particular activity, attitude, or idea through time. An example of a historical study would

Studying the culture of white-water river guides is an example of ethnographic research design.

be to historically document the development of in-line skating. The researcher would gather information about the introduction of in-line skates and what they were used for initially. The researcher would then investigate and document the explosion of recreational in-line skating, in-line hockey leagues, and competitive sports that use in-line skates.

Another historical study could focus on documenting the development of snowboarding, from the development of the first snowboard to becoming an Olympic event. Many topics or studies could be explored through a historical study design. If the purpose of the study is to research and document the development of something—such as a phenomenon or trend—the historical design should be used. The historical design allows the researcher to investigate the factors that influenced the development of a phenomenon. This enables the researcher to understand how the phenomenon developed through time and to predict where this particular phenomenon may progress to in the future. In this type of qualitative design, the researcher must dedicate time to interviews and must examine other data sources to fully capture and understand the developmental process of what is being studied. As with the ethnographic research design, the historical design has a distinct purpose that can provide valuable information to guide future programs and services in the parks and recreation industry.

Case Study Design

The **case study** design is used frequently within the field of parks and recreation. A case study focuses on gathering very comprehensive data about an individual or a small group of individuals. An ethnographic study examines a culture as a whole, while the case study focuses on only a limited number of individuals within a subculture. An example of a case study project is conducting a study of low-income single mothers in the local community. The researcher would interview a limited number of low-income single mothers to identify their needs, desires, and preferences for recreational services and programs. The park and recreation programmer would then take this information and use it to guide the agency's future plans for serving this particular section of the community.

The case study design focuses on gathering extensive data from a limited number of people in order to comprehensively understand the topic. This type of study can be used with one individual, such as a disabled child, or with a small group of individuals. Case study research provides foundational knowledge about a particular individual or a group of people who have not been previously studied. In other words, there is limited or no information available within the literature about people similar to those who the case study will research. The information gathered during a case study and the conclusions from the case study will help guide future research efforts regarding the same individual or group of individuals.

The qualitative study designs all have distinctly different purposes, and they use different processes to gather data. Each study design focuses on gathering data to document the development of a phenomenon or to understand the cultural components of a subgroup of people. These qualitative designs, as well as the quantitative designs discussed earlier, generally focus on components within the community that are external to the agency. To investigate and resolve a problem that is internal to the agency, a researcher would use the action research design.

Action Research

Every park and recreation agency has very specific problems, issues, and needs that are unique to that agency. Agencies struggle with customer service issues, park management issues, and resources issues that are unique to each particular agency. The **action research** design is the method used in situations that are internal concerns within the agency. Action research can be either a quantitative or qualitative study design, but the study focuses on answering a research question that is unique to the agency. The study has limited application to other agencies because each agency is different. Additionally, an action research study can use an experimental, correlation, survey, case study, ethnographic, or historical design. The focus of the study is always on a current problem for the organization.

For example, at one agency, the registration process for classes and programs has generated a large number of customer complaints each registration cycle. The director decides it is time to identify the issues causing the complaints so that the agency can develop a plan to try to eliminate the sources of the complaints. Each park and recreation agency has a variety of registration options for its customers. In this case, the director determines that the complaints focused on the telephone registration option for the agency. With this information, the director decides to set up a

PROFESSIONAL PERSPECTIVES

■ The real world of parks and recreation

A goal of many park and recreation agencies is to develop a broad range of partnerships with local school boards, the chamber of commerce, private companies, nonprofits, and federal agencies. One such example is a university park and recreation department formalizing a partnership with the U.S. Forest Service regarding a recreation area. In this partnership, the academic community agreed to manage the property, conduct programs, and provide service while giving their students real work experiences to help develop their professional skills. The two organizations formalized their partnership by signing a memorandum of understanding, which is a type of government contract. The faculty and students (undergraduate, graduate, and doctorial) managed the facility year-round for four years without revisiting the goals, objectives, and vision of this partnership.

By the end of the fourth year, the relationship between the agencies had deteriorated. The students believed that their responsibility focused too much on maintenance, cleaning, and bookkeeping instead of program development and research. A doctorial student decided to investigate the intent of the partnership, the desired outcomes of the partnership, and the perception of each partner concerning the role of each as specified in the memorandum of understanding. The student unearthed a can of worms that highlighted a vast difference between the university's perception of what they should be doing and the active role of the Forest Service in this partnership. These perceptions and expectations were vastly different from the views of the Forest Service regarding its relationship with the concessionaire (the university).

Why was research important in this case?

The research conducted to analyze this partnership after four years was critical to defining the problem areas within the partnership. Without identifying the problem areas, there would be no plan to bring both partners to the table to resolve the issues, and the partnership would have been dissolved. The use of research and evaluation is vitally important when working with partners. The purpose, intent, and outcomes of the partnership should be evaluated on an annual basis to optimize the benefits for both partners, to build sustainable relationships, and to resolve problems or issues.

phone bank and to have one call-in number with 15 staff members available to answer questions and register individuals for programs. In the past, customers called in to four different sites for this service, and at any given time, only four people were available to answer questions and register people for programs. With the implementation of this new telephone registration operation, the complaints about registration dropped by 75 percent.

Obviously, this was an effective strategy for this particular agency, but it may not be feasible for other agencies. This is a key feature of action research; the results are not expected to be applicable to any other agency than the agency that conducted the study. This focused effort assists agencies in investigating agency-specific problems, issues, and needs. The agency can then develop a plan of action that uses the available resources of that agency. In this example, a type of correlation study was used. The researchers examined the relationship between the frequency of customer complaints and increased staff working registration with a centralized process in place. In action research, the researcher has the option of choosing any type of study design while trying to resolve a problem for the agency.

Table 3.1 provides a summary of the research designs that are used most frequently in the field of parks and recreation.

■ *TEST YOUR SKILLS WITH EXERCISES 3.1 THROUGH 3.6.*

• *TABLE 3.1* •
Research Design Options

Study design	Purpose	Variables	Type
Experimental	Cause and effect	Manipulate variables	Quantitative
Correlation	Relationships	No manipulation of variables	Quantitative
Survey	Descriptive	No manipulation of variables	Quantitative
Ethnographic	Understand culture	No variables used	Qualitative
Historical	Document development	No variables used	Qualitative
Case study	Understand one person or small group	No variables used	Qualitative
Action research	Solve internal problem or issue of the agency	No manipulation of variables	Quantitative or qualitative

Conclusion

The research problem and research questions focus the intent of the study for the researcher. These two initial steps in the scientific research process guide the remaining steps of the planning process for a study. The research questions are a way to clearly communicate whether the study is being conducted using the scientific method of inquiry, evaluation research, or action research. In addition, the research questions communicate whether the study is a quantitative or qualitative study. The research questions also communicate and guide the study procedures, no matter what study design is being used. The research design of the study determines the methods that are used to gather and analyze data. These foundational steps are critically important because they help ensure that the study examines what it is intended to examine. They also help ensure that the study provides the results needed to answer the research questions.

EXERCISES

■ Exercise 3.1: Identifying Types of Research

For each statement, note what type of research is being referred to. Choose from the following research designs:

Experimental   Survey   Case study   Historical
Correlation   Action   Ethnographic

1. Researchers examine the cause-and-effect relationship between variables.
2. Researchers manipulate a variable in the study.
3. Researchers examine the strength of a relationship.
4. Researchers gather numerical data on two variables, but they do not manipulate the variables.
5. Researchers control the environment of the study, as in a laboratory.
6. Researchers gather data on beliefs, attitudes, and preferences.

7. Researchers gather data to describe a population.

8. Researchers gather numeric data. (three answers)

9. Researchers gather data in the form of words or observations. (four answers)

10. Researchers measure variables. (three answers)

11. Researchers use artifacts to trace the development of the activity.

12. The study is used to understand a culture or a subculture.

13. The study is used to address a problem within an agency.

14. The results of the study do not apply beyond the agency.

15. Researchers study one individual or a small group of individuals.

16. Researchers seek to understand the "whole" of something, not specific variables. (three answers)

▪ Exercise 3.2: Applying the Types of Research Design

For each of the seven research designs, use the following problem statement regarding obesity to complete the information for a study that will address the problem.

The investigators are concerned about the increasing rate of childhood obesity among 11- to 14-year-old girls. The recreation department's largest program is the aquatic program. This area includes swimming lessons, open swim, and an outdoor pool. The agency wants to use the aquatics program to combat the obesity problem for this group.

Problem: Obesity epidemic

1. Experimental design: What experimental study could be conducted to address the problem? Describe the study:

   What is the treatment variable?

   What is the outcome variable?

   The purpose of this study is to measure the effect of _____ on _____.

2. Correlation design: What correlation study could be completed to investigate the obesity problem? Describe the study:

   What is variable 1?

   What is variable 2?

   The purpose of this study is to measure the strength of the relationship between _____ and _____.

3. Survey design: What descriptive information should be gathered about the needs of the group? Describe it:

   Variable 1:

   Variable 2:

   Variable 3:

   The purpose of this study is to _____.

4. Ethnographic design: What could be examined in an ethnographic study in order to better understand this subgroup? Describe it:

   Subculture to investigate in relation to the problem:

   The purpose of this study is to _____

   _____.

5. Case study design: How could a case study assist in investigating the obesity problem in 11- to 14-year-old girls? Describe the case study:

   What person will be studied?

   What will be investigated?

   The purpose of this study is to _____

   _____ .

6. Historical design: What historical elements are important to the investigation of the obesity problem? Describe these elements:

   The purpose of this study is to _____

   _____ .

7. Action research design: What can the agency do in relation to the problem? Describe the action research study:

   The purpose of this study is to _____

   _____ .

■ Exercise 3.3: Qualitative Research Questions

For each of the following research designs, write a research question related to the problem of gang activity in the local community. For example, the research question could address the gang culture, gang recruitment, gang criminal activity, or the recreational needs or preferences of gangs.

1. Ethnographic research question:
2. Case study research question:
3. Historical research question:
4. Action research question:

■ Exercise 3.4: Quantitative Research Questions

For each of the following research designs, write a research question related to evaluating the agency's day camp program. For example, the research question could address staff, location, program content, or the registration process.

1. Case study research question:
2. Correlation research question:
3. Survey research question:
4. Action research question:

■ Exercise 3.5: What Type of Research Question?

For each of the following research questions, identify the type of research study that should be used to answer the question. Select from these research designs:

Experimental	Survey	Ethnographic	Historical
Correlation	Case study	Action	

1. What is the effect of participation in a Junior Ranger program covering Leave No Trace practices on the amount of litter in the national park?
2. What is the relationship between taking swimming lessons and purchasing a season pass for the aquatic facility?
3. What types of recreation programs do parents in the community prefer for their children?

4. How did snowboarding become an Olympic sport?

5. What recreation activities does John (an autistic boy) prefer?

6. Why do teenagers join a gang instead of some other community group?

7. What is the best method for advertising the programs of the XYZ recreation center (mail, e-mail, or online)?

8. What recommendations do parents have to improve the day camp program?

9. Which of the previous questions are from quantitative studies? (List the question numbers.)

10. Which of the previous questions are from qualitative studies? (List the question numbers.)

■ Exercise 3.6: Article Review

Review the research articles used in exercise 1.2 and complete the following:

1. Article:
   a. What is the research problem?
   b. What is the purpose of the study?
   c. What are the research questions for the study?
   d. Is the research design in the study quantitative or qualitative?
   e. What research design is used in the study?

2. Article:
   a. What is the research problem?
   b. What is the purpose of the study?
   c. What are the research questions for the study?
   d. Is the research design in the study quantitative or qualitative?
   e. What research design is used in the study?

CASE STUDY

Many public park and recreation agencies partner with the local school district to run recreation programs and services through local community schools. The current challenge is that the recreation department's use of the school facilities has become increasingly limited. The number of days and number of hours per day that the recreation department has use of the school are decreasing. The department's access to school facilities falls very short of what is needed to meet the needs of the local community for afternoon, evening, and weekend programs. What would you do about this deteriorating relationship?

FOR THE INVESTIGATOR

The Health and Leisure Survey examines drug and alcohol use as well as recreation and fitness activities. The majority of the questions come from the CDC's Control Risk Assessment Survey that has been used nationally to analyze risk-taking behaviors in adolescents. This instrument was modified to meet the needs of the college campus and to provide the data needed for exercise and recreational interests. With this in mind, review the Health and Leisure Survey and answer the following questions:

1. What is a research problem that could be addressed using this survey?

2. What is the purpose of the study in which this survey would be used?

3. What are the research questions for this study?

4. What is the research design for this study? Why was this design selected?

5. Write a justification for this study. Do not describe what you think the solutions are; rather, explain why the resources should be dedicated to this study.

• OBJECTIVES •

After completing this chapter, you will be able to

- describe what a review of literature is,
- identify five benefits of conducting a review of literature, and
- understand the process used to identify literature related to a research topic.

Review of Literature

At the recreation facility where you work, the staff has been perplexed about the low involvement of the local Latino immigrants in the programs and services provided by the agency. The staff has tried various marketing techniques to inform the residents about the facility. However, all these efforts have failed to motivate the residents to take advantage of the programs, services, and facilities within walking distance of their homes. During a staff meeting, this topic was discussed, and the group decided that some type of research needed to be conducted. The research project would need to identify cultural elements within the Latino community, leisure interests and preferences of the community, and barriers to participation. The director appointed you as the leader of the team for this research project. You realize that your knowledge about the local Latino community and their culture is limited at best. You decide that the first step is to gather information to build the research team's foundational knowledge about this minority group. To do this, you must conduct a review of literature.

The review of literature sounds very intimidating, but it serves a very valuable purpose for every study. All researchers begin the research process with very limited or no information related to the research problem. The review of literature enables you to gain the necessary background information on the problem; otherwise, you would wander blindly through the research process. You cannot move forward in the research process until you complete this step. In this step, you should develop a good understanding of the problem, the issues related to the problem, and what has been done in the past to study and resolve the problem.

What Is a Review of Literature?

A **review of literature** is a comprehensive examination of information that exists related to the research topic. In the sample study, you are searching for information about the local Latino community, including the culture, recreational interests, and barriers to participation in recreational activities. For the review of literature, your goal is to gather "scholarly" information about the topic so that the research team can build their foundational knowledge related to the research project. In this case, you are seeking scholarly information or previous research on the Latino community. What is **scholarly literature?** Scholarly literature may be original research from a professional journal, information from textbooks and other books related to the research topic, or relevant information from professional trade journals. An example of a professional journal is *The Journal of Park and Recreation Administrators*. This journal has current research articles that can assist recreation professionals in the operations of their agency. Textbooks or other books that are available through a local bookstore can provide valuable information about the topic in more gen-

eral terms than a research journal article. Finally, professional trade magazines, such as *Parks and Recreation* (a monthly magazine from the National Recreation and Park Association), are filled with valuable information from different areas in the field. This provides you with information about programs, services, and operational considerations based on what is currently being done by park and recreation agencies. The process of evaluating the quality of information is covered in more detail within this chapter.

Why Conduct a Review of Literature?

As the team leader on the research project, you know that your knowledge (and the team's knowledge) about the Latino community is very limited. You cannot move forward in the research process until you develop knowledge about the study topic. The process of reviewing the literature provides a number of benefits that assist the researcher in planning a study. Figure 4.1 identifies many of these benefits.

By reviewing research articles and other forms of literature, the researcher can identify factual information and theories that have been documented in relation to the research topic. This information can assist the researcher in developing the research problem, the focus of the study, and the justification for the study. By reviewing the existing research on the topic, the researcher is better informed about the focus of previous research and how previous studies have been conducted. If valuable knowledge about the research topic already exists, the researcher saves time and resources by not repeating a study that has already been conducted. On the other hand, previous research studies can provide valuable information to assist researchers in developing the

- Identifies theories and factual information related to the research topic
- Clarifies the problem, focus, and justification for the study
- Helps develop research questions
- Identifies what has been studied or needs to be investigated further
- Saves time and effort in the development of the research or instrumentation plan

Figure 4.1   Benefits of a review of literature.

research plan and process for their study. Through the review of literature, the researcher can often identify how to conduct the study, what data to collect, what data collection techniques to use, and how to analyze the data. The information obtained from the literature can serve as a map to guide the planning process for the current study. The review of literature is a critical step in the research process. This step builds the researcher's knowledge on the topic and provides valuable information to assist the researcher in the planning process for a study.

How to Find Literature

The literature review should focus on gathering information from three sources:

1. General references
2. Primary sources
3. Secondary sources

By gathering information from these three areas within the literature, you can develop a comprehensive understanding of your research topic. These sources will provide valuable information to assist you in developing your research topic and your research plan.

General References

The first step in the review of literature is to search through **general references**—which serve as an index or database—for books, articles, and research studies related to the topic of the study. This initial search enables you to identify primary and secondary literature components that you may want to review. Searching the general references can save you valuable time in your review of literature. This step provides you with a list of abstracts containing descriptions of articles, books, or other documents. You can review the descriptions to determine how relevant or usable the sources are for the study you are conducting.

To search general references, you must familiarize yourself with the academic electronic database at your local university by making an appointment with a reference librarian. Academic electronic databases are search engines that are specific to scholarly works, such as books, journals, and other documents. Institutions subscribe to individual databases and then organize those databases into discipline clusters such as psychology, sociology, and recreation or leisure. Most databases also include multidisciplinary search engines, such as EBSCO, that have multidisciplinary clusters of information.

To search the databases, you use key terms related to the literature that you're looking for. The research librarian can assist you in identifying the key terms and how to search the various databases. The term or terms that you use to search a database may yield a limited number of hits or an abundance of hits. If the number of hits is limited, you should examine the key words that are listed for a number of the sources found in the initial search. This is a good way to identify other key terms that you can use to search for literature. The research librarian can help you identify alternative search terms to either expand or narrow your search so you can locate relevant pieces of literature. The results of the database search may identify a wide variety of options, including citations, abstracts, and full-text articles. Many times the database or library will not have a hard copy or electronic copy of the article or publication that you want to review. In these cases, your best option is to use the interlibrary loan option to acquire the article or book that you need for your study.

Secondary Sources

The best examples of **secondary sources** are textbooks and books. The information contained in books is not new knowledge; rather, it is current and existing knowledge that is presented in a different manner. For example, you could search the general references for publications related to Latino culture, recreational interests, and barriers to recreational participation. This search will result in books and textbooks that examine the Latino culture. These books can help you gain a general understanding of the Latino culture, which serves as the foundational knowledge you need for planning your study.

By reviewing the secondary sources, you begin to develop a general understanding of the Latino culture, but you need more specific information about recreational interests and barriers to participation in recreational activities. Where do you look for more specific information? One resource for this information is the references or bibliography list within the books you reviewed. This is a process that works backward through the literature, beginning with a current book and working backward through the resources used to develop the content of the book. Reviewing the references of a book will often help you identify primary sources of literature to examine.

Primary Sources

What is a **primary source** of literature? An example of a primary source of literature is a research article published in a professional journal. The person who conducted the research is the author of the journal article. Every profession has research journals, and the field of park and recreation is no exception. Most professional organizations within this field have some type of journal that provides information about current research in the field; the articles are written by the people who conducted the study. These journals are reviewed by peers before publication. A peer review is when an expert panel reviews the submitted work to ensure that the work is written according to publication guidelines. The panel will also verify that the researchers followed the professional standards that guide the research process and the reporting of research. The traditional format of a peer-reviewed article includes the same components as a completed academic thesis. These components include the abstract, introduction, materials and methods, results, discussion, acknowledgments, and references. With this being said, you must remember that all research journal articles are not created equal. As a researcher, you must evaluate the quality and relevance of each journal article. Each article should be evaluated separately on its own merits using the criteria listed in figure 4.2.

As a researcher, you should begin your review of literature by first searching general references. From there, you identify secondary sources. And finally, you move on to primary sources of literature to discover more specific information about how to conduct your research study. If you approach the literature review in this manner, you will move from more general knowledge of your research area to more specific information about how to conduct the study. This is a logical progression that ensures that the researcher has the information needed to plan and conduct a research project.

Internet Information

Without question, the Internet is the easiest and fastest source of information in today's technological society. But, not all Internet sites are equal. Your search for information during the literature review should be focused on professional journals, books, and scholarly research articles that are of the highest quality possible. A general search engine such as Google, Yahoo, or Dogpile can provide you with hundreds of links from a basic keyword search; however, there is no way to evaluate the quality of this information. Information located through these search engines does not undergo the quality assurance checks that occur with scholarly journals, books, and professional publications. Another source of information from the Internet is referred to as RSS (Really Simple Syndication). RSS can provide higher-quality information than is found using a general search engine.

RSS is an Internet-based communication process that is essentially equivalent to publishing a want ad. When you subscribe to an RSS feed, a selected Web site will automatically forward information to you about your chosen topic. Any information related to the topic is forwarded to

- Who is the author?
- What are the author's qualifications to write on this subject?
- Is the author affiliated with an institution? Is the author writing to push the institution's agenda or opinion?
- Is the information reliable and accurate? To judge this, you must determine the sources used in writing the article. Were they journals, trade magazines, or something Googled from the Internet? Check the bibliography of the article.
- Was the publication reviewed by an editor, or was it peer reviewed?
- Does the information appear to be unbiased, or does it appear to be pushing a particular opinion or agenda?

Figure 4.2 Criteria used to evaluate literature.

■ The real world of parks and recreation

I have to admit that literature review is not the most exciting use of my time, but it is the most rewarding in the long run. Obviously, the literature review is a critical element in any research endeavor, but I also use it in curriculum and program planning. My first research professor said, "There is no such thing as original research." I couldn't understand how he could say that. Every month the professional journals I read were loaded with "original investigations." Once I began my research project, I realized that every published research article was built on research that had preceded it. And as much as I relied on the works that helped steer me through my first research project, I became even more dependant on reviewing professional literature when I was out in the field building educational and promotional programs. Let me share an example of how a review of literature helped me in the program planning process.

I was working for a reproductive health clinic in a small midwestern town. Our client population was predominantly low-income women and teens. The data we kept indicated that there was an increasing rate of unintended pregnancies among adolescents. We were naturally concerned, not only because of the multiple health risks to the young mothers and infants, but also because of the long-term socioeconomic impact on families and the community. We shared our concerns with the local health department. Their data, which were pooled with data from private practices, indicated a larger community-wide increase in adolescent pregnancies. The result was the formation of an adolescent pregnancy task force that included local health care practitioners, business leaders, school personnel, social workers, clergy, parents, and youth.

Our first order of business was to determine how best to address the problem. Obviously, education was identified as a key component, but the schools were limited in their ability to expand the sex education curriculum. Educational and promotional literature could be used, but distribution venues were limited because of the conservative nature of the community. Results from our focus groups indicated that the adolescent population was very interested in learning more about sexuality and safe sex. The results also indicated that the adolescents didn't think they got what they wanted and needed from schools or home. They wanted someplace they could go—outside of the classroom, home, or church—where they could get the information they need from trusted sources who would not ask, "Why do you want to know about *that*?" We decided to hold a one-day workshop for teens to coincide with a teachers workshop (no school) day.

Why was research important in this case?

We had already reviewed some of the relevant literature related to the nature and scope of the problem. This helped us build our case with the community regarding the need for a program. Next, we had to identify the social, cultural, and environmental factors affecting adolescent sexual behaviors. This information, in addition to the information we received through our focus groups, helped us clearly define our objectives, identify appropriate tools and resources, and construct both impact and outcome evaluation tools. It also helped us produce effective marketing and promotional materials and develop a grant proposal to fund our program.

Without making a long story longer, the result was a SUCCESS! We got a grant. We had a great turnout. Participants loved the program, learned a lot, and retained the information and knowledge for at least 6 months. Parents, teachers, and other members of the community were satisfied. (We had a lot of requests to make it an annual event.) I moved from the community to take another job, but colleagues whom I kept

(continued)

(continued)

in touch with told me that data for the next three years showed a decrease in the rates of adolescent pregnancy AND sexually transmitted infections. Best of all, 15 years later, two of my nieces recalled the event, and they said that not only were they grateful for the opportunity but their parents were grateful as well.

you as soon as it is posted on or becomes available through the Web site. To help you sort incoming information, you can set up several accounts through various feed readers. This enables you to categorize incoming content. After a preliminary analysis of incoming information, you can choose to print, save, delete, or forward the feeds for storage. Once the review of literature is completed, you will have a large volume of information that needs to be organized for the research project.

Synthesizing the Literature

When completing a review of literature, one of the greatest challenges is trying to pull together or synthesize the information in a logical and coherent manner. Researchers often want to list a summary of each book or article reviewed. This is the wrong approach to synthesizing the information; instead, you should present the information by concept or topic. This presents a more logical progression through the information collected during the review of literature. To do this, you must synthesize information from all the sources of literature topic by topic, and you must present each topic individually. The information for each topic area is then presented in one or more paragraphs. For example, in the research study about the Latino community, you would take all the information about the culture and weave it together, noting similarities and differences in the literature. You may find 10 or more sources on the topic and discover similar things stated in each source. You can take this information and write a few paragraphs highlighting the more important cultural considerations for your study. This information is used in developing the research problem, research question, and justification for the study. After pulling together or synthesizing the most important information from the literature, you are prepared to plan the study and educate others about the importance of conducting the proposed research project.

For the proposed study of the local Latino community, the review of literature will educate the team about the Latino culture and assist the

1. Read the article or publication.

2. Take each piece of literature and divide the information by topic, such as background, methods, conclusions, and recommendations.

3. Put like items from the literature together by topic. This can be done by cutting and pasting sections of articles (either on hard copy or electronically). You may also use note cards.

4. Revisit each topic area and further divide the information into subtopics. This puts all like items together so you can begin to see similarities and differences within the literature.

5. Now you can write each section of the review of literature and present both sides of the issues or topic.

Figure 4.3   Guidelines for synthesizing literature.

team in planning and conducting the study. This information helps ensure that the research team has the knowledge to efficiently and effectively plan a study that will answer the research questions. Figure 4.3 provides guidelines to follow when synthesizing literature from various sources. These steps help you organize the information you have gathered into a form that is manageable and that allows you to focus on the most important pieces.

■ TEST YOUR SKILLS WITH EXERCISES 4.1 AND 4.2.

Conclusion

As you can tell, no researcher should begin the planning process for a research or evaluation study without conducting a review of literature. The literature provides a wealth of information to educate the researcher about the research topic, which helps focus the researcher's efforts in the study. The scholarly literature from other researchers provides information that can assist you in determining what type of study to conduct, how to conduct it, and what variables to measure. If you skip or neglect this step in the research and evaluation process, you will be blindly wandering through the research process, wasting your time and the agency's resources. Take time to learn about your research topic and what has been published in relation to your topic. This effort can provide you with a guiding light that will make your research journey an enjoyable expedition without any detours or dead-end trails.

EXERCISES

■ Exercise 4.1: Review of Literature

Review the research articles used in exercise 1.2. For each article, select two articles from the bibliography of research article 1 and two from research article 2 and review those articles for the following information.

1. Article 1 from bibliography:
   a. What is the research problem in the article?
   b. How is this article useful to the study for which the articles was used as a source? Describe how.
2. Article 2 from bibliography:
   a. What is the research problem in the article?
   b. How is this article useful to the study? Describe how.
3. Article 1 from bibliography:
   a. What is the research problem in the article?
   b. How is this article useful to the study? Describe how.
4. Article 2 from bibliography:
   a. What is the research problem in the article?
   b. How is this article useful to the study? Describe how.

■ Exercise 4.2: Literature Search

Visit your campus library and complete the following scavenger hunt.

1. Identify two books related to recreational trends. (List the title, author, and publisher.)
   a.
   b.

2. Search a database (such as ERIC, Psylit, or Solit) to identify three scholarly articles that would be useful in identifying recreational trends on college campuses, drug and alcohol use on campus, or programs that have been conducted to combat drug and alcohol use on campus. List the following information for each scholarly article.

Article 1:
    a. Database searched:
    b. Key terms used in the search:
    c. Title of the article:
    d. Purpose of the study:
    e. Conclusion reached in the study:

Article 2:
    a. Database searched:
    b. Key terms used in the search:
    c. Title of the article:
    d. Purpose of the study:
    e. Conclusion reached in the study:

Article 3:
    a. Database searched:
    b. Key terms used in the search:
    c. Title of the article:
    d. Purpose of the study:
    e. Conclusion reached in the study:

Now return to the database and locate two articles in the National Recreation and Park Association *Park and Recreation Magazine* related to the obesity epidemic.

1. Article:
    Month of publication:
    Title of article:
    Summarize key points from the article in one paragraph:

2. Article:
    Month of publication:
    Title of article:
    Summarize key points from the article in one paragraph:

CASE STUDY

Pick a particular problem that your community is faced with, and explain how you would use the literature to assist you in addressing the problem.

FOR THE INVESTIGATOR

The review of literature is the most interesting exploration you will undertake during the research process. Revisit the research problem and research questions to determine what type of information you need to build your knowledge of the topic area.

1. For the sample study, several topics should jump out at you. What topics do you need to learn more about in relation to the study?

2. Now that you have identified the topic areas, it is time to search the literature for additional information. Visit the library and consult with the research librarian to complete the following:

    a. List five scholarly articles on the topics you have identified.

    b. List five secondary sources or articles on the topics you have identified.

    c. Visit the CDC Web site to learn more about the risk-taking behaviors of adolescents in your state. List the most significant ones here.

    d. Visit the Web site of the National Recreation and Parks Association to learn more about health and obesity issues nationally. Discuss the most significant issues here.

CHAPTER 5

• OBJECTIVES •

After completing this chapter, you will be able to

- describe how the different types of variables are used in research and evaluation,
- summarize the use of hypotheses and the advantages and disadvantages of using hypotheses,

- describe the various measurement scales and their relationship to variables and data analysis, and
- compare and contrast the use of variables, hypotheses, and data analysis in quantitative study design versus qualitative design.

Variables and Hypotheses in Study Designs

You are a young professional at your first job, and your boss asks you to develop an evaluation plan for the agency's swimming classes. The agency is preparing for the CAPRA accreditation process, and class evaluations are a required standard for accreditation. You try not to panic as you reflect back to your research methods class. The immediate questions you have are as follows: Should any type of relationship be examined? What variables should be measured? What measurement scale should be used for each variable during data analysis? Should a hypothesis be used? These questions are important steps in the research and evaluation process.

In research and evaluation, variables and hypotheses play a critical role in the design of the study. Variables and hypotheses provide a focused purpose for the study by determining what is being examined and why. A variable is a concept that can vary within the group of people being studied. A hypothesis is an educated guess about the outcomes of the study. The use of variables and hypotheses differs between quantitative and qualitative studies and can affect the design of the study. As discussed earlier, the design of a study can be experimental, correlation, survey, case study, historical, ethnographic, or action research. This chapter explains the purpose and use of variables and hypotheses. In addition, this chapter explores issues related to variables that can affect the analysis of data and the conclusions of the study. The use of variables and hypotheses hinges on what is being studied, which is often some type of relationship.

Relationships

In many research projects, the researchers study relationships. This can be done using the scientific method of research or the evaluation method. For example, an experimental study can be conducted to examine how exercise affects blood pressure. The researcher wants to determine if swimming five days a week lowers blood pressure. Another researcher wants to examine the relationship between people participating in the Step Up to Health program and their commitment to exercising in the future. Another park and recreation director wants to evaluate the customers' satisfaction with the new online registration procedures for the agency's programs. The director plans to do this by comparing the online procedures with the other methods for registration (mail-in, telephone, and walk-in registration). Each of these studies is examining relationships in some way.

Not all research questions address a relationship. A research question that asks "What are the demographic characteristics of the participants who register for the yoga class?" will not involve examining a relationship. The researchers for this study are simply looking to describe yoga participants by their demographic characteristics, such as age, sex, or socioeconomic status.

How does one examine relationships? The first step in this process is to identify the variables of the relationship that the researcher wants to investigate. Again, variables are concepts or items that vary within a group being studied. To better understand

variables, let's revisit the previous examples of relationships stated as research questions.

Within parks and recreation, programmers often want to determine what type of exercise would be best for specific groups of people. In this case, the programmer must conduct an experimental study with a particular group. One such study could be based on the experimental research question "Does swimming an hour a day five days a week lower blood pressure?" For this study, the researcher needs to determine who swims and who does not. The people selected to participate in the study would be people who have borderline high blood pressure. These people are not on medication for high blood pressure, but they are very likely to need this type of medication in the future. This study is examining how swimming affects blood pressure. The variables of the study are swimming and blood pressure. The researcher is investigating if swimming decreases a person's blood pressure or has no effect on the person's blood pressure.

Another situation that a programmer may face is studying relationships between specific variables where the variables are not manipulated. This type of study requires a correlation research question. Consider the question "What is the relationship between participating in Step Up to Health programs and the participant's commitment to exercising three times a week in the future?" This is a correlation research question that examines the relationship between participation in a program and commitment to exercising in the future. The variables that this study will examine are participating in the program and committing to exercise in the future. The researcher wants to determine how one is related to the other in hopes of identifying ways to increase people's commitment to exercise.

Another common situation for park and recreation professionals is the need to evaluate operational functions of the agency, such as the registration process, customer service, and staff training. The question "What is the level of customer satisfaction with the new online registration process for programs?" is an evaluation question related to the registration process of the agency. The variables that this study will examine are the levels of customer satisfaction and the registration process. The customers have several options that they can use for registration, but the park and recreation director is most interested in the new online registration option. The registration options that will be evaluated are the online process, mail-in process, telephone process, and walk-in registration. The director can compare the customer satisfaction levels for all these registration options.

Relationships serve as the foundation for a multitude of research questions within the field of parks and recreation. Experimental, correlation, and evaluation studies all examine relationships between variables, as demonstrated in the three examples in this section. The variables that are being studied are clearly stated in the research questions (i.e., swimming, blood pressure, participation in a program, commitment to exercise, customer satisfaction, and the online registration process). The relationships stated in these research questions focus the efforts of the study and specify the variables that will be examined in the study.

Variables

Variables determine what data will be collected and analyzed to answer the research question. The research question states the relationship that is being studied, but the variables are the precise items that will be measured. The measurements of these variables are done through the data collection process during the course of the study. Park and recreation professionals must be able to identify relationships, variables, and the types of variables used within quantitative studies to gather numeric data. Qualitative studies also use variables, but not in the same manner. Qualitative studies use variables to breakdown data by variables but not as numbers for statistical analysis of the data. The variables are used to sort and regroup the data for further analysis in order to develop themes within the data and to serve as the foundation of conclusions of the study.

Each of the sample research questions specifies a relationship that involves examining specific variables. The variables noted in the research question guide the study design and the data collection process. The variables stated in each question further focus the purpose of the study or evaluation. To better understand how variables are used in research and evaluations, you must look beyond the research question. The variables are used as a means to provide numeric data for analysis. To conduct statistical analysis, numbers are needed to represent the data for each variable. Several types of variables are used within research, including quantitative, categorical, independent, dependent, constant, and extraneous variables. As a future researcher or evaluator, you must understand the different types of variables and how they are used in research.

■ *TEST YOUR SKILLS WITH EXERCISE 5.1.*

Quantitative Variables

Within the park and recreation industry, one type of variable that is frequently used in research and evaluation is the **quantitative variable.** Quantitative variables are used within experimental studies, correlation studies, and evaluation studies. This is a variable that exists in varying degrees or is represented by an amount on a scale indicating more or less of something. The numbers indicate how much of that variable is present, such as weight, height, or a rating on a five-point scale of whether someone likes or dislikes something. In the previous section, several quantitative variables were included within the sample research questions.

In the first sample research question, the variables being studied are swimming and blood pressure. Swimming is not a quantitative variable. The subjects will either swim or not, which is a yes or no question. There is no variance with this variable; therefore, it is not a quantitative variable. Blood pressure is a quantitative variable because it varies in degree or on a continuum among people. The variance in blood pressure is represented by numbers.

In the second research question, the variables are participation in the program and commitment to exercise. Participation in the program is not a quantitative variable because it does not vary in amount or degree. A person either did or did not participate in the program. The other variable in this question—commitment to exercise—is a quantitative variable. This variable will be measured as a level of commitment on a five-point scale. People could range from having no commitment to having some commitment to being highly committed to future exercise.

The variables noted in the third research question are the level of customer satisfaction and the online registration process. The level of customer satisfaction is a quantitative variable. It will vary widely in degree among the people who complete the survey. The online registration process is not a quantitative variable because it does not vary in degree or amount. A person either did or did not use the online registration option.

Categorical Variables

A study within parks and recreation will often use one or two **categorical variables.** Experimental studies can use one quantitative variable and one categorical variable. Correlation studies can use one quantitative variable and one or two categorical variables. Evaluations and surveys frequently use one categorical variable within the study.

Categorical variables do not vary in degree, amount, or quantity. The numbers do not represent more or less of something but rather a category that can be used to sort data for analysis. The most frequent use of categorical data is to represent demographic data, such as sex, ethnicity, age, socioeconomic status, and marital status. For example, in a survey, participants may respond with 1 for male or 2 for female to indicate their sex. The 2 does not mean that women are twice as good as men; rather, it allows the researcher to break down data based on sex. The researcher can then analyze the differences between the responses of males and females on a particular issue. In addition, the researcher can look at how many males and females participated in the study. The responses for particular items may or may not vary based on sex.

In the study of customer satisfaction with the new online registration, the park and recreation director discovered that males prefer to use the online registration and females prefer to use the telephone registration option. Categorical variables—such as sex, age, marital status, and socioeconomic status—also permit the researcher to better understand the characteristics of the study group. Finally, statistical analysis cannot be performed using words, such as *male* or *female.* The use of numbers allows the researcher to perform statistical analysis that otherwise could not be performed with the data.

Categorical variables are included in each of the previous examples of research questions. In the first research question, the variable of swimming is a categorical variable; the participant either swims or does not swim. In the second research question, the categorical variable is participation in the Step Up to Health program; the study participants either participated in the program or did not participate in the program. In the third research question, the customer satisfaction with the new online registration process is a different use of a categorical variable. Within the agency, the customers can choose between

A participant either swims or doesn't swim, so swimming is a categorical variable.

mail-in registration, telephone registration, walk-in registration, or the new online registration process. The categorical variable is actually the registration process used by the customer. The data may be divided into the four different options or categories. The registration process does not vary in degree, but rather in the kind or type of registration process the customer used to register for programs.

Within evaluation, the categorical variable can also be the type of program the person participated in during the session. To evaluate programs and services of the agency, a number can be assigned to each type of class, program, or service. For example, a 1 is assigned to all beginner swimming classes, a 2 to all intermediate swimming classes, a 3 to stroke and turn clinics, a 4 to water aerobics, and a 5 to arthritis water aerobic classes. This use of a categorical variable permits the programmers to evaluate the classes and programs within each program type instead of all aquatic classes together. These results allow the programmer to compare different types of classes (e.g., compare beginner swimming to water aerobics) and to examine customer satisfaction with the content of the class, the instructors, and the facilities. The programmer can then determine which programs or classes are most liked and which ones are most disliked by the customers. This helps the programmer develop recommendations for changes to the program schedule or to the content of the classes for the next program cycle.

Experimental Variables

The next types of variables that must be discussed are the variables that are only used in experimental research. These variables are called independent variables and dependent variables, and they are always used together within experimental studies.

Independent Variables In an experimental study, only one variable is manipulated. This variable is often considered the "treatment" administered to the subjects. The **independent variable** can be either a quantitative variable or a categorical variable. For example, the treatment may be the exercise program a person participates in, such as swimming. The variable that the researcher purposely manipulates is the independent variable. In the research question "What are the effects of swimming five days a week on a person's blood pressure?" the independent variable is swimming. The researcher purposely assigns people to a swimming group and a nonswimming

group. The treatment is to swim five days a week. The researcher then wants to measure the effects of swimming on each person's blood pressure at the end of six weeks.

Dependent Variables The variable that is measured to determine the effect of the treatment is the **dependent variable.** This is also called the **outcome variable.** In the research question "What are the effects of swimming five days a week on a person's blood pressure?" the dependent variable is blood pressure. The results of the dependent variable are dependent on the independent variable. In this case, the difference in blood pressure is dependent on whether the person swam five days a week or not. The dependent variable is not manipulated but rather serves as the indicator of the effect of the treatment. The dependent variable in experimental studies is usually a quantitative variable, which measures changes that other types of variables cannot measure. The terms *dependent variable* and *independent variable* are not used in evaluation research because the environment of the evaluation study cannot be controlled for the experiment.

Experimental research generally occurs in a clinical setting where the researcher can determine what to manipulate (independent variable), who will participate in the study, and what outcome to measure (dependent variable). Residential training centers for people diagnosed with mental retardation can be found throughout the United States. A recreation therapist is employed as part of the treatment team, which includes psychologists, direct care staff, social workers, and other professionals. In one of these centers, the team identified a problem that involved a group of residents showing a marked increase in aggressive and disruptive behavior during the evening hours and during the weekends. This particular group of residents was physically active and appeared to enjoy physical activities. The treatment team decided to try an experiment that would provide these individuals with additional recreation time every evening to determine if this would decrease the incidence of aggressive and disruptive behavior. In this study, the independent (or manipulated) variable was additional time at the gym where the residents were engaged in physical activities (the majority of their day was spent passively sitting in classes). The dependent variable was the frequency of aggressive or disruptive behaviors displayed by the selected residents each day. The results of this experiment concluded that the additional active recreation time in the gym significantly decreased the incidence of aggressive and disruptive behaviors for these residents. As a result of this study, the training center hired an additional employee whose job is to plan, organize, and conduct evening and weekend recreational activities that involve physical activity for specific groups of residents at the training center. In this particular example, the independent variable was a categorical variable, and the dependent variable was a quantitative variable.

■ *TEST YOUR SKILLS WITH EXERCISE 5.2.*

Constant Variables

Within certain studies, a researcher wants to have one variable that is the same for all subjects in the study, such as sex or age. This type of variable is a **constant variable.** This is a simple concept that is useful within research and evaluation studies. A constant variable is a variable that is held constant or is the same for all people within the study. The research question will generally state the constant variable to be used in the study. For example, a fitness center director notices that people who attend aerobics classes are all female and that the majority of people using the free weights are male. The center director wants to identify fitness classes that would attract men; however, the director is not sure what would be appealing to men. The director decides to survey the center's male members to identify what fitness classes the men want at the center. The constant in this study is men. This is done because the fitness center director wants the study to focus specifically on men only, not women. Constants can be selected from a wide variety of characteristics beyond sex, including age, geographic area, marital status, parental status, or membership. The constant is identified through the research problem and research question, and it serves as a key variable within the study. The use of a constant variable allows equal comparisons among the group being studied (in other words, the study is comparing apples to apples rather than apples to oranges).

Extraneous Variables

The variable that presents a challenge in all research projects is an **extraneous variable.** Research projects may include many variables that are being studied, but researchers also need to identify other variables that may affect the study. Extraneous variables are present in every type of study, and they can influence the results of the study without the researcher's knowledge.

In other words, the changes seen in the study may be due to the effects of the extraneous variables, not the variables being studied. Researchers need to identify these variables and minimize their impact within the study. An example of the impact of extraneous variables can be seen in an outdoor adventure program that works with at-risk youth. The program staff takes the teens through a specific sequence of outdoor activities. These experiences are used as the foundation for the teens to reflect on their own paths and the choices they are facing in their lives. The goal of this program is to move the teens onto a path that is productive for their future, not destructive. The staff begins to see progress regarding the behaviors of the teens and the focus in their lives. Then the teens go home to the same environment that created this at-risk youth. The home environment is the extraneous variable that the program staff cannot control; they do not know what occurs inside the home. Is the teen neglected, verbally abused, or physically abused? Does a parent abuse drugs or alcohol? The home environment affects the results of this program as an extraneous variable that the researchers cannot control.

Some steps can be taken to control extraneous variables. In this case, learning more about the home environment of the teens can better equip the staff to directly address these negative influences in their lives. Another option for controlling extraneous variables is to treat them as a constant within the study. For example, sex, ethnicity, or age can be an extraneous variable that affects the results of the study or evaluation. The researcher can easily use these variables as constants by only including people with predetermined characteristics in the study. This enables the researcher to control the impact of the extraneous variables on the results of the study.

Use of Variables

Researchers and evaluators can use many combinations of variables to study relationships or gather data. A study can use two quantitative variables, two categorical variables, or one quantitative variable and one categorical variable. The purpose of the study and the research question will identify the variables that are being investigated in the study. The researcher gathers data on the identified variables for statistical analysis to formulate conclusions. This entire process falls within the quantitative study design. For qualitative studies, the use of variables is very different than for quantitative studies. The data collected in qualitative studies tend to be "words" and are analyzed using a coding process, not statistical analysis. The variables identified in qualitative studies come from the data analysis process and are not identified at the beginning of the study, as in quantitative studies. This difference is critical to keep in mind when developing a study or evaluation plan.

Hypotheses

At this point in the study, the researcher has determined the research design, has developed the research question, and has specifically identified the variables to study. Depending on the study design, the researcher now has a choice to make—whether or not to use a hypothesis. **Hypotheses** can be used in experimental studies and correlation studies, but they are not used in survey studies. Survey studies do not involve studying a relationship, but rather developing descriptions.

What is a hypothesis? A hypothesis is a prediction about the outcome of the study or the relationship between the variables. Using a hypothesis is not appropriate in some studies, such as a survey or qualitative study. When a hypothesis is used, the researcher has two choices: a **directional hypothesis** or a **nondirectional hypothesis.** A directional hypothesis predicts a specific change in a variable. A nondirectional hypothesis predicts that there will be a difference but does not predict the direction of the difference.

Table 5.1 provides research questions to examine regarding the use of hypotheses in research. Research questions 1 and 2 do not involve studying relationships of variables; therefore, a hypothesis is not used within either study. For research question 1, the researcher is seeking to describe customers based on key characteristics, not a relationship. For research question 2, the researcher is examining programs offered in relation to CAPRA accreditation standards. Research question 3, which is from a correlation study, has a directional hypothesis. The purpose of a correlation study is to examine the strength of the relationship between two variables. Therefore, a directional hypothesis is an appropriate choice within a correlation study. In the example in

• *TABLE 5.1* •

Research Questions, Variables, and Hypotheses

Research question	Variables	Hypothesis
1. What are the characteristics of our season pass holders (Idlewild Amusement and Water Park)?	Sex, age, socioeconomic status, geographic location, number of children in household, children's ages, number of season passes in household, number of visits per season	A hypothesis is not appropriate for this research question. The research will not involve studying a relationship.
2. What are the programs being offered for each age group as required in the CAPRA standards (park and recreation department)?	Programs, age groups (preschool age, elementary school age, middle school age, high school age, young adults, older adults, and seniors)	A hypothesis is not appropriate for this research question. The research will not involve studying a relationship.
3. What is the relationship between participation in the leisure education program and the rate of alcohol relapse after discharge (alcohol residential treatment program)?	Participation in the leisure education program and alcohol use relapse after discharge	As the rate of participation in the leisure education program increases, the rate of relapse will decrease.
4. Which of the following methods of encouraging Leave No Trace practices is most effective in reducing the amount of trash being left at campsites? Having rangers visit the site Providing the visitors with a brochure on Leave No Trace when they check in at the campground	The methods being tested: (1) a ranger or staff member visiting the campsite and talking with people about Leave No Trace and (2) providing the visitors with a brochure on Leave No Trace when they check in at the campground	There will be a difference in the amount of trash left at the campsite depending on the method used to communicate the Leave No Trace practices.

table 5.1, the researcher is making a directional prediction that participation in a leisure education program will decrease the frequency of relapsing. Research question 4 has a nondirectional hypothesis. This hypothesis predicts a difference but does not predict a decrease in the amount of trash being left at the campsite. The hypothesis allows for the possibility that there could be an increase of trash being left, depending on the method used to communicate the Leave No Trace practices. A better hypothesis for this research question would be to specifically predict which of the two methods will yield the best results (such as the ranger visiting the campsite to explain the Leave No Trace practices).

Advantages of Using Hypotheses

The use of a hypothesis within a study presents both advantages and disadvantages to the researcher (table 5.2). An advantage of using a hypothesis is that it requires the researcher to narrowly focus the study and dig deeply into all the possible results of the study. The review of literature assists the researcher in narrowing down the scope and focus of the study. By reviewing previous studies on the topic, the researcher can examine the variables used and can learn from the recommendations the researchers made for future studies. In the example of the Leave No Trace efforts at campsites, the researcher learns from the literature that several methods are used in the field to educate visitors on Leave No Trace practices. The most frequently used methods are providing a brochure at check-in and having a staff member visit each campsite to talk about Leave No Trace practices. The previous studies did not examine each method independently of each other through the course of the entire campground season with different users. This information helps the researcher identify the variables that need to be studied. It also helps the researcher

determine how to study the relationship and make a prediction about the most effective way to educate campground visitors.

Disadvantages of Using Hypotheses

Some disadvantages are also associated with the use of a hypothesis in research. The greatest drawback of using a hypothesis in a study is that it can lead the researcher to bias the data collection and analysis. When this occurs, the researcher conducts the data collection and analysis in a way that proves the hypothesis to be true. This could be done unconsciously where the researcher only looks for data that verify or validate the hypothesis. Bias is a significant disadvantage that leads into the second disadvantage—overlooking other important data. In the study regarding Leave No Trace practices, the aspect of educating children is overlooked as a possible means of educating campers. This could be a critical component because children can influence their parents' behavior at the campsite, thus reducing the amount of trash left at the campsite. When developing quantitative studies, the researcher must first determine if using a hypothesis is appropriate within the study. If a hypothesis is used, steps must be taken to minimize any biases in data collection and the likelihood of overlooking other critical variables of the study. These steps are done during the planning stage of the study and are specified within the research procedures.

■ *TEST YOUR SKILLS WITH EXERCISE 5.3.*

Quantitative and Qualitative Studies

The use of hypotheses differs between quantitative and qualitative studies. In quantitative studies, the hypothesis is stated at the beginning of the study. This is not the case in qualitative studies. Not all qualitative studies conclude with a hypothesis, but if a hypothesis is used, it is the

• *TABLE 5.2* •

Advantages and Disadvantages of Using a Hypothesis

Advantages	Disadvantages
Requires the researcher to narrowly focus the study	May cause the researcher to use bias in the data collection and analysis
Requires the researcher to deeply study and research the topic area	May cause the researcher to be too focused and to overlook other important variables
Allows the researcher to learn from other similar studies	

conclusion of the study. In qualitative studies, data are gathered and analyzed so that the researchers can form a hypothesis about what is being studied. Qualitative studies begin with a very broad focus; through the research process, the researcher begins to narrow down the focus to formulate a hypothesis. In contrast, quantitative studies begin with a narrowly focused hypothesis and specific variables to investigate. Through the data collection process, the researcher seeks to apply the results of the study to a broader group of people. Regarding how hypotheses are used, the bottom line is that quantitative studies begin with a hypothesis and qualitative studies end with a hypothesis. Figure 5.1 provides a visual illustration of the use of hypotheses in quantitative and qualitative studies.

The Leave No Trace study could be conducted as a qualitative study. The researcher can include a limited number of people in the study but may want to apply the results to all visitors at the campground. In this qualitative study, the researcher wants to identify how educating children about the Leave No Trace practices influences the behavior of their parents. This study would provide ranger programs for the children. In these programs, the children learn about Leave No Trace and what they should and should not do at the campground. The researchers will then interview the parents of the children who attended the program before their departure from the campground. This interview would focus on how the parents' children influenced their behavior in applying the Leave No Trace practices. The researchers would then take the data and formulate a hypothesis that could be tested through future research efforts.

When deciding whether or not to use a hypothesis, the researcher should first consider the type of study being conducted (quantitative or qualitative). Then the researcher should consider the study design. Using a hypothesis is not appropriate in all studies. The researcher must determine whether the study design is appropriate for the use of a hypothesis. If a hypothesis is used, the researcher must also take steps to ensure that the data collection and analysis are not biased in order to validate the hypothesis. Once these decisions are made, the researcher must go back and further examine what type of variables are being used in the study.

Measurement Scales

Variables serve as the foundation within every study or evaluation that is performed using quantitative techniques. The variables in studies are

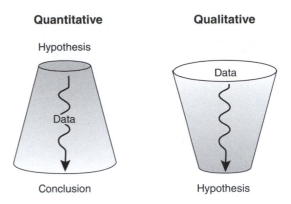

Figure 5.1 Visual illustration of the use of hypotheses in quantitative and qualitative studies.

either quantitative, categorical, or constant. They identify what is being studied, focus the efforts of the study, and determine the type of statistical analysis that can be performed with the data. To determine what analysis can be performed with the variables—both individually and in combinations—the researcher must identify the **measurement scale** for each variable. This is done during the planning process before any data are collected, not after the data collection. The type of analysis to be used in the study is specified in the research procedures for the research project. Four measurement scales are commonly used for variables: nominal, ordinal, interval, and ratio.

Nominal Measurement Scale

A **nominal measurement scale** is applied to categorical variables. The numbers serve the purpose of assisting the researcher in breaking down data by categories only. The categories could be sex, age, ethnicity, or any type of program. Research question 1 in table 5.1 has a multitude of variables. Each variable is a nominal measurement scale. The people taking the survey check the characteristic that applies to them. For example, for the variable "sex," the person either checks male or female. Nominal data provide the researcher with limited options for analysis. The data related to one nominal variable can be presented as the frequency, or the total number, within each category. The data can also be presented as a percentage of each option within the categorical variable. For example, a researcher surveyed 100 people; 54 of the participants were males, and 46 were females. The total number for each response option within the sex variable is the frequency. The percentage within the sex variable is 54 percent male and 46 percent female. Table 5.3 presents this information. Nominal data are most frequently used for summarizing demographic

● *TABLE 5.3* ●

Frequency Table and Percent for Descriptive Questions

	Male	Female	Total
Frequency	54	46	100
Percentage	54%	46%	100%

information in research, evaluation, or survey studies in order to describe the characteristics of the study participants. When a categorical variable is analyzed with another categorical variable or quantitative variable, more advanced statistical analysis can be performed with the data.

Ordinal Measurement Scale

The second type of measurement scale is the **ordinal scale.** This type of data is ranked in order (first, second, third, and so on) based on some attribute. The intervals between first, second, and third vary; they are not a standard interval. For example, the finish times for swimmers in a race represent an ordinal scale of measurement. The time between first, second, and third place varies from .09 second to several seconds. This variation in the intervals limits the type of statistical analysis that can be performed with the data because the intervals between the places are not a standard unit of measure. Table 5.4 provides ordinal data on the results of a swimming event. Another example of the ordinal measurement scale is a listing of exam scores in order. The instructor usually lists scores from highest to lowest. The number of points between first, second, and third highest score is not the same. This is the case for many of the test scores. This rank order listing of scores allows the instructor to view the scores and

● *TABLE 5.4* ●

Scores From the 100-Meter Freestyle Race

Lane	Time
2	57.0 seconds
3	57.3 seconds
1	58.0 seconds
4	58.5 seconds

determine how many students scored an A, B, C, D, and F on the exam. The instructor is then able to gauge how the class as a whole is performing.

Interval Measurement Scale

The third type of measurement scale is an **interval measurement scale.** This measurement scale has very distinct features that are different from nominal and ordinal scales. First, in an interval scale, the interval between 0 and 1, 1 and 2, and 2 and 3 is the same unit of measurement. The second feature is the use of a zero. The twist of using a zero is that it is not a true zero, meaning a total absence of something. A thermometer for measuring the outside temperature uses an interval scale. The interval between each degree is equal, and the thermometer also has a zero. When the temperature outside is 0 degrees, there is not an absence of temperature, but rather it is very cold.

In research and evaluation, the Likert five-point scale is used to find out if people agree or disagree with a series of statements. The number the person associates with each statement indicates the person's level of agreement or disagreement with the statement (a 5 means the person strongly agrees; a 0 means the person strongly disagrees). The numbers for each statement are added together, and the sum represents the individual's attitudes or beliefs in relation to the topic being investigated. An example of this is provided in figure 5.2. For a Likert scale, it is assumed that the intervals between each number are equal and that 0 represents an opinion. Data that measure a quantitative variable using an interval scale can be analyzed using more advanced statistical analysis than frequency and percentages.

Ratio Measurement Scale

The fourth measurement scale is the **ratio scale.** This scale has equal intervals between points (such as 1, 2, and 3) and uses a zero in the measurement scale. The difference between interval and ratio scales is that the zero in the ratio scale means the absence of something. If a bowler scores a zero in one frame, the zero means that the bowler did not knock down any pins.

In the Likert scale shown in figure 5.3, the zero means an absence of something—the absence of an opinion. Using this type of Likert scale is common within research and evaluation studies. This measurement scale can be used to quantify variables, and it permits the researcher to use more advanced statistical analysis with the data. The correlation research question (question 3) in

I believe that the recreation programs are meeting the recreational needs of my children.

Strongly agree		Agree			Strongly disagree
5	4	3	2	1	0

Figure 5.2   Interval Likert Scale

I believe that the recreation programs are meeting the recreational needs of my children.

Strongly agree		Agree		Strongly disagree	No opinion
5	4	3	2	1	0

Figure 5.3   Ratio Likert scale.

table 5.1 has the rate of relapse as a quantitative variable. If the person does not relapse by using alcohol, the rate of relapse is zero. This represents an absence of the variable being measured.

Experimental Study Variables

What type of analysis can be performed with independent and dependent variables? To determine what measurement scale applies to these variables, the researcher must first determine what types of variables they are—categorical or quantitative. Independent variables could be either categorical (such as two different types of programs) or quantitative (such as time spent lifting weights). The dependent variables are almost always quantitative variables. To accurately measure the impact of the independent variable on the dependent variable, the data must be collected on a continuum that measures changes or variances. In a study of how the amount of time spent each week lifting weights affects body fat density, body fat density is measured by percentages. This number is a numeric representation of the data that is used for analysis. In table 5.1, research question 4 is an experimental question. The methods being tested serve as a categorical variable and a nominal measurement scale. The

dependent variable is the amount of trash left at the campsite. This variable is a quantitative variable and uses a ratio measurement scale where 0 represents no trash left at the campsite. In experimental studies, the researcher has a variety of statistical analysis options that may be used to analyze data and formulate conclusions. These options will be covered in chapter 11 of this text.

Table 5.5 provides a summary of how each type of variable relates to a measurement scale and analysis options.

● *TABLE 5.5* ●

Variables and Measurement Scales

Variable	Measurement scale	Analysis
Categorical	Nominal	Frequency or percentages
Quantitative	Ordinal	Rank order
Quantitative	Interval	All of the above plus more advanced statistical analysis
Quantitative	Ratio	All of the above plus more advanced statistical analysis

PROFESSIONAL PERSPECTIVES

■ The real world of parks and recreation

Currently, within the U.S. Armed Forces, there is a growing concern regarding the increased use of drugs and alcohol as well as deaths related to motorcycle use among the veterans returning from the Gulf War. These areas were identified as the variables to study through various federal agencies. The researchers hypothesized that these service members had operated for such an extended time on an "adrenaline high" or "adrenaline rush" in the combat zone that they were trying to maintain this feeling through drugs, alcohol, and motorcycle riding once they left the combat zone. The researchers had to figure out how to bring these service members down from these highs and introduce them to other activities that were not so destructive. The Department of the Army decided that adventure recreation activities would be the best choice. In addition, a team approach including counselors,

recreation therapists, and outdoor recreation staff would develop and conduct a combat transitional program for soldiers transitioning from the combat zone to their next duty station. The research began in 2009, and at the time of this publication, the data were being gathered from the program and analyzed to determine the effectiveness of the program.

Why was research important in this case?

Evaluation and research are critically important to this initiative. The effectiveness of the program can save lives, keep families intact, and retain good service men and women in the armed forces. If this program is not effective, people will die unnecessarily trying to maintain an adrenaline high instead of managing it. What could be more important than saving the lives of those who defend our democratic society?

■ TEST YOUR SKILL WITH EXERCISES 5.4, 5.5, AND 5.6.

Conclusion

An intertwined relationship exists between research questions, variables, hypotheses, and measurement scales. All these factors affect the results of the study and the significance of those results. Researchers and evaluators must take time to think through the process of planning these elements so that the results of the study are significant to the organization. A common mistake that occurs with inexperienced researchers is that they skip these important steps in the planning process. This results in data that cannot be analyzed or yield results that are meaningless to the organization. As a result, the researcher has wasted the valuable resources of time and manpower without producing a meaningful product. If this process is done properly, it yields meaningful results in an efficient and effective manner for the organization.

EXERCISES

■ Exercise 5.1: Relationships and Variables

What variables are being examined in each of the following research questions? List the variables after the research question.

1. What pottery and fitness classes do the community residents prefer?

2. Which type of recreational activity—basketball or yoga—controls impulse behavior better?

3. What is the relationship between the age of a person and the total amount of time spent on the computer during a seven-day period?

4. What is the relationship between a person's sex (male or female) and the type of outdoor activities the person chooses to participate in?

5. What is the impact of participating in a six-month health program on the individual's blood pressure?

6. What is the relationship between the amount of time spent playing outside and obesity among children ages five to seven?

7. What are the leisure preferences within the Latino community?

8. What is the impact of participating in arthritis water aerobics on the individual's range of motion?

■ Exercise 5.2: Independent and Dependent Variables

For each statement, identify which variable is the independent variable and which is the dependent variable.

1. The programmer wants to test two methods of teaching rock climbing in order to determine which method is most effective for helping people learn five basic skills.

   Independent variable:

   Dependent variable:

2. A recreation therapist wants to try two types of adult bikes to determine which bike is easier for the residents to ride.

   Independent variable:

   Dependent variable:

3. The aquatic supervisor wants to determine which type of guard training (lecture or pool sessions) is more effective in refreshing lifeguards' rescue skills.

   Independent variable:

   Dependent variable:

4. The park ranger wants to determine which method (ranger visiting the campsite, posters, or a brochure provided at check-in) is most effective in reducing the amount of trash left at the campsite.

   Independent variable:

   Dependent variable:

■ Exercise 5.3: Hypotheses

Write a directional hypothesis for each of the following research questions.

1. What is the relationship between childhood obesity and time spent watching television?

2. What is the effect of a staff member being present in the fitness room on customer satisfaction?

3. What is the relationship between participating in the Hearts N' Parks program and the likelihood that the person will continue to exercise in the future?

4. What is the relationship between participating in a soccer camp and participating in the fall soccer league?

5. What effect does cleaning the locker rooms two times during the day have on customer satisfaction?

■ Exercise 5.4: Variables, Types of Variables, and Measurement Scales

For each research question, do the following:

a. Identify the variables noted in the question.

b. Identify the type of variable for each one listed in *a* (quantitative, categorical, or constant).

c. Identify one possible extraneous variable for the study.

d. Identify the measurement scale for each of the research variables noted in *a* (nominal, ordinal, interval, or ratio).

1. What is the relationship between participating in soccer and a person's sex (male or female)?

a. Variables:

b. Type of variable:

c. Extraneous variable:

d. Measurement scale for each variable:

2. In the camp evaluation, what rating do campers give to the day camp program and counselors on a five-point Likert scale with no zero option?

a. Variables:

b. Type of variable:

c. Extraneous variable:

d. Measurement scale for each variable:

3. What fitness classes do the female seniors at the recreation center desire in the future?

a. Variables:

b. Type of variable:

c. Extraneous variable:

d. Measurement scale for each variable:

■ Exercise 5.5: What Type of Variables?

Identify the type of variable (quantitative, categorical, or constant) for each of the following variables. Then note the appropriate measurement scale (nominal, ordinal, or interval and ratio) for each variable.

1. Age of person

   Type of variable:

   Measurement scale for the variable:

2. The program that a person participated in at the facility

   Type of variable:

   Measurement scale for the variable:

3. Customer satisfaction on a five-point scale

   Type of variable:

   Measurement scale for the variable:

4. The ethnicity of an individual

   Type of variable:

   Measurement scale for the variable:

5. The type of registration option used by a person (mail-in, online, or phone)

   Type of variable:

   Measurement scale for the variable:

6. The number of laps swam during one month

   Type of variable:

   Measurement scale for the variable:

7. Level of commitment to future exercise

   Type of variable:

   Measurement scale for the variable:

8. Only including eight-year-old boys in the study

   Type of variable:

   Measurement scale for the variable:

9. Number of programs a person participated in last year

   Type of variable:

   Measurement scale for the variable:

10. Only customers who registered for a program are included in the study

    Type of variable:

    Measurement scale for the variable:

■ **Exercise 5.6: Article Analysis**

Review the research articles used in exercise 1.2 and complete the following.

1. Article:
   a. What were the variables in the study?
   b. How were they examined? Measured?
   c. Was a hypothesis used in the study? Why or why not?
   d. What type of measurement scale was used for each variable studied?

2. Article:
   a. What were the variables in the study?
   b. How were they examined? Measured?
   c. Was a hypothesis used in the study? Why or why not?
   d. What type of measurement scale was used for each variable studied?

CASE STUDY

What if the combat transitional program discussed on page 64 only had the soldiers for a week and they were only introduced to one adventure activity? What would you do differently with this program?

FOR THE INVESTIGATOR

It is time to examine the Health and Leisure Survey (found in the Online Student Resource) in a more detailed manner in relation to variables, hypotheses, and relationships. Each question on the survey (except question U) represents a variable that can be examined independently or correlated with a second variable. The first challenge is to identify the variables examined in each question. The next challenge is to identify what type of variable each one is (either quantitative or categorical). Finally, you must determine what measurement scale is appropriate for each variable (either nominal, ordinal, interval, or ratio).

1. Complete the following table to identify the variables, the type of variable, and the measurement scale for each question.

• **TABLE 5.6** •

Identify the Variables

Question	Variable	Type of variable	Measurement scale
A			
B			
C			
D			
E			
F			

Question	Variable	Type of variable	Measurement scale
G			
H			
I			
J			
K			
L			
M			
N			
O			
P			
Q			
R			
S			
T			

2. After identifying the variables, you need to determine if hypotheses can be developed to predict the relationship between variables.

    a. What variables should be examined as a pair to determine if there is a relationship? Choose four pairs of variables from the table that you would like to examine.

        Pair 1:

        Pair 2:

        Pair 3:

        Pair 4:

Numerous combinations of relationships can be examined through a correlation analysis, such as the relationship between GPA and frequency of drug use. A researcher might hypothesize the following: "As the frequency of drug use increases, the GPA will decrease." This hypothesis predicts a negative relationship between the variables.

3. What are the hypotheses for the four pairs of variables identified in question 2?

    Hypothesis 1:

    Hypothesis 2:

    Hypothesis 3:

    Hypothesis 4:

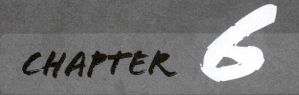

• OBJECTIVES •

After completing this chapter, you will be able to

- identify the purpose of the internal review board (IRB) at colleges and universities,

- describe the six ethical concerns for all research studies,

- discuss what steps can be taken to ensure that a research project complies with the six ethical concerns, and

- explain the elements that a consent form can contain and why each element should be included.

Ethics
in Research

As the programmer, you have been dedicating a large amount of time to developing the evaluation process for the classes that you coordinate at the recreation department. You have identified research questions, reviewed the literature, and identified variables to investigate through the evaluation process. Your supervisor reviews your work and compliments you on the high quality of your work to date. Both of you begin to discuss how to conduct the evaluation of the classes. Your supervisor then asks, "Will anything that you are planning to do within the evaluation process have the potential to cause the agency to be sued?" Your eyes widen with a look of panic as you realize that you have totally overlooked the ethic guidelines for research. You vaguely remember a discussion in class on this topic, and you decide to go back and review the ethical guidelines for research. During your review of the information, you discover that there are a number of guidelines for ethics in research. You also discover that internal review boards on college and university campuses use specific guidelines to review research projects of students in regard to ethics. Because the agency you work for does not have a research review board, you decide to use the ethical guidelines that apply to all research projects. You also decide to visit the research Web site of the local university to review their guidelines for research projects.

Every person conducting research and evaluation must ensure that the study is being done ethically and within established guidelines. Researchers must follow the guidelines that serve as the national standards for research and evaluation. These guidelines provide all universities and research agencies with ethical rules on how to conduct research. In the real world of recreation, many of the research projects conducted are action research or evaluation. Generally, these types of studies will not harm people; they tend to be a paper-and-pencil exercise or an interview, both of which are very straightforward for you and the subject. This does not reduce the importance of examining every research and evaluation project in terms of ethical guidelines and ethical considerations. At a minimum, you need to revisit the basic ethical considerations for research that are contained in this chapter. This will ensure that the study, the handling of the data, and the data analysis are done properly and ethically.

Every college or university across the United States has students or faculty conducting research as part of their graduation requirements or as part of their job. Within the environment of higher education, research is a normal activity pursued by both faculty and students. To ensure that the research projects are being conducted appropriately or in an ethical manner, every institution has some type of committee that reviews the plans for research studies. This committee is often called the internal review board (IRB). The IRB's job is to review the plan for a research study to ensure that all institutional and ethical guidelines are met. If you review the research guidelines at your institution, you will probably discover very explicit criteria for the application process, consent forms to participate in the study, and ethical considerations. At a college or university, a person cannot begin a research study until the IRB has reviewed and approved the plan.

As a professional working in the field, you will probably not have an IRB within your agency. What can you do to ensure that the research or evaluation project you are planning adheres to ethical guidelines and will not result in legal action against your agency? The first thing you should do is become familiar with the IRB guidelines at your local colleges or universities. This refreshes your memory on the topic and provides you with concrete information about things you should keep in mind while developing your research plan. The second thing you should do is take this information and discuss it with your supervisor. Your supervisor can serve as a second set of eyes to review the information and can help answer any questions you may have about legal issues associated with the research project. At this point, if you are uncertain about your research plan, it is time to contact your agency lawyer to discuss your concerns. The lawyer can answer your questions about the legal implications of the research project. By consulting these three resources, you can ensure that your overall research plan is appropriate and legal. With that being said, what are the general guidelines that all researchers are expected to follow?

Across every field of study, researchers must consider six ethical guidelines when planning a research study. These guidelines help ensure that the people who are involved in the study are treated appropriately and that the researchers conduct themselves appropriately. The ethical guidelines that all researchers must adhere to are as follows:

1. The researcher must ensure that the people involved in the study are protected from harm.

2. The researcher must ensure that the identity of the people involved in the study remains confidential.

3. The researcher must obtain permission from the parents of children involved in the study.

4. The researcher must avoid the use of deception during the study.

5. The researcher should use all the data collected for analysis.

6. The researcher must not pressure or coerce people to participate in the study.

These six ethical guidelines may or may not apply to the research projects you will be conducting, but they should all be reviewed for every project to determine if the study presents an ethical problem. If a problem is identified, then steps must be taken to revise the research plan in order to eliminate that particular problem. To help you fully understand the six ethical considerations, each guideline is reviewed in more depth in the following sections.

Protection From Harm

The first ethical consideration is ensuring that the people involved in the study are not harmed. How can participating in a research study harm a person? Harm can happen in several ways. The first way is when a person experiences physical harm. For example, the study may involve participating in an indoor climbing program where an artificial rock wall is being used for the program. The people in the program could be harmed while participating in a high-rope element of the course. Participants could experience muscle strains, muscle tears, or even a broken bone. In this case, every possible safety guideline for climbing should be followed to minimize or eliminate the potential for physical harm.

Harm can also occur in other forms, such as financial harm. If a person is physically injured during the climbing program, the person could also suffer financial harm or loss due to doctor bills or being unable to work because of the injury. The final two considerations related to harm are emotional and psychological harm. These types of harm are more difficult to identify. Inadvertently, a researcher could emotionally or psychologically harm a participant. This could occur in many ways, such as trying to force a person to complete a climb without addressing the person's fear or concern. This type of harm can also occur if a person's personal information is not kept confiden-

tial, particularly if the information is of a sensitive nature (such as drug use or mental illness). Every step should be taken to protect the people who are participating in the research study.

Confidentiality

The second ethical consideration that a researcher must consider is confidentiality. As mentioned, this ethical consideration can also be related to protecting the people involved in the study from harm. The researcher must ensure that the identities and information for the people involved in the study remain confidential. To ensure this, only the researchers should have access to this information. If people other than the researchers have access to this information, the people in the study could be subjected to retaliation or a hostile environment. An example of this is the use of peer evaluations in class to evaluate the performance of other group members on a project. The reality of group projects is that one person often ends up doing a majority of the work while another group member does a minimal amount of work. A per-

One ethical consideration is to ensure that the subjects in a study are not physically harmed.

son's evaluation of other group members should accurately reflect who contributed and who did not contribute to the project. If other group members discover that a person said something negative about their work, the person could be confronted in a hostile manner or threatened by these group members. This could result in harm to the person as the victim of the other group members' anger. As a researcher, you must protect the identity of the people in the study and the information obtained from these people.

Several steps can be taken to ensure confidentiality within the study. First, the names of the individuals involved in the study should only be known by the researcher. The researcher should use numbers or letters to represent each person involved in the study instead of using the participants' names. A researcher can create a list of people who have been selected to participate in the study and then assign a letter or number to each person on the list. Table 6.1 is an example of this technique. By using this technique, the researcher tracks the participation of people in the study and their data by numbers instead of names. The general rule for ensuring confidentiality is to never use the participants' names. By doing this, confidentiality is maintained, and the participants are protected from harm.

Another step that can be taken to ensure confidentiality is to keep all the data-gathering devices in a locked container (such as a file cabinet), particularly if names are on the data sheets. This ensures that no one will gain access to this information. Also, make sure no one has access to the data except the researchers. This helps ensure that sensitive information is not seen by or shared with people who should not have access to it. For example, if you are conducting a survey on drug and alcohol use, the content of the survey is very sensitive. If people other than the researchers have access to this information, there could be consequences for participants based on their information.

Parental Permission

When children are involved in the research project, the researcher must obtain permission from their parents for the children to participate in the research study. The parents must understand the focus of the study, the purpose of the study, how their child will be involved in the study, and any risks that are associated with participating in the study. This guideline is a requirement—if children are to be involved in the study, the researcher *must* have their parents' permission. The best way to communicate information about the study and to obtain parental permission is to use a consent form. If your study does not involve children, this is not a concern.

Avoiding Deception

Deception occurs when the researcher leads the people in the study to believe something that may not be true. For example, deception is frequently used in studies that test new medicine for particular health issues. A group of people volunteer to participate in the study to test a new medicine for treating asthma. All the people believe that they are taking the new medicine, but in reality, that is not true. Half of the people are receiving their regular medicine, and the other half are receiving the new medicine. The people have been deceived in order to determine how effective the new medicine is in controlling asthma. This type of practice is frowned on within the field of park and recreation as well as within higher education. Researchers in these settings are advised to avoid the use of deception. When deception is used, it is usually included within the structure or plan for the study. The best way to avoid deception is to plan a study design that does not use deception.

Using All Data

At times researchers may be tempted to exclude some of the data collected during the study because the data do not "fit" with the rest of the data collected. This is an ethical issue as well as an integrity issue. The fifth ethical consideration

• **TABLE 6.1** •

Tracking System for Subjects

Numeric system to track participants	
Subject	Number
John Smith	1
Brice Blankenship	2
Kelly Jones	3
Davis Cason	4
Callie Collins	5

PROFESSIONAL PERSPECTIVES

■ The real world of parks and recreation

Many agencies are faced with problems that cannot be explored through a survey or questionnaire. Some problems need to be explored using an interview format. A focus group is one technique used by agencies to conduct a group interview to discuss a problem. The Fairfax County Park Authority did this to explore the reasons why women who participate in the aerobics program do not use the weight room or the swimming pool in the facility for additional fitness activities. Several focus groups were conducted with groups of women who participated in aerobics but were not using any other fitness activities and services at the agency and did not use the weight room and pool. Maintaining confidentiality with the participants in the focus groups was vitally important. Their identity was only known by the researchers who conducted and videotaped the focus groups. The researchers analyzed the video and formulated the conclusions of the study. These conclusions were the only items shared with the staff of the agency. The results of the focus groups included identifying barriers to using the weight room and swimming pool. One of these barriers was the cleanliness of the locker room. This particular item had not crossed the minds of the staff, and plans were made to ensure that the locker rooms were cleaned two times a day.

Why was research important in this case?

The research process was very important in this example because the barrier to participation would have never been identified and addressed. This particular issue had not crossed the minds of the staff during discussions about the reasons why women do not use the weight room and the swimming pool. The only way to learn these reasons was to talk to users of the facility to learn their perceptions, concerns, and barriers.

focuses on the researchers using all the data in the analysis phase. Omitting data from the analysis can result in conclusions that are not true. Some researchers also omit data that do not verify their opinion. In this case, the results only include data that validate the researcher's opinions, preferences, and beliefs. This type of manipulation of the data is not ethical. Research is conducted to discover the truth within the data, not to manipulate the data to validate a researcher's opinion. In the analysis phase, the researcher should use all the data collected to formulate the conclusions of the study. If some of the data do not seem to fit with the majority of the data, the researcher should try to discover why and should address this in the study results.

Avoiding Coercion

The researcher should never pressure or require a person to participate in a study. These actions are considered coercion and are not ethical. A more specific example of coercion is a professor telling students that they must participate in a research project as part of a class. In other words, participation is a requirement of the class. This is coercion and violates one of the principles of using humans as participants or subjects in a study. The principle violated is that all participants or subjects have a right not to participate or to withdraw from the study at any time. To try to force or require people to participate in a study or remain in a study is considered unethical. What steps can a researcher take to avoid coercion and to increase the likelihood that a person will participate in the study and complete the study?

The most common step taken by researchers to avoid coercion is the use of a consent form. A consent form is developed by the researcher and is given to the people who have been selected to participate in a study. These people will review and sign the form. Consent forms can contain various pieces of information. Universities and colleges have very specific guidelines about the format and content of the consent form. Generally, consent forms provide information about who is conducting the study and the purpose of the study. The form also contains information asking for the consent of the person to participate in the study (figure 6.1). Here are some other items that can be included in the consent form:

- List of potential risks to the participants in the study
- Time commitment needed to participate in the study
- A statement about the person's right to withdraw at any time

- Whom to contact to ask questions or address concerns about the study

Researchers may or may not use consent forms depending on the research project. A researcher distributing a customer satisfaction survey to people who have completed the swimming class will most likely not use a consent form. Surveys are used frequently in parks and recreation agencies to evaluate programs and services, and most customers will view these surveys as part of the operations of the agency. Another researcher may be conducting a health and fitness study that requires people to participate in fitness classes during a defined time

1. Purpose and description of study: This states the purpose of the study, when the study will be conducted, how long the study will be conducted, the dates of the study, the number of participants, and how the person will participate in the study.

2. Procedures: This describes the procedures for the study, any discomfort or risks associated with participating in the study, and the specific amount of time required to participate in the study.

3. Participant benefits: This describes any benefits the person may receive personally from participating in the study.

4. Participant risks: This describes any risks (psychological, emotional, physical, and so on) that are possible as a result of participating in the study.

5. Voluntary participation and withdrawal: A statement is included to communicate that participating in the study is voluntary and that the participant can withdraw from the study at any time. This section also states the consequences of withdrawing from the study.

6. Confidential or anonymous: This states if the study is confidential or anonymous. Confidentiality means that the information provided by the participant will be protected and will not be able to be connected with the individual. The steps taken to ensure confidentiality must be stated, such as coding responses and keeping data in a locked container.

7. Contact information: The contact information for the study and agency is listed in this section. This includes names, telephone numbers, and address.

8. Informed consent statement: This statement includes wording such as, "I have read and understand the explanation provided to me and have been given a copy of this consent form. I have had all my questions answered to my satisfaction, and I voluntarily agree to participate in this study."

9. Signature and date lines for participant

Figure 6.1 Consent form components.

period. A consent form is usually used for this type of study. The consent form helps ensure that the participants in the study understand the purpose of the research project, the risks of participating in the study, the time commitment of the study, and their right to withdraw at any time. Consent forms ensure that participants understand their role, risks, and rights while participating in the study; the form can serve as a legal document for the agency in case legal actions are taken against the agency as a result of the study. A general guideline to remember is that participating in a research project is always a person's choice, not a requirement. Second, if you are conducting a study that involves people, you should consult with your supervisor to determine whether a consent form is necessary for the study.

■ *TEST YOUR SKILLS WITH EXERCISES 6.1, 6.2, AND 6.3.*

Conclusion

Researchers must ensure that all research and evaluation studies are conducted in an ethical manner and with the highest level of integrity. The ethical concerns reviewed in this chapter bring together legal concerns and integrity concerns within the ethical guidelines. If research is conducted ethically, the participants in the study, the agency, and the researchers are all protected—and the results of the study will be true and valid.

EXERCISES

■ Exercise 6.1: Ethical Guidelines

Identify the ethical concern that is being violated in each of the following situations. Choose from these options:

Protection from harm	Coercion
Confidentiality	Deception
Parental permission	Use of all data in analysis

1. The professor tells his class that they must participate in the research study or they will fail the class.

2. The researcher discovers data that do not fit what she thinks is accurate for the group. She decides to exclude those data from the data analysis phase.

3. The researcher requires subjects to place their name on the survey and then shares the surveys (with names on them) with a group of graduate students who are assisting with the study.

4. The researcher wants to study the social interaction of third graders on the playground. The researcher begins the study without the parents' knowledge of the study and their child's involvement.

5. The researcher tells the students that the questionnaire is 30 percent of their grade, but in reality, the exam is just a test run for a survey.

6. The adventure therapist allows her clients to climb boulders that are 15 feet (4.5 m) above the ground without any spotting or belaying.

7. The park and recreation director requires parents to place their name on the customer satisfaction survey.

8. The day camp coordinator has decided to conduct a study to determine how healthy snacks affect behavior during each camp. This is done without the parents' knowledge.

9. The day camp director did not like some parents' comments about the staff, so he did not include them in the final report.

10. The recreation programmer told parents that if they completed the program evaluation they would be included in a drawing for a free program of their choice; however, there is no such drawing.

■ Exercise 6.2: Ethical Decision Making

Describe what should be done in each of the following situations in order to comply with the ethical guidelines presented in this chapter.

1. The professor tells his class that they must participate in the research study or they will fail the class.

2. The researcher discovers data that do not fit what she thinks is accurate for the group. She decides to exclude these data from the data analysis phase.

3. The researcher requires subjects to place their name on the survey and then shares the surveys (with names on them) with a group of graduate students who are assisting with the study.

4. The researcher wants to study the social interaction of third graders on the playground. The researcher begins the study without the parents' knowledge of the study and their child's involvement.

5. The researcher tells the students that the questionnaire is 30 percent of their grade, but in reality, the exam is just a test run for a survey.

6. The adventure therapist allows her clients to climb boulders that are 15 feet above the ground without any spotting or belaying.

7. The park and recreation director requires parents to place their name on the customer satisfaction survey.

8. The day camp coordinator has decided to conduct a study to determine how healthy snacks affect behavior during each camp. This is done without the parents' knowledge.

9. The day camp director did not like some parents' comments about the staff, so he did not include them in the final report.

10. The recreation programmer told parents that if they completed the program evaluation they would be included in a drawing for a free program of their choice; however, there is no such drawing.

■ Exercise 6.3: Article Analysis

Review the research articles used in exercise 1.2 and evaluate the studies in terms of ethical practices by completing the following.

1. Article:

   a. Which of the ethical concerns **are not** an issue in the study (protection from harm, confidentiality, minors as subjects, coercion, deception, or use of all data in analysis)? Explain why.

   b. Which of the ethical concerns **are** an issue in the study (protection from harm, confidentiality, minors as subjects, coercion, deception, or use of all data in analysis)? Explain why.

   c. What do you think was done to ensure that the ethical concerns in item 2 were not violated?

2. Article:

a. Which of the ethical concerns **are not** an issue in the study (protection from harm, confidentiality, minors as subjects, coercion, deception, or use of all data in analysis)? Explain why.

b. Which of the ethical concerns **are** an issue in the study (protection from harm, confidentiality, minors as subjects, coercion, deception, or use of all data in analysis)? Explain why.

c. What do you think was done to ensure that the ethical concerns in item 2 were not violated?

CASE STUDY

Arthritis water aerobics programs are a huge success at recreation centers across the United States. These programs service people who need exercise and movement but have difficulty doing this on land. Many doctors tell their patients who are age 65 and older that they must go exercise. This is a shock to many of these patients, and it is often the first time they have been "ordered" to exercise. The arthritis water aerobics is a perfect exercise for these individuals. However, many of them are very hesitant to sign up. What would you do to identify the barriers, concerns, and issues for these people? What do you think some of the barriers might be for these individuals, particularly women?

FOR THE INVESTIGATOR

In every research project, you must be concerned about the ethics involved in conducting a study. In this chapter, ethical concerns and guidelines were reviewed.

1. Which of the ethical concerns are not an issue in the sample study? Explain why.
2. Which of the ethical concerns are an issue in the sample study? Explain why.
3. What can be done to ensure that the ethical concerns are not violated and do not result in the agency being sued?

CHAPTER 7

• OBJECTIVES •

After completing this chapter, you will be able to

- differentiate between the various random and nonrandom sampling techniques that can be used in research and evaluation,
- identify when to use random and nonrandom sampling techniques,
- assess the advantages and disadvantages of random and nonrandom sampling techniques, and
- summarize the impact that sampling issues have on external validity and identify the options that are available to enhance external validity.

Sampling

The president of the university has approached your research methods class and asked the group to conduct a study to assess the recreational needs of the student population on campus. The class accepts the challenge and then begins discussing how to approach such a large study. The group decides to use a quantitative study design to identify the recreational needs of the students on campus. The next step in the research or evaluation process is to define what individuals, groups, organizations, or artifacts will be involved in the study. The research question and research problem help the class in this decision. This decision is dependent on the unit of measurement that is specified in the research problem, the research question, and the hypothesis, if used. An additional consideration in this decision is whom or what group the class wants the results to apply to at the conclusion of the study. The class wants the results of the study to apply beyond those involved in the study. The broader the class wants to apply the results of the study, the more critical the decision becomes regarding whom and what group to involve in the study. To properly make this decision, the class must understand three terms: *population, sampling,* and *sample.*

The three simple concepts, population, sampling, and sample are foundational to all research and evaluation studies. They help define who will be involved in the study and the focus of the study beyond the research question. In this chapter, each of the concepts will be discussed independently, although their interrelatedness will be addressed as well.

Defining the Population

The first step in this decision-making process is to identify all the individuals who could be involved in the study. This group is referred to as the **population.** A population is the group of all individuals, organizations, or artifacts that could be involved in the study. The population is also the group that the researcher wants the results of the study to apply to at the conclusion of the study. Before determining who will participate in the study, the researcher must define the population. For example, colleges and universities across the United States are becoming increasingly concerned about alcohol use and the incidence of accidents, injuries, and deaths that occur while students are intoxicated. Administrators have also noted low participation rates in recreational programs offered on campus. This has led administrators to ask the following question: "What are the recreational needs and interests of today's students?" If these needs can be identified and programs can be provided to meet these needs, maybe the alcohol-related incidents on campus will decrease. At a university, all the students currently enrolled in classes serve as the population. The administrators want the results of this study to apply to the student population as a whole, not just the selected few who participate in the study. If the administrators were primarily concerned about fraternities and sororities, then the unit of measurement would be groups and all the fraternal organizations on campus that make up the population.

Sampling Techniques

Once the population is clearly defined and identified, the next step is to determine who will participate in the study. The process used to do this is called **sampling.** A wide variety of sampling techniques can be used in a study, and each will be explored in this chapter. The sampling process leads to the selection of a **sample.** A sample is the subset of individuals, groups, or organizations selected through the sampling process to participate in the study. Each individual person selected for a sample is referred to as a *subject.* The individuals or groups selected as the sample will participate in the study, and data will be gathered from them to formulate the conclusions of the study. In a research project, the researcher does not have the time, money, or resources to gather data from every person, group, and organization identified in the population; therefore, sampling is used to select a sample that is representative of the population as a whole.

Random Sampling Techniques

As mentioned, the sample represents the population from which it was selected for the study. The first sampling options are **random sampling** techniques. All random sampling techniques are based on the probability of each individual, group, or organization being selected as part of the sample. In random sampling techniques, the probability of being selected is more equalized than in nonrandom sampling techniques among the individuals, groups, or organizations in the population. To determine which sampling technique to use, the researcher must reexamine the research question. The researcher must also determine what technique is feasible to use in terms of time and money and how accessible the population is to the researcher. (In other words, the researcher needs to identify how much time and money can be spent on gathering data and what sampling technique is best in relation to the research question.) For random sampling techniques, the researcher can choose from simple random sampling, systematic random sampling, stratified random sampling, cluster random sampling, and two-stage random sampling. Each sampling technique has different features that may make it the best choice for a particular study based on the purpose of the study.

Simple Random Sampling The first random sampling technique to consider is **simple random sampling.** To use this sampling technique, the researcher must be able to identify every individual in the population. The distinguishing feature of this technique is that every person in the population has the same chance of being selected. To identify a random sample, the researcher must first determine the number of people to include in the sample and identify every person in the population. The researcher then uses random sampling to select the sample. For example, the administrators at a local university want to determine the

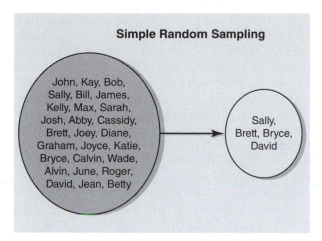

Simple Random Sampling

John, Kay, Bob, Sally, Bill, James, Kelly, Max, Sarah, Josh, Abby, Cassidy, Brett, Joey, Diane, Graham, Joyce, Katie, Bryce, Calvin, Wade, Alvin, June, Roger, David, Jean, Betty

Sally, Brett, Bryce, David

Figure 7.1 Simple random sampling.

recreational needs of the undergraduate students at the institution (they want to do this because of the increase in incidents occurring on campus that involve alcohol). The administrators want a sample of 400 students to include in the study. To come up with this sample, the administrators must first obtain an alphabetical list of all undergraduate students (this list is the population). The administrators will number the students on the list from 1 to 4,000. The numbers are then individually written on small sheets of paper and put in a hat. To draw the sample, the administrators pull 400 sheets of paper from the hat. The numbers drawn identify the students on the list who are selected to be the sample for the study. Figure 7.1 gives an illustration of this process.

Another technique that can be used to select a random sample is the table of random numbers. When using the table of random numbers, the researcher's first decision is to identify the sample size. In the recreational needs study, the desired sample size is 400. The same alphabetical list of students is used to identify the sample for the study. Instead of drawing numbers out of a hat, the table of random numbers is used. Table 7.1 provides a sample of a table of random numbers. A table of random numbers can generally be located in many research text books or can be generated through the Excel spread sheet. To begin sample selection, the administrators randomly select a series of numbers in the table. The total number of people in the population is 4,000, which is a four-digit number. Therefore, the first four digits of the number series selected from the table are used to identify the first person selected for the sample. For the number series 32154, the first four digits are 3215. The administrators then go to

the alphabetical list of students to identify which student is number 3215. The administrators move to the next series of numbers and use the first four digits of this set to identify the second person in the sample. The series of numbers is 00921, and the second person selected for the sample is number 0092. This process continues until 400 students have been selected to be included in the sample for the study.

Simple random sampling can also be used in evaluation. In the evaluation study of customer satisfaction with the recreation programs, a list can be developed of all customers who are currently enrolled in programs at the agency. The programmers can then use the table of random numbers to identify 100 customers who will be mailed evaluation surveys regarding their experience in the program. This sampling technique can be used within research and evaluation studies to ensure that every person in the population has an equal chance of being selected for the sample.

Systematic Random Sampling Systematic **random sampling** is the second type of random sampling technique that a researcher can use in a study. This is an alternative technique that can be used when all individuals within the population can be identified (as in the simple random sampling process). The researcher must begin with a list of all people in the population. The administrators at the university can again use the alphabetical list of all students enrolled at the university. The first person identified for the sample is selected randomly, and then the remaining sample is completed by selecting every 40th person on the list from the beginning point. The interval of 40 was selected to ensure that the entire list would be used, not just a section of the list. The interval of 40 students is usually referred to as selecting every "nth" name; the researchers determine what the "n" stands for in the sampling process to ensure that every person's chance of being selected remains equal.

● *TABLE 7.1* ●

Excerpt from
Table of Random Numbers

32154	12389	83278
00921	71239	01678
99432	00097	63191
05338	50215	40154

If a recreation programmer is interested in evaluating customers' satisfaction with the programs they have completed, systematic random sampling can be used. The programmers can also use a systematic random sampling technique to mail an evaluation to 100 randomly selected customers. For the population list, the programmers can simply obtain a list of all people who have completed programs in the past session. The important consideration is determining what the value of "n" will be. The programmers need to select an interval that ensures that the entire list of people is used in the sampling process. Systematic random sampling can be used in evaluation and scientific methods of research if all the individuals of the population can be identified; if they cannot be identified, then another technique must be used.

Stratified Random Sampling The third type of random sampling that a researcher could use is **stratified random sampling.** A **stratum** is a concept or characteristic that is used to subdivide the population into smaller groups. For example, the administrators want to study the recreational needs of the undergraduate students, and they want to ensure that the sample has equal representation from each class (freshmen, sophomores, juniors, and seniors). The stratum for this study is class. To properly use the stratified random sampling technique, the researcher must be able to identify all individuals in the population and then subdivide the population based on the stratum of class. The administrators divide the population into groups based on class and then develop a list of all students in each class. The sample is drawn from these four lists. In this study, the administrators want a sample of 400 students. They would randomly draw 100 names from each group (freshmen, sophomores, juniors, and seniors) using the hat technique or a table of random numbers. By using the stratified random sampling technique, the administrators ensure that each class has an equal voice in the results of the study. This prevents any single group from dominating the results that will guide the future planning for recreational activities on the campus. This technique can also be used in the example of the programmers evaluating customers' satisfaction with the programs that they have just completed. In this case, the population can be divided by program type, such as aquatics, dance, preschool programs, and seniors programs. To choose people for the sample, the programmer can randomly select people from the lists for each class type.

Another use for the stratified random sampling technique is to ensure that the sample represents the population in equal proportions. For example, in figure 7.2 a campus population could consist of 30 percent freshmen, 30 percent sophomores, 20 percent juniors, and 20 percent seniors. In a study, the researcher may want to maintain these percentages in the sample. To do this, the researcher divides the population by class and determines that a sample of 100 subjects is needed for the study. The researcher would randomly select 30 freshmen, 30 sophomores, 20 juniors, and 20 seniors to make up the sample. This ensures that the sample is in the same proportions as the population based on the stratum. In other words, the sample is representative of the population based on class at the university.

This technique is frequently used when communities survey residents. The strata that could be used include ethnic origin, age, socioeconomic level, and family situation (single, single parent, and so on). Both uses of the stratified random sampling technique can be helpful in making sure that specific characteristics within the population are accurately reflected in the sample. In a community that has a small percentage of minorities, the use of the simple random sampling process could result in no minorities being included within the sample. To ensure that the sample represents the population, the stratified random sampling process should be used. The minority residents are identified as a stratum, and then an appropriate number could be selected to provide them with an equal voice in the study. This is commonly done in studies conducted to identify needs within communities.

Cluster Random Sampling The fourth random sampling technique that a researcher can use is

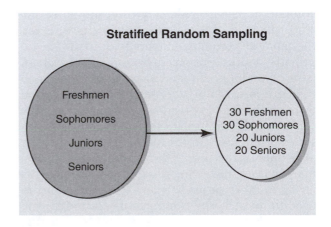

Figure 7.2 Stratified random sampling.

cluster random sampling. The previous techniques focused on identifying individuals first and then applying a random sampling technique. The cluster random sampling technique is used when the researcher cannot easily identify all the individuals in a population but *can* easily identify groups or organizations within the population. The cluster technique focuses on using preexisting groups or organizations and randomly selecting entire groups to include in the sample instead of individuals. For example, the administrators at the university are concerned about the dramatic increase in alcohol-related incidents among the fraternities and sororities on campus. The university currently has 100 recognized fraternal organizations, and the administrators want to use 10 fraternities and 10 sororities within the sample. The names of all the fraternities are put into a hat, and 10 are selected randomly. The same is done for the sororities. This provides a total sample of 20 fraternal organizations. Once this is done, all the members of the 20 organizations are included in the sample for the recreational needs study. Figure 7.3 provides an illustration of this process.

This sampling technique is also very useful in the evaluation process, such as the evaluation of customers' satisfaction with their experience in an agency's recreation programs. In any recreation center, the groups involved in programs can be easily identified—they are the classes themselves. The programmer gets a list of all the classes being offered during that session and randomly selects 30 classes. The people enrolled in the selected classes make up the sample for the customer satisfaction survey. Programmers use cluster random sampling as a means to assess customer satisfaction without the cost of trying to identify all the people in the population. Programmers

often want customers to evaluate a new instructor for a class. In this case, all the classes that the instructor teaches will be selected for the sample. Cluster random sampling is a useful technique when the population is large and is organized in preexisting groups, such as class in college, class at a recreation center, or a particular program.

Two-Stage Random Sampling   The final random sampling technique is **two-stage random sampling.** This sampling technique combines cluster random sampling and individual random sampling. Two-stage random sampling saves time for the researcher when the population includes a large number of individuals contained within preexisting groups. The first step is to identify preexisting groups (or clusters), such as fraternal organizations on a campus. As in the previous example, 20 fraternal organizations are selected in the first step of the sampling process. Instead of including all the members of the selected fraternal organizations in the study, the administrator obtains complete lists of membership for each fraternal organization. The administrator then randomly selects 15 individuals from each fraternal organization to be in the sample. Figure 7.4 illustrates how this process moves from groups to individuals.

This technique is also used in the evaluation process when the population includes a large number of individuals within preexisting groups. In the program evaluation study, the programmer has selected 30 classes randomly from a list. The total number of people enrolled in these classes is still too large—in other words, it is not financially feasible to include every individual from each class in the sample. The programmer generates a list of all the individuals registered in the

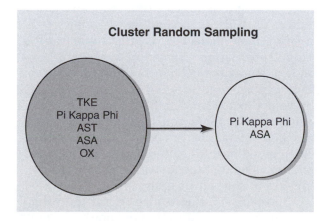

Figure 7.3   Cluster random sampling.

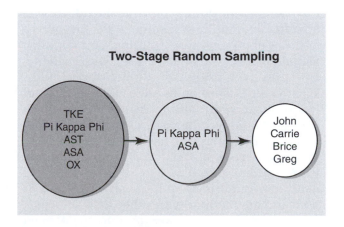

Figure 7.4   Two-stage random sampling.

30 classes. Then the programmer uses the table of random numbers or the systematic random sampling process to select 100 individuals from the list. The selected individuals make up the sample for the evaluation. The two-stage random sampling technique is more time consuming, but it is a useful technique when the total number of individuals within the groups is too large to include in the sample (because of financial reasons, time constraints, or other factors in the research or evaluation project).

■ *TEST YOUR SKILLS WITH EXERCISE 7.1 AND 7.2.*

Nonrandom Sampling

Sometimes random sampling techniques are not a good choice for a study because of the researcher's needs for data, the available time, or the manpower available to collect data. In these cases, researchers can choose from a second group of sampling options: the **nonrandom sampling techniques.** All random sampling techniques are based on a fairly equal probability that each individual, group, or organization has of being selected to be part of the sample. This is not the case with nonrandom sampling techniques. In nonrandom sampling techniques, the probability of being selected is not the same for each individual, group, or organization in the population. When choosing a nonrandom sampling technique for a study, the researcher must determine which technique is appropriate based on the research question, the amount of time and money available for the study, and how accessible the population is to the researcher. For nonrandom sampling techniques, the researcher can choose from purposive sampling, convenience sampling, volunteer sampling, and snowball sampling.

Purposive Sampling Within the category of nonrandom sampling techniques, the first option to consider is **purposive sampling.** This sampling technique is most frequently used with a qualitative study, such as a case study or historical study. This type of sampling provides a focused effort in gathering rich data to answer the research question. It allows the researcher to identify the specific individuals who have the information the researcher needs related to the research question; the researcher is then able to focus on collecting data from these people. Purposive sampling is used in combination with other data sources—such as the literature, agency documents, and artifacts—to gather relevant information related

to the research question. In purposive sampling, the researcher uses her judgment to select the sample. Researchers use purposive sampling in two ways; one is expert sampling, and the other is the selection of subjects based on their representation of the population. With expert sampling, the researcher identifies the experts who have the information the researcher needs to answer the research question. The selection of subjects is based on the purpose of the study.

In the study of the recreational needs of students (being conducted to combat the alcohol-related incidents involving students), the administrators would review the literature to identify other universities across the nation that have successfully completed a similar study. The administrators would then contact several of the universities that have implemented recreational programs that decreased the frequency of alcohol-related incidents at their university. It does not make sense to include universities that have not conducted a similar study because these institutions have no valuable information to share. The researchers contact several institutions and gather information about how they conducted their study, the results of their study, the programs that they implemented, and the results of their effort in reducing alcohol-related incidents. The researchers will take all this information from several institutions and analyze it through a process of coding. This process allows the researcher to combine the information in various ways to formulate conclusions. The researchers will use this information as the foundation to develop the plan at their own institution.

The administrators can also use another type of purposive sampling to select a small number of students to include in the sample based on specific characteristics. In the recreational needs study, the administrators would select a limited number of students to conduct interviews with based on their characteristics that represent the student population. Instead of surveying hundreds of students to obtain limited information, the researchers select a small number of students and gather extensive data from them. The small number of students can be interviewed in a manner that is similar to a two-way conversation. This method enables researchers to gather more comprehensive data about perceptions, attitudes, beliefs, and needs from each person.

Purposive sampling is also useful in evaluation. The program directors may not know how satisfied their repeat customers are with a specific class, such as the arthritis water aerobics. The written surveys are good, but the programmer needs additional information from a small group of people who have registered for the class for many sessions. The programmer purposely interviews several of these people about their satisfaction with the program, what benefits the class is providing for them, and any suggestions they have for future improvements to the class. This type of rich data cannot be collected with a written survey. Purposive sampling provides researchers with an option for digging much deeper into the information and specifically identifying the people or organizations that have the information the researcher needs for the study. Figure 7.5 gives an illustration of this process.

The size of the sample in purposive sampling is influenced by the group being studied. If the group members are very similar, or **homogeneous,** then the number needed in the sample is smaller than if the group varies widely on the characteristics being studied. In the example, the number of institutions selected for the sample is smaller than the number of students selected to be interviewed. Only a limited number of institutions had conducted a similar study and were also similar in size and geographic location to the university where the study is being conducted. This resulted in a smaller number for the sample. For interviewing students, researchers had to consider that there are many characteristics that vary across a student population. This requires a larger sample to ensure that the students interviewed possess the characteristics that the researchers have determined to be important within the study.

The primary disadvantage of using purposive sampling is that the researcher's judgment in identifying the population members and selecting the sample can be flawed or biased. To control biases and limit errors in judgment, a team of people should be involved in the selection process instead of one individual. The team can check and double-check the purposive sampling criteria and sampling process to minimize errors in the selection process.

Convenience Sampling and Volunteer Sampling The second option in nonrandom sampling technique is **convenience** and **volunteer sampling.** In this type of sampling, the researcher selects subjects from whoever is available at a given place at a given time. For example, a researcher wants to study students' attitudes about a new recreation complex on campus. The researcher goes to the student center at lunchtime on Monday for three hours; the researcher asks the first 50 students he sees to complete the survey about a new recreation complex. This type of sampling method should be avoided if possible because the results of the study are not valid beyond the people who complete the survey. This type of sampling creates a bias in the results and does not represent the population as a whole. Volunteer sampling is also a type of convenience sampling where people are asked to volunteer to participate in the study. With this type of sampling, no mechanisms are used to ensure that the sample represents the population of the study. An additional disadvantage to volunteer sampling is that individuals who want to complain tend to volunteer; individuals who may provide positive information or the other side of the issue might be less likely to volunteer. This is also a problem with surveys that are sent to subjects by mail or e-mail. The responses can be a volunteer sample that only provides information from people who want to complain, not a comprehensive picture. Figure 7.6 provides an illustration of this process.

Snowball Sampling A third option in nonrandom sampling techniques is **snowball sampling.**

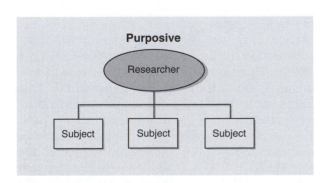

Figure 7.5 Purposive sampling.

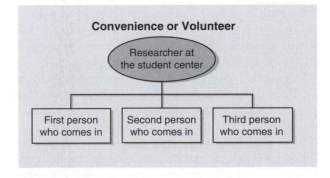

Figure 7.6 Convenience or volunteer sampling.

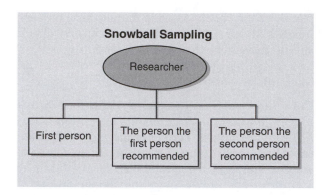

Figure 7.7   Snowball sampling.

This begins with the researcher identifying one person for the sample. The researcher uses her judgment to select this individual based on the perception that this individual has information to help answer the research question. The researcher interviews this person, and at the conclusion of the interview, the researcher asks this person who else should be interviewed in the data-gathering process. The researcher then interviews the other people whom the first person recommended to include in the study. This process continues like a snowball rolling downhill, getting bigger the longer it rolls. Figure 7.7 gives an illustration of this process.

The results of this technique can also be invalid because of the uncontrolled bias introduced by the particular subject's perception. The person's recommendations for others to interview could be based on trying to confirm that person's opinion. This can prevent the researcher from receiving opinions on the other side of the issue. In the recreational needs study, students who are interviewed and then asked to recommend others to interview may only recommend people with similar interests. This referral does not represent the vast recreational interests across a campus, but rather only one small subculture on the campus. It is difficult to control this type of bias with the referral system used in snowball sampling. One option to help control this bias is to gather information from other sources to formulate the conclusions of the study, not just from the people interviewed in the snowball process.

As you can see, researchers have many options available within the sampling step of the research process. The research design, the purpose of the study, and the population help you determine which sampling technique to use in the study. Before you select a sampling technique, you need to closely examine the advantages and disadvantages of each technique. Table 7.2 provides a summary of how each sampling technique is used and the advantages and disadvantages of each one.

■ *TEST YOUR SKILLS WITH EXERCISES 7.3 AND 7.4.*

Sampling Issues

When developing procedures for sampling, the researcher must be aware of the potential for sampling bias and sampling error. These two factors can result in invalid conclusions from a study. The sampling plan should include steps to ensure that sampling bias and sampling error are minimized.

Bias

Sampling bias occurs when one type of individual, group, or organization is overrepresented in the sample, resulting in a sample that does not represent the population as a whole. Sampling bias can occur in random and nonrandom sampling. If a researcher uses simple random sampling to select a sample in order to assess students' opinions about a new recreation complex, the sample could have an overrepresentation of freshmen and an underrepresentation of seniors. The type of sampling used can also help minimize the sampling bias. If the researcher used a stratified random sampling technique, the likelihood that the sample would represent the population on key characteristics is much greater. Sampling bias does not just occur in quantitative studies; it can also occur in qualitative studies. If the researcher's judgment of who should be included in the sample is flawed in any way, the sample will be biased.

To control sampling bias in research and evaluation, the researcher should ensure that the sample size is large enough to accurately represent the population and should use the sampling techniques that will minimize sampling bias. In addition, the researcher should use multiple sources of data to formulate the conclusion of the study instead of just using the data from the sample. Other sources of data could be the literature, agency records, program enrollment information, facility usage, or the director of the agency. The results from the various types of data are analyzed to formulate the conclusions. This helps to control sampling bias by confirming key points through the multiple sources of data. Finally, the researcher could repeat or replicate the study to see if the results are the same as the first study. This is one additional technique that can help minimize the impact of sampling bias in a research or evaluation project.

• TABLE 7.2 •

Summary of Sampling Techniques

Sampling technique	Use	Advantages	Disadvantages	Study type
RANDOM				
Simple random sampling	Used when every individual in the population can be identified	*Easy to use *Allows researcher to calculate sample error	Researchers must identify all population members.	Quantitative studies
Systematic random sampling	Used when every individual in the population can be identified	*Easy to use *Allows researcher to calculate sample error	Researchers must identify all population members.	Quantitative studies
Stratified random sampling	Used when every individual in the population can be identified and divided based on strata	*Ensures specific representation from the population in the sample	Researchers must identify all population members and subdivide the list into strata groups.	Quantitative studies
Cluster random sampling	Used when it is not feasible to identify every member of the population, but the researcher can identify preexisting groups.	*Works well with a large population that has identifiable groups *More cost effective than other techniques	This technique can increase sampling bias and often must be used with another random sampling option.	Quantitative studies
Two-stage random sampling	Used when it is not feasible to identify every member of the population, but the researcher can identify preexisting groups.	*Works well with a large population that has identifiable groups *More cost effective than other techniques	This technique can be difficult to explain to others.	Quantitative studies
NONRANDOM				
Purposive	Used to identify people who have the information needed	*Enables researcher to get information from experts *Allows researcher to use time efficiently to gather rich data	Researchers' judgment can be wrong in selecting experts.	Qualitative studies
Convenience or volunteer	Used when the researcher selects whoever is available at a certain place or time	*Easy to use	This technique causes sampling error and lacks external validity.	Avoid using
Snowball	Used when people are selected based on personal referral	*Easy to use	Referrals can involve judgment error and biases.	Avoid using

PROFESSIONAL PERSPECTIVES

■ The real world of parks and recreation

Within parks and recreation, programmers are constantly wondering what programs and services are appealing to specific minority groups in their community. This was a question explored by a programmer in Prince Georges County, Maryland. She was concerned that she was not seeing African American females in the 6th through 12th grade at her facility. She decided to conduct a focus group study using a purposive sampling technique. She worked with the local school counselors to identify good subjects to participate in the study. The focus groups were conducted, and the results were formulated in three major areas: (1) what the participants do in their free time after school and on the weekends, (2) what obligations they have after school, and (3) what programs and services they want to see offered at their local recreation center. The results provided very valuable information that the programmer would have never known without conducting this study.

The programmer learned that most of these girls had obligations after school to take care of their younger siblings, which prevented them from visiting the recreation center. She also discovered that the main focus of their recreational activities revolves around their church, not the recreation center. Finally, the programmer discovered that the girls wanted more pragmatic programs about job hunting, education, and vocational training—not sport leagues.

Why was research important in this case?

The programmer finally got the information she needed to serve this section of her community. She was able to identify partners for programs (churches), what days and times to provide the programs, and what programs and services to plan. Without this study, she would have continued to only guess about these items and plan programs that did not draw these girls into the facility.

Error

The second consideration in sampling is how to minimize the effects of **sampling error.** Sampling error is the statistical calculation of sampling bias that occurred in the sampling process for the study. The larger the sample, the smaller the sample error will be; this is because a larger sample is a better representation of the population. The steps taken to control sampling bias also help minimize sampling error. The best way to control sampling error is to ensure that the sample is large enough to minimize the statistical calculation of sampling error.

The **sample size** is directly related to sampling error and sampling bias. How big should the sample be? Sadly, there are no clear guidelines for the sample size of individuals, groups, or organizations. A number of issues will guide the decision about sample size. First, the sample size is influenced by the research question, the purpose of the study, and the type of study being conducted. A correlation study requires a larger sample than a case study. The size of the population and the characteristics of the population also influence the sample size. A population that is homogeneous (members are very similar) requires a smaller sample than a population that is **heterogeneous** (members vary widely). A homogeneous population could be preschoolers enrolled in programs at a community facility. The age group serves as a constant variable and narrowly focuses the study. This requires a smaller sample than a needs assessment within a community. An entire community represents a heterogeneous population that varies widely by age, marital status, parental status, and income level. The needs assessment would require a larger sample to ensure that the community is accurately represented in the sample. This is also related to the size of the population; the larger the population, the larger the sample needs to be. Finally, in determining the sample size, the researcher must look at what is feasible or possible considering the time needed, money required, and manpower available to conduct the study. The economic issue of cost is a reality of the study and is a critical component in determining the sample size.

External Validity

One final issue of concern related to the sampling process is **external validity.** The sampling process is a critical step in the research or evaluation process because it affects the external validity of the study. External validity refers to the extent to which the results of the study can be applied to the population that the sample represents. If the study results can only be applied to the sample, the study has no external validity. This limitation is caused by the study design and the sampling process used to gather data. A convenience sampling method provides little to no external validity. Therefore, the results of a study using convenience sampling cannot be applied beyond the sample itself. When a study has good external validity, the results can be applied to the population as a whole. Random sampling techniques and purposive sampling can give the study better external validity than when the researcher uses convenience, volunteer, and snowball sampling techniques.

Qualitative studies pose an additional challenge for the researcher when it comes to enhancing external validity. A researcher must revisit the purpose of the qualitative study, which is focused on documenting the phenomenon as a whole. The researcher can also examine what is unique about the group being studied. The results of the study can be generalized to other groups, settings, and times based on how similar these other elements are to the original study group. The ability to generalize is based on similarities of the study group with other groups, places, or situations.

To enhance the external validity of qualitative studies, the researcher can conduct the study in a variety of places, with different people, and at different times. This extended study method may not be possible because of limitations of time, money, and manpower. The researcher should gather extensive descriptive information about the group, setting, and time in which a study is conducted. This extensive documentation of the process, place, people, and time allows the researcher to repeat or replicate the study. The process of replicating a study is a technique that can be used to enhance external validity in both quantitative and qualitative studies.

■ *TEST YOUR SKILLS WITH EXERCISE 7.5.*

Conclusion

Choosing which sampling technique to use is a significant decision in the research and evaluation process for all researchers. The time involved in identifying the population of the study is a key factor that affects this decision. The type of study will also guide this decision—quantitative studies generally use a random sampling technique, while quantitative studies use a nonrandom sampling process. By reviewing these two critical elements, the researcher will logically select the sampling process that best meets the purpose of the study and the available resources for the study. The primary concern in the sampling decision is the external validity of the study. A study for which the results are only applicable to the sample may be a waste of the limited resources within the agency. The agency should always consider the resources needed to conduct a study so that the results are meaningful to the future operations of the agency.

EXERCISES

■ Exercise 7.1: Random Sampling Characteristics

Answer the following questions by identifying which type or types of random sampling technique are being referred to (simple random sampling, systematic random sampling, stratified random sampling, cluster random sampling, or two-stage random sampling).

1. Which sampling techniques give each person an equal probability of being selected? List all techniques that this applies to below.

2. Which sampling techniques require the researcher to identify all subjects in the population before drawing a sample? List all sampling techniques that this applies to below.

3. Which sampling techniques use groups during the process of drawing a sample? List all techniques that this applies to below.

4. Which sampling technique involves dividing the population into groups based on a characteristic before drawing a sample?

5. Which sampling technique involves using groups and then individuals during the process of drawing a sample?

6. Which sampling technique is used to ensure that the sample represents the population on a key characteristic?

■ Exercise 7.2: Sampling Techniques Application

This is an exercise on how each type of random sampling can be used within one study. The recreation programmer wants to evaluate all the classes in the current session. The type and number of classes are as follows:

3	Adult yoga classes	30 enrolled
10	Step aerobic classes (adults)	300 enrolled
10	Wiggles and Giggles (preschool)	100 enrolled
3	Ballet (children)	30 enrolled
2	Dog obedience	20 enrolled
15	Sport classes for children	15 enrolled
25	Beginner swimming classes	250 enrolled
20	Intermediate swimming classes	200 enrolled
10	Advanced swimming classes	100 enrolled

1. How could simple random sampling be used?

2. How could systematic random sampling be used?

3. How could stratified random sampling be used?

4. How could cluster sampling be used?

5. How could two-stage random sampling be used?

■ Exercise 7.3: Nonrandom Sampling Techniques

Answer the following questions by identifying which type of nonrandom sampling technique is being referred to (purposive, convenience, volunteer, or snowball).

1. Which sampling technique is used as a sampling method for qualitative studies?

2. Which sampling technique relies on the researcher's judgment to select additional subjects?

3. Which three sampling techniques can create a bias in the results of the study?

4. Which sampling technique involves having one subject make a referral about other subjects to collect data from?

5. Which sampling technique is conducted at a certain place and certain time to collect data?

6. Which sampling technique specifically identifies the subjects who have the information needed?

7. Which sampling technique involves asking for people to volunteer for the study?

■ Exercise 7.4: Identify the Sampling Technique

Which sampling technique is being used in each of the following statements? The answer could be a random sampling option (simple, systematic, stratified, cluster, or two-stage) or a nonrandom sampling option (purposive, convenience, volunteer, or snowball).

The study that is being discussed in these statements is a needs assessment to identify additional arts classes and programs needed in the community.

1. The programmer identifies the key community leaders in the arts and then interviews them.

2. The programmer obtains a list of public schools (K-12) and randomly selects three classes from each school. The researcher sends a survey home with all the children in the selected classes.

3. The programmer interviews the director of the local arts council and asks her who else in the community should be interviewed.

4. The programmer obtains a list of all households in the community and decides to send a survey to every 30th household on the list.

5. The programmer obtains a list of all households within the community and then divides them into groups based on ethnicity. Then the programmer randomly selects the same number of households from each group to ensure that all ethnic groups have an equal voice in the study.

■ **Exercise 7.5: Article Analysis**

Return to the articles used in exercise 1.2 and complete the following questions related to sampling for each article.

1. Article:

   a. What is the population of the study?

   b. What is the sampling technique used in the study?

   c. What are the strengths of the sampling technique used?

   d. What are the weaknesses of the sampling technique used?

   e. How far can the results be generalized beyond the study?

2. Article:

   a. What is the population of the study?

   b. What is the sampling technique used in the study?

   c. What are the strengths of the sampling technique used?

   d. What are the weaknesses of the sampling technique used?

   e. How far can the results be generalized beyond the study?

CASE STUDY

One of the current challenges in many park and recreation agencies is serving the Hispanic and Latino population within their community. The current programs and services do not attract this group into the recreation center, which is within walking distance from their homes. What would you do?

FOR THE INVESTIGATOR

Now you are back in the shoes of the head researcher on the Health and Leisure Survey study team. The challenge facing you today is determining the population and the sampling method for the study. Let's assume that this study is being conducted on your college or university campus with undergraduate students. You must specifically define the population for the study. Is it enough to simply state undergraduate students? What about part-time students? Students who live off campus, in the dorms, or at home? These subgroups must be considered in the definition of the population for the study.

1. Now that you have thought about the various types of undergraduates on your campus, define the population for the study.

2. Now that you have defined the population, review the numerous options for sampling. Select a sampling process and explain your selection in terms of representation, the research questions, and the purpose of the study.

CHAPTER 8

• OBJECTIVES •

After completing this chapter, you will be able to

- apply the options that are used in deciding who will lead the research and evaluation process,

- understand that the CAPRA standards specify the need for internal staff to conduct research and evaluation,

- examine the decisions that need to be made in developing the instrumentation plan, and

- classify the various types of data available for researchers to collect.

Instrumentation

You are doing your internship at your dream agency, and your supervisor has assigned you the task of conducting a study. The purpose of the study is to identify what factors lead people to purchase a summer season pass for the agency's outdoor pool. You are both scared and thrilled about this assignment and have worked diligently preparing for this study. Now, you are faced with developing the data collection plan for the study, and you feel overwhelmed with all the decisions. These decisions relate back to the research problem, research questions, and research design. These three areas help guide you through the decision-making process for the data collection plan, which is called the instrumentation plan.

The **instrumentation** phase serves as the road map for sampling, data collection, data analysis, and the sharing of information from the study. This step requires the researcher to "make a plan and then work the plan." This plan is guided by the purpose of the study and the research question. It serves as the step-by-step guide on how to conduct the study. The researcher has a number of critical decisions to make in the planning process. First, the researcher must determine who will be in charge of the study. Will internal staff conduct the study or will an external agency be hired to conduct the study? Second, the researcher must determine the financial requirements for conducting the study. Finally, the researcher needs to determine the personnel requirements for conducting the study. In addition to these decisions, a number of decisions must be made in relation to gathering data. These decisions determine what data are needed, whom to collect the data from (the population), the sampling process to be used, how to collect data, when to collect data, and where the data will be collected. The last decision in the plan is to determine how the data will be analyzed and shared with others. These decisions must be made before conducting the study. Park and recreation professionals often skip many of these critical decisions and rush to gather data—then they are not sure what to do with the data once they have the data in hand. By dedicating time to the instrumentation decisions, the researchers will work efficiently and effectively, which will save time and money in the long run.

Selecting a Leader

Park and recreation agencies have two choices when determining who will be in charge of the research or evaluation project. The agency can hire an external company to conduct the study, or the agency can appoint someone from the internal staff to lead the study. Each option has advantages and disadvantages, which are summarized in table 8.1.

Using an External Agency

An advantage of using an external agency to conduct research projects is that the agency brings experts to the organization who are unbiased and objective in their views of the organization. The experts are also likely to have broader knowledge and skills related to research procedures than internal staff members have. External researchers also bring a "fresh set of eyes" to examine the agency and conduct the study. This unbiased review can be difficult for internal staff to complete because they work within the internal culture of the agency.

A disadvantage of using an external agency to conduct a study is the cost associated with the service. This additional cost must be paid by the recreational agency and is a budgetary consideration. The cost for this type of service can vary widely depending on what external agency is providing the service. A private company that does nothing but research studies for others will likely cost more than working with a local college or university. A variety of agencies and organiza-

• TABLE 8.1 •
Research Options for an Agency

	External agency	Internal agency
Advantages	External researchers serve as a fresh set of eyes and provide an unbiased review of the agency.	Staff members know the agency and their particular area better than anyone.
	External researchers are experts in the area of research or evaluation.	Researchers can set up an internal training program to assist others in conducting small studies in their area.
	External researchers bring different experience and knowledge to the agency.	The study can lead to ongoing research and evaluation projects.
Disadvantages	The process is more costly than using internal staff to conduct the study.	Personnel may not have the proper training, knowledge, or skills to lead research and evaluation projects.
	The person or group conducting the research is not part of the agency in the future.	The scope of the project may be beyond the skills of the staff.

tions provide services in the area of research and evaluation within local communities. To identify these agencies, one must investigate the local resources to identify the options that are available. Finally, the last disadvantage of using an external agency is that when the study is completed, the relationship is terminated. The experts and their knowledge, skills, and abilities leave the organization and are no longer available to assist with research projects.

Many CAPRA accredited organizations use a mix of internal staff and external agencies to meet the requirements of the evaluation standards. For example, Mammoth County Parks Department used an external research agency to conduct the community needs assessments. The scope of this type of study was beyond what the internal staff of the agency could independently conduct. The scope of the research project helps guide the decision on whether to use internal resources or an external agency to conduct the study. At Mammoth County Parks Department, internal staff members were used to conduct evaluations of programs and services, as well as studies related to the feasibility of new services (such as the therapeutic riding center in the county).

Using Internal Staff

As mentioned, internal staff can also be used to conduct research and evaluation studies. There are several advantages to using internal staff to conduct research projects. First, the staff members of the agency are very knowledgeable about their particular area of the agency—more knowledgeable than any other person within the organization or others external to the organization. The staff members know intimate details and facts about the organization and their area (including the organizational history) that are not documented within the records of the organization. Second, the recreation center director knows the customer base of the center better than others in the organization. The staff members of the center have the most current knowledge about their customers, programs, services, and events that affect the participation rates at their facility. An additional benefit of using internal staff to conduct research is their year-round availability, as opposed to the "one shot" availability of an external agency.

The CAPRA accreditation standards related to evaluation and research are very explicit; there must be a staff member of the organization who is in charge of managing the evaluation and research efforts. Montgomery County Recreation

Department has a part-time staff member employed for the sole purpose of heading up research projects and evaluation efforts. This allows the employees to dedicate their time and energy to projects instead of trying to "find time" to do what is needed. In addition to having an employee dedicated to research and evaluation, the CAPRA standards also specify that an on-going training program should exist to train the staff of the agency in research and evaluation methods. This type of training allows staff to conduct research or evaluation projects that are focused on their scope of responsibility, such as day camps or therapeutic programs.

The challenges that an agency faces in identifying research staff include (1) identifying staff who have advanced degrees (a master's or above); (2) locating an individual who is knowledgeable about the process and procedures of research and evaluation; and (3) identifying an individual who has the organizational skills to lead these projects. The first critical decision in the instrumentation plan is to determine who is in charge. This decision is also affected by financial limitations and the staff's skills, knowledge, and abilities in the area of research.

Defining the Population

The second decision that needs to be made is identifying the population of the study. The population is the group that the researcher wants the study results to apply to. The research question helps to define the limits of the population, the study design, and the sampling process. The research design can either be a research project or an evaluation project. Each has a specific purpose and outcome. To guide the decision on defining the population, the next consideration is whether the study is a quantitative study or a qualitative study.

An example of a research question for an aquatic facility is as follows: "What is the relationship between taking swimming lessons and purchasing a season pool pass for the summer at Martin Luther King Aquatic Center?" This question defines the population as the people who have taken swimming lessons at this facility from January through June. When a research question examines a relationship, the study is a correlation study and requires a quantitative study design. To enhance the validity of the study, the sample should consist of a large portion of the population. This study is simple to conduct by cross-referencing the list of swim lesson participants with the list of season pass holders.

If a second research question asks, "What are the factors that lead a person to purchase a summer season pass for the pool?" the research question approaches the season pool pass from a different perspective. This question explores the factors that lead the customer to purchase a season pass. The population for this question is all summer season pass holders; this research question would be best explored through a qualitative research design. The researcher needs to deeply explore the customers' decision-making process and the factors that lead to the purchase of summer season pool passes. This type of data cannot be gathered numerically. The best way to gather this data is through interviews in a qualitative design. In qualitative designs, the sample is small, and the researcher uses a purposive sampling process. The researchers can identify the new season pass holders and then select a limited number of these pass holders to interview.

A third example of defining the population is a local fitness center director who wants to have clients evaluate their personal trainer. This is an evaluation study that defines the population as all customers working with a personal trainer. The question is "How satisfied are clients with the performance of their personal trainer?" The personal trainer evaluation would be given to every customer so that 100 percent of the population is included in the study. This evaluation design is a quantitative design used to gather numeric data on each of the personal trainers (these data serve as the evaluation of the trainers' jobs). These examples demonstrate how each decision in the research process influences the following decisions in the process: research questions, study design, population, and sample. Table 8.2 summarizes the three examples in this section by noting the research question and population.

Making an Instrumentation Plan

The **instrumentation plan** is composed of a number of decisions that need to be made before beginning the study. These decisions are made to determine

- what data are needed to answer the research questions,
- how to gather the data,
- when to gather the data,
- where to gather the data, and
- how to analyze the data.

These decisions must be made as part of the instrumentation plan for the study. They help guide the progress of the study to the ultimate goal of gathering data and formulating conclusions to answer the research question.

Selecting Data

The previous decisions help define what data need to be gathered and why the data are important. What is data? **Data** refers to the information that is gathered to answer the research question. Data can be numbers, words, or actual objects, such as photos, articles, or video. The instrumentation process defines what data need to be collected and the timing of the data collection process.

What data are needed if the researcher is examining the relationship between taking swimming lessons and purchasing a summer session pass? The researcher needs the records of swimming lesson participants and season pass holders. Examining any other type of data, such as instructor evaluations, is a waste of time if it does not focus on answering the research question. If the researcher is examining the factors that lead a person to purchase a summer pass for the pool,

• TABLE 8.2 •
Identify the Population

Question	Population
What is the relationship between taking swimming lessons and purchasing a season pool pass for the summer at Martin Luther King Aquatic Center?	All people who have taken swimming lessons from January to June
What are the factors that lead a person to purchase a summer season pass for the pool?	All season pass holders
How satisfied are clients with the performance of their personal trainer?	All clients who work with a personal trainer

interview data are needed to fully understand the factors in the decision-making process of the customer. By using the interview process, the researcher can conduct a two-way conversation in order to explore the factors that lead to purchasing the season pass. This type of data is very comprehensive in exploring the decision-making process, and it is more effective than looking at only one or two variables. In the example of the fitness center evaluating the personal trainers, a written survey will provide the data needed to evaluate the performances of the trainers. By identifying the specific type of data needed to answer the research question, the researchers' efforts are properly focused. Table 8.3 summarizes what data are needed in relation to the previous decisions in the instrumentation plan.

Gathering Data

The next natural question is, how will the data be collected? To answer this question, the researcher needs to identify whether the study is an evaluation, a quantitative study, or a qualitative study. This helps determine how to collect data. What instrument will be used to collect data? The researcher has a variety of options that may be used as a data collection instrument, such as surveys, interviews, observations, or rating instruments. Table 8.4 summarizes the decision of how to gather data along with the previous pieces of the instrumentation plan.

Determining When to Collect Data

Once the researcher decides what data to collect and how to collect them, the researcher must determine when to collect the data, where to collect them, and who should collect them. The results of the study can be influenced by the time that data are gathered, where the data are gathered, and who gathers the data. Studies that only use literature

• TABLE 8.3 •
Determining What Data Are Needed

Question	Defining the population	Selecting data
What is the relationship between taking swimming lessons and purchasing a season pool pass for the summer at Martin Luther King Aquatic Center?	All people who have taken swimming lessons from January to June	Records of swim lesson participants and season pass holders
What are the factors that lead a person to purchase a summer season pass for the pool?	All season pass holders	Interview data on the customers' decision-making process
How satisfied are clients with the performance of their personal trainer?	All clients who work with a personal trainer	Evaluation rating of performance

• TABLE 8.4 •
Determining Where Data Are for Collection

Question	Defining the population	Selecting data	Gathering data
What is the relationship between taking swimming lessons and purchasing a season pool pass for the summer at Martin Luther King Aquatic Center?	All people who have taken swimming lessons from January to June	Records of swim lesson participants and season pass holders	Agency records
What are the factors that lead a person to purchase a summer season pass for the pool?	All season pass holders	Interview data on the customers' decision-making process	Interviews
How satisfied are clients with the performance of their personal trainer?	All clients who work with a personal trainer	Evaluation rating of performance	Survey

or the records of the agency are not influenced by these decisions. This is the case with the first research question concerning the relationship between taking swimming lessons and purchasing a summer season pass. Once the majority of season passes have been sold, the data should be gathered at the beginning of the summer.

This is not the case when data are being gathered from human subjects. Timing considerations that must be addressed are the month, the day of the week, and the time of day that the data are collected. In the example of identifying what factors lead a person to purchase a season pass to the pool, the interview should be conducted as soon as possible after the purchase of the pass. If the researchers wait weeks or months after the purchase, the subjects may not recall what factors led them to make the purchase. This interview could be done over the phone or in a small group.

For the fitness center evaluating the personal trainers, a specific time frame is necessary in order to ensure a high response rate. The manager decides to give the clients an evaluation form to complete after their last session with their personal trainer (before they leave the facility). This is a better plan than mailing the surveys to the clients' home weeks after the clients' last session with their trainer. The timing of data collection can affect the quality of the data received from the subjects. Table 8.5 presents this information, along with the previous decisions in the instrumentation plan.

Determining Where to Collect Data

The place that data are collected and the person collecting data must be specifically defined in the instrumentation plan. The best plan is to standardize the place and person for the data collection. This standardization helps enhance the truthfulness and validity of the data. The subjects should be in an environment where they feel at ease so that they will answer questions honestly. These two considerations are not an issue for the first research question because the data are coming from the documents of the agency and not from individuals.

In the case of identifying the factors that lead to purchasing a season pass for the pool, the interviews will be conducted by telephone. The people conducting the interviews should be trained in how to conduct an interview and how to record the information accurately. Each person being interviewed will be at home while participating in the interview, which is a comfortable environment for that individual.

In the example of evaluating personal trainers, having the clients' trainer administer the survey in the gym will most likely provide invalid data. The ideal situation would be to have one staff person provide the clients with a quiet room to complete the survey. Then the subject should return the survey to the same staff member who gave the survey to the subject. This standardizes where the data are collected and by whom.

• TABLE 8.5 •
Determining When to Collect Data

Question	Defining the population	Selecting data	Gathering data	When to collect data
What is the relationship between taking swimming lessons and purchasing a season pool pass for the summer at Martin Luther King Aquatic Center?	All people who have taken swimming lessons from January to June	Records of swim lesson participants and season pass holders	Agency records	At the beginning of the summer
What are the factors that lead a person to purchase a summer season pass for the pool?	All season pass holders	Interview data on the customers' decision-making process	Telephone interviews	After the purchase of the season pass
How satisfied are clients with the performance of their personal trainer?	All clients who work with a personal trainer	Evaluation rating of performance	Survey	After the last training session

• TABLE 8.6 •
Summary of Instrumentation Plan Steps

Question	Defining the population	Selecting data	Gathering data	When to collect data	Where and who
What is the relationship between taking swimming lessons and purchasing a season pool pass for the summer at Martin Luther King Aquatic Center?	All people who have taken swimming lessons from January to June	Records of swim lesson participants and season pass holders	Agency records	At the beginning of the summer	Only documents and records; data collected at the office
What are the factors that lead a person to purchase a summer season pass for the pool?	All season pass holders	Interview data on the customers' decision-making process	Telephone interviews	After the purchase of the season pass	Phone interview with person at home by a trained interviewer
How satisfied are clients with the performance of their personal trainer?	All clients who work with a personal trainer	Evaluation rating of performance	Survey	After the last training session	At the fitness center by a staff member, not the trainer

Table 8.6 provides a summary of all the instrument pieces and provides examples of each decision that needs to be made in developing the instrumentation plan for a study.

Analyzing Data

The next planning decision to make is how to analyze the data and what to do with the information once the analysis is completed. The type of analysis used with data is determined by whether the data are quantitative or qualitative data. To analyze quantitative data, some type of statistical analysis is used to provide the results. The type of statistical analysis used with data must be thought out and documented in the instrumentation plan.

Some of the most frequently used options for statistical analysis will be covered later in this text. Qualitative data are analyzed through a coding process that identifies themes; these themes become the foundation for the conclusions of the study. This type of data analysis will also be covered later in this text. The results of the data analysis should be summarized and presented in a report to supervisors and other parties for review. Research and evaluation efforts yield a wealth of information that can be used to educate commissioners, city councils, customers, and other decision makers. Studies that document outcomes of the programs and benefits to the community

serve as a powerful tool that allows the agency to document its benefits to the community through facts and data, not perceptions and speculations. In today's cost-conscious society, the agency must prove that it is contributing to the quality of life of the community and must document the outcomes from the programs. This type of documentation and evidence is also a requirement for CAPRA accredited agencies and represents an ongoing evaluation process within the agency. Table 8.7 summarizes the key decisions that need to be made in the development of the instrumentation plan.

Kinds of Data

Researchers can collect various kinds of data. Data can be collected regarding attributes, facts, attitudes, preferences, and beliefs. Table 8.8 provides a definition of each type of data and how each type of data can be used in research or evaluation. For a research project, the researchers can use one of these types of data or a combination of the types. Most studies include gathering some type of attribute data, which is demographic data. These data allow the researcher to describe the sample based on key demographic characteristics. In the example of the evaluation of personal trainers at the fitness center, researchers will also gather

• TABLE 8.7 •

Parts of the Instrumentation Plan

1. Leadership	Internal or external?
2. Cost	What funds are available?
3. Population	Define the population for the study.
4. Research design	Quantitative, qualitative, or evaluation?
5. Sampling process	Choose one of the random or nonrandom sampling options.
6. What data are needed?	What information is needed to answer the research question?
7. How will data be collected?	Quantitative or qualitative methods?
8. When will data be collected?	Identify the month, day of week, and time of day.
9. Where will data be collected?	Specify the location.
10. Who will collect the data?	What staff members are responsible for data collection?
11. Data analysis	How will data be analyzed?
12. What will be done with the results?	Who should get the report?

Reprinted from NRPA.

• TABLE 8.8 •

Types of Data

Data type	Definition	Use
Attributes	Characteristics of people	Demographic information (e.g., age and sex)
Facts	Behaviors of people	Past or present participation in activities (e.g., frequency of participation in swimming lessons)
Attitudes	Likes and dislikes	Which art project did you like best?
Preferences	Used in comparisons	Which of the two class times do you prefer?
Beliefs	Perception of what is true or important	The mission, vision, and goals of the organization

facts in relation to their customers' behavior (in addition to demographic data).

The type of information gathered to evaluate the personal trainers could include (1) how many days this week the client worked out with the personal trainer, (2) what physical activities were done during the training session, and (3) how many training sessions the customer received. These pieces of factual data allow the researcher to better understand the subjects' interaction and satisfaction with their personal trainer. Data related to subjects' attitudes assist the researcher in determining how satisfied the clients are with their personal trainer and the results from their workout sessions.

Another use of data related to attitudes is in planning programs and services to meet the needs of the group being studied. A fitness facility can survey customers about what new programs or services the customers like and dislike. Gathering this type of data assists the researcher in accurately expanding programs and services based on the attitudes of the customers (instead of the perceptions of the management). The fitness center manager takes the data on the customers' attitudes and then develops a list of suggested programs and services. This list is then given to the customers so they can indicate which programs or services they prefer. The staff realizes that it is not possible to provide every program and service that the customers like, so the

PROFESSIONAL PERSPECTIVES

■ The real world of parks and recreation

The local department of natural resources has struggled with the goose population that remains year-round at a local lake. This creates problems for visitors and creates sanitation issues within the lake because of the runoff from the goose poop. The staff was struggling with the question of how to encourage the geese to move along and migrate; the staff wanted to avoid killing the animals. A ranger decided to review trade magazines and located several useful articles. These articles described techniques that were used to control the geese population and encourage migration at several agencies across the nation. The ranger contacted two of the agencies to determine how they instituted this control program, to learn if the program is still successful, and to obtain any recommendations on how to alter the program to ensure success. The ranger learned that the most effective technique is using firecracker-type devices that create noise and scare the geese. This has to be done repeatedly to ensure that the geese move to another location for the season and migrate. The ranger was thrilled to learn of this nonlethal method of controlling the geese population and limiting their length of stay at the park. The staff developed a plan to run the program and then gather data to evaluate whether the program was effective.

Why was research important in this case?

Without following up with other agencies that have a similar problem, evaluating the frequency of firing noise makers, and the number of geese at the park, the ranger would not have been able to accurately determine the effectiveness of the program. The ranger could have easily decided to organize hunters to eliminate the geese that stay at the park.

---

preference data are critical in making the decision about what new programs should be provided.

The last type of data that can be collected is data about beliefs. This type of data can be documented within an agency. Information about the agency's vision, mission, and objectives guides the operation of the agency. Most park and recreation agencies state in their mission that the organization's purpose is to "enhance the quality of life within the community." Every individual has beliefs about quality of life. Learning what the community residents believe about issues related to quality of life can assist the agency in moving the mission statement from an abstract concept into programs and services. For example, a current national concern is the obesity epidemic among children. This concern is reflected in parents' beliefs that a wide variety of physical activities are important to the future health of their children. This belief can be incorporated into the operation of the agency by providing a wide variety of programs and services that involve physical activity. In addition, the programs can introduce children to a variety of lifetime fitness activities to combat obesity through their life span. The type of data to be collected by the researchers must be documented in the research plan to ensure that the data answer the research question. Once this decision is made, the researcher then selects an instrument for collecting the data.

■ *TEST YOUR SKILLS WITH EXERCISES 8.1, 8.2, AND 8.3.*

Conclusion

Developing the instrumentation plan is a multi-step process that guides the focus and effort of the study. The numerous decisions in this step are time consuming, but this is time well spent. The time dedicated to this step of the research process will save time in the long run because all the critical decisions have been made and documented. In other words, the researcher makes the plan and works the plan. This effort will also help unify, focus, and coordinate the efforts of the research team in an efficient and effective manner. Everyone will know what the plan is, what they must do within the plan, and when tasks must be completed. The instrumentation plan is the road map from the beginning of the project to the end.

EXERCISES

■ Exercise 8.1: Quantitative Instrumentation Plan Practice

Complete the table to develop the instrumentation plan for the following study. Quantitative research question: What is the relationship between registering for summer day camp and participation in YMCA youth programs (i.e., swimming, soccer, baseball, after-school care)?

• TABLE 8.9 •

Instrumentation Plan Practice

Element	Decision for element	Researcher's decision
1. Leadership	Internal or external?	
2. Cost	What funds are available?	
3. Population	Define the population for the study.	
4. Research design	Quantitative, qualitative, or evaluation?	
5. Sampling process	Choose one of the random or nonrandom sampling options.	
6. What data are needed?	What information is needed to answer the research question?	
7. How will data be collected?	Quantitative or qualitative methods?	
8. When will data be collected?	Identify the month, day of week, and time of day.	
9. Where will data be collected?	Specify the location.	
10. Who will collect the data?	What staff members are responsible for data collection?	
11. Data analysis	How will data be analyzed?	
12. What will be done with the results?	Who should get the report?	

■ Exercise 8.2: Qualitative Instrumentation Plan Practice

Complete the table to develop the instrumentation plan for the following study.

Qualitative research question: What aspects of the youth swimming lessons at the YMCA do the parents like the most and the least?

(The programmer wants more in-depth responses so she can identify the successful elements and the elements that need to be changed. She wants to sit down and talk with several parents during their child's swimming lesson.)

• *TABLE 8.10* •

Instrumentation Plan Practice

Element	Decision for element	Researcher's decision
1. Leadership	Internal or external?	
2. Cost	What funds are available?	
3. Population	Define the population for the study.	
4. Research design	Quantitative, qualitative, or evaluation?	
5. Sampling process	Choose one of the random or non-random sampling options.	
6. What data are needed?	What information is needed to answer the research question?	
7. How will data be collected?	Quantitative or qualitative methods?	
8. When will data be collected?	Identify the month, day of week, and time of day.	
9. Where will data be collected?	Specify the location.	
10. Who will collect the data?	What staff members are responsible for data collection?	
11. Data analysis	How will data be analyzed?	
12. What will be done with the results?	Who should get the report?	

■ **Exercise 8.3: Article Analysis**

Return to the research articles used in exercise 1.2 and complete the following questions related to instrumentation of each study.

1. Article:
   a. What was the population for the study?
   b. What data were needed?
   c. How were the data collected?
   d. When were the data collected?
   e. Where were the data collected?
   f. Who collected the data?
   g. How were the data analyzed?

2. Article:
   a. What was the population for the study?
   b. What data were needed?
   c. How were the data collected?
   d. When were the data collected?
   e. Where were the data collected?
   f. Who collected the data?
   g. How were the data analyzed?

CASE STUDY

The naturalist staff at Rocky Gap State Park is in charge of running interpretive programs and educational programs, including wildlife education programs. The staff members want to update their Junior Ranger program because the material is outdated and does not really engage the child completing the packet. In addition, the naturalists have noticed that they have a large number of repeat visitors and only one Junior Ranger program. How could the naturalists use the instrumentation process in their efforts to create several different Junior Ranger programs for park visitors?

FOR THE INVESTIGATOR

Now that you have identified the population and the sampling process, it is time to develop the instrumentation plan. This involves determining how to collect data, when to collect data, where to collect data, and who will collect data. What options can you identify for each area of data collection? Determining when to collect data is critical on college and university campuses. In these settings, many events and holidays are considered "party time," such as Spring Fling, homecoming weekend, or St. Patrick's Day, to list a few. The place where data are collected is critical in gathering honest information. Think about the places that would negatively influence the truthfulness of the data and the places that would positively influence the truthfulness of the data. The last consideration in gathering data is who will gather the data. Who could gather data? How does this selection influence the truthfulness of the data collected? Would students in class be honest in their responses to the questions if their professor gave them the survey and collected it? Think about who would be a better choice for collecting data and why this person (or people) would be a better option. These are all critical decisions to ponder because they can influence the truthfulness of the data collected.

Now that we have reviewed these items, it is time to make the decisions about when and where the data will be collected and who will collect the data.

Explain your decision for each of the following elements and why you have selected the noted option.

1. When will data be collected?
2. Where will data be collected?
3. Who will collect the data?

• OBJECTIVES •

After completing this chapter, you will be able to

- analyze the differences between subject-completed instruments and researcher-completed instruments,

- evaluate the instruments that a researcher may select for producing quantitative data or qualitative data,

- explain the factors related to validity and reliability that must be considered when choosing an instrument, and

- recommend what type of evidence to gather to enhance the validity and reliability of an instrument that the researcher creates for a study.

Data Collection Tools

You have been approached by the director to conduct a study to determine what factors led people to purchase a season pass for the outdoor aquatics complex. The director wants to identify these factors so that they can be included in the marketing efforts for the season passes. You are now faced with developing a study and making the critical decisions about what information is needed, whom to collect it from, and when and where to collect the information.

One of the more challenging decisions within this plan is what to use to gather data. A large variety of options are available to the researcher. This decision is influenced by the type of study being conducted, the purpose of the study, the population, and the time available to gather data. The purpose of the study is to identify the motivational factors that led individuals to purchase a season pass. The data need to be collected from the season pass holders shortly after they have purchased the pass. The data that are needed center on the individual's attitudes and preferences in relation to the season pass. One of the most important factors in this decision is whether an appropriate data collection instrument already exists or whether the researchers must develop the instrument themselves.

This chapter explores the various data collection tools that a researcher can use in a research project. Data collection tools serve as the primary method of gathering data for a study beyond the literature and records. Part of the time spent in developing the instrumentation plan must be dedicated to learning about data collection tools. This effort permits the researcher to learn what data collection tools were used in similar studies. If this type of information is not available, numerous books can be found that specifically address data collection tools. These references assist the researcher in identifying the options that are available for data collection in a study.

Types of Instruments

A variety of tools are available for researchers to use in collecting data for a study. The first category of data collection tools, or instruments, is the **subject-completed instruments.** Subject-completed instruments are given to the subjects involved in the study to complete and return to the researcher. A survey is one of the most commonly used subject-completed instruments in the field of parks and recreation. In the case of the season pass sales, the programmer would mail out surveys to the season pass holders. These surveys would be designed to gather the data needed to identify what factors led the individual to purchase the season pass.

Subject-Completed Instruments

Within the category of subject-completed instruments, the researcher has three options:

1. Written questionnaires or surveys that generally force the person to select from a limited number of response options
2. Written questionnaires or surveys that ask for a written response
3. Self-checklists

These instruments are all completed by the subject and returned to the researcher.

Written Questionnaires With Forced-Choice Questions Written questionnaires or surveys may contain **forced-choice** or **closed-ended** questions. In other words, the instrument provides the only choices that the subject can select for each question. Questionnaires and surveys can gather data related to attributes, facts, attitudes, preferences, or the beliefs of the subjects. Two examples of closed-ended or forced-choice demographic questions are provided in figure 9.1.

The subjects select the number for their age category. If the subject is 22 years old, then he would select number 1. This type of data takes variables, such as age, and converts them into numeric data for analysis. Instead of gathering data on the exact age of the person, the researcher gathers data based on 10-year intervals, which simplifies the data analysis process. Data related to ethnic origin can be gathered in the same manner. Instead of collecting words, the researcher assigns a number to each category in the ethnic origin question; this allows the researcher to analyze numbers instead of words. The numbers assigned to each category are typically assigned in ascending order, such as 1, 2, 3, and 4. For the age data, the interval of

What is your age?

1. 20-29
2. 30-39
3. 40-49
4. 50-59
5. 60-69
6. 70-79
7. 80 or older

What is your ethnic origin?

1. African American
2. Caucasian
3. Latino or Hispanic
4. Pacific Islander
5. Asian American
6. Native American

Figure 9.1   Examples of closed-ended or forced-choice demographic questions.

ages used for each response category provides a uniform interval for each response. The researcher determined the size (age range) of each interval for this question. The numbers assigned to the ethnic question in figure 9.1 are also assigned by the researcher and are typically seen in this order in the question.

Each closed-ended question provides a limited number of response choices to the subject. Other questions in questionnaires can ask the person to select from one of five response categories. A Likert scale is a common scale used to gather opinion data to evaluate programs, services, and events. A Likert scale question is an instrument that lists statements and asks the subjects to indicate their level of agreement or disagreement with the statement. In the scale shown in figure 9.2, the researcher chose a five-point scale (instead of a seven-point scale) with a range of strongly agree to strongly disagree with the statement. The researcher assumes that the number selected in agreement or disagreement reflects the subjects' attitude. The example in figure 9.2 is a Likert scale question that is commonly seen in program evaluations.

Questionnaires and surveys provide quantitative data that can be summarized and analyzed in a timely fashion. If the researcher knows what variables to measure and has a limited time frame to gather and analyze data, forced-choice questionnaires and surveys are often used to gather the data.

Written Questionnaires With Open-Ended Questions   Subject-completed instruments can also be designed to provide qualitative data. A survey or questionnaire that asks **open-ended questions** can provide this type of data. An open-ended question allows the subjects to write a response in their own words, instead of forcing subjects to choose a response from a limited number of options. Open-ended questions should be used when the researcher wants more in-depth information than a forced-choice questionnaire can provide.

For example, the following open-ended questions are commonly seen on evaluation forms used by day camps:

1. What did your child like the most about his or her day camp experience?
2. What suggestions do you have to improve the day camp for next year?

The information gathered from parents from these questions provides valuable marketing information that can be used the next summer in the promotion of the day camps. Open-ended questions are also used when the researcher does not want to limit the information coming from the subject. In the question asking for suggestions for the following year, the parents may provide ideas that the camp staff would have never considered. This type of data does take longer to analyze, but the results provide more in-depth information than closed-ended questions.

Many park and recreation departments use both types of questions on evaluation forms for programs and events. The closed-ended questions focus on the specific variables that the agency wants to evaluate, such as the person's level of satisfaction with a class instructor, the facilities, front desk assistance, or the cleanliness of the facility. The open-ended responses provide additional information beyond a limited number of variables, such as elements of a program that the individual liked or disliked, or suggestions for improving a program or service. This type of data requires more time to summarize and analyze than numerical data. On the flip side, this type of response provides a higher quality of data than forced-choice responses.

State the degree to which you agree or disagree with these statements.

	Strongly disagree	Disagree		Agree	Strongly agree
(1) The instructor was well-prepared for every class.	1	2	3	4	5

Figure 9.2   Example of a Likert scale.

Which of the following activities would you be interested in doing with your teenager during the **spring and fall**? Please check your top **five** choices.

___ **1.** Archery

___ **2.** Biking

___ **3.** Canoeing

___ **4.** Paddle boating

___ **5.** Sailing

___ **6.** Kayaking

___ **7.** White-water rafting

___ **8.** Nature programs

___ **9.** Fishing

___ **10.** Swimming (indoor)

___ **11.** Field day (variety of sports and outdoor activities

___ **12.** Climbing wall

___ **13.** Rock climbing

___ **14.** Hiking

___ **15.** Orienteering (map and compass)

Figure 9.3   An example of a self-checklist.

Self-Checklist   A **self-checklist** is used to gather factual information about behaviors, attitudes, and preferences from the subject. This data collection tool is useful if the agency is trying to decide how to expand programs and services to meet the needs within the community. These subject-completed instruments can be used to gather quantitative data for analysis to answer the research question. A preference checklist is provided to the customers so they can indicate which programs they would prefer the agency to add at the facility. The customers may also be asked to indicate a limited number of preferences, such as their top five choices on the checklist. Figure 9.3 contains a sample preference list used to identify future programs for a local Teens Outside program series.

Table 9.1 provides a summary of the uses, advantages, and disadvantages of the three subject-completed instruments. Each of these options provides advantages and disadvantages. If you choose a closed-ended or forced-choice data collection instrument, the data are easy to collect and analyze, but you lose the richness of data collected. If you select a data collection instrument that has open-ended responses, you collect rich data, but the data are more complicated to synthesize and analyze. When making this decision, you must consider the tradeoffs of time versus richness of the data. This decision should be made when developing the research plan.

■ *TEST YOUR SKILLS WITH EXERCISE 9.1.*

Researcher-Completed Instruments

The second category of instruments is the **researcher-completed instruments.** These instruments are completed by the researcher, and the researcher serves as the primary data collector. An example of a researcher-completed instrument is a performance checklist used during swimming lessons. The student is asked to perform a variety of swimming skills, and the instructor checks off the skills that the student can perform. The researcher-completed instruments include the following options:

1. Focus groups
2. Unstructured interviews
3. Observations
4. Structured interviews
5. Performance checklists
6. Product evaluation forms
7. Rating scales
8. Documents and records

The options within researcher-completed instruments can provide quantitative or qualitative data for analysis. The type of data needed will guide the decision on what type of data collection instrument to use within the study.

• TABLE 9.1 •
Subject-Completed Instruments

Instrument	Use	Advantages	Disadvantages
Written questionnaire or survey with closed-ended questions	Used to gather information about attitudes, attributes, preferences, or facts (e.g., sex, ethnic origin, evaluation of an instructor)	Data are easy to collect and analyze because of the forced choice among options listed.	Data gathered are limited in scope (limited to the response categories).
Written questionnaire or survey with open-ended questions	Used to gather information about attitudes, attributes, preferences, or beliefs (e.g., likes, dislikes, or recommendations for improvement)	Rich, in-depth data can be collected from the subjects (who can write down anything they desire).	This instrument requires an extensive amount of time for summarizing and analyzing data through a coding process.
Self-checklist	Used to gather information about facts, attitudes, or preferences (e.g., preferences for new programs)	Data are easy to gather and analyze.	Data gathered are limited in scope (limited to the response options listed on the instrument).

Focus Groups and Interviews The first two options within the researcher-completed instruments are **focus groups** and **unstructured interviews.** These instruments provide qualitative data that allow the researcher to dig much deeper than forced-choice questions. Focus groups and unstructured interviews are conducted in a face-to-face situation where a facilitator asks open-ended questions. For example, a researcher could ask, "What are the factors in your decision-making process that led you to purchase a season pool pass?" This goes far beyond a "yes" or "no" response. It permits the researcher to gather extensive data related to the decision-making process and the subjects' preferences. A focus group is a group interview on a specific topic. A two-way conversation is conducted to explore a topic in an in-depth manner. An interview, on the other hand, is conducted with only one person. The questions asked in an interview can also be asked in a focus group. The data from a focus group or interview will assist the agency's leadership in making decisions related to programs, services, budget allocations, and personnel needs. This type of instrument provides a large amount of qualitative data that require analysis through a coding process. More time is required to analyze this type of data compared to quantitative data because the data are composed of words instead of numbers. These techniques provide valuable information related to individuals' attitudes, beliefs, and preferences.

Observations During a study, a researcher sometimes does not want to gather data based on interview questions; instead, the researcher wants to record more holistic data. **Observations** are an option that a researcher can use to collect this type of data. The data from observations document what occurs within the natural environment as it happens. The researcher records what is observed through her own perceptions over an extended amount of time. Observation requires the researcher to watch the subjects and take notes on what is seen during the observation session. Researchers can use four techniques for observation; these options are summarized in table 9.2. In the first option, the researcher observes the group as a full participant in the experience, and the participants do not know they are being observed. In the second option, the researcher observes as a complete participant, but the people do know they are being observed.

In the other two options for observation, the researcher observes the group as an outsider and not as a member of the group. The group members either know they are being observed or do not know that they are being observed. Observing the group in an unobtrusive manner can be an advantage. When the subjects don't know that they are being observed, the researcher will not influence the subjects' behaviors. If the group knows they are being observed, the individuals may change their behavior because of the observer's presence. To ensure that the data are correct, observations should be conducted by at least two researchers. The two researchers can then compare their data for accuracy.

• TABLE 9.2 •

Observation Options

Observer options	Obtrusive observer	Unobtrusive observer
Observation as a complete participant: Researcher is considered a member of the group and participates as a group member.	Subjects know that they are being observed by the researcher who is a member of the group.	Subjects **do not** know that they are being observed by the researcher who is a member of the group.
Observation as a nonparticipant: Researcher is not considered a member of the group and does not participate with the group.	Subjects know that they are being observed by an outsider or researcher.	Subjects **do not** know that they are being observed.

An example of the use of observation is at a residential camp for adjudicated youth. The researcher wants to investigate how the program operates and the effects of the program on the youth. The researcher can be an observer by working daily as a staff member and collecting data on the program and the process. The campers may or may not know they are being studied depending on the researcher's preference. Another option would be for the researcher to follow the campers through the program on a daily basis without acting as a staff member. The researcher again determines whether the campers should know they are being observed.

Observations allow the researcher to witness or take part in the experience that is being investigated. This is a different approach than interviewing people about the experience. Through observations, the researcher obtains a firsthand account of the events and experiences of the subjects.

Structured Interviews In many studies, the researcher may not have the time or resources available to collect and analyze qualitative data from focus groups, unstructured interviews, or observations. Many studies require researcher-completed instruments that gather quantitative data to answer the research question. For these studies, the first option for the researcher to consider is a structured interview. In this technique, the researcher can use the subject-completed questionnaire or survey as the interview tool. The researcher reads the interview questions and the closed-ended response options to the subject. The subject selects from the options, and the researcher records the selection on the instrument. This option is used when the researcher has data collectors to collect data on a one-on-one basis.

Checklist-Type Instruments Some studies require a different type of data other than attitudes or preferences. These studies need data related to a person's performance or product after a series of instructional sessions. Performance checklists, product evaluations, and rating scales are all researcher-completed instruments that are generally administered at the end of a program or to evaluate a product. A **performance checklist** documents what a person can and cannot perform. For example, a swim instructor uses a performance checklist to determine if the swimmer is ready for the next level of swimming classes. A beginner swimmer must perform a variety of swimming skills, which may include swimming the front crawl for 20 yards (18.3 m) without stopping. The swimmer either can or cannot perform this skill. The instructor tracks the individual's progress with a skills checklist through the series of classes.

A **product evaluation form** is an instrument that is similar to a checklist. However, instead of documenting whether a person can do something, this tool is used to evaluate a product. For example, a product evaluation form may be used within an art class. The art teacher provides guidelines and instructions on how to make a bowl on the potter's wheel. The students practice making bowls, and then they submit their best bowl for the instructor to evaluate based on the specified criteria. The instructor has a checklist of the particular evaluation criteria, such as roundness, height, thickness of the sides, and thickness of the base. The instructor then provides feedback to the student on how to improve the product.

A **rating scale** is another option that goes beyond simply documenting whether the person did or did not do something. The rating scale allows the researcher to document the quality of a product or performance. An example of a performance rating scale is a diving competition. Judges provide a number after each dive, which represents their rating of the performance. Rating scales are frequently used in sport events, such as ice skating competitions and gymnastics competition, to evaluate each athlete's performance.

These researcher-completed instruments provide a different type of data that is more factual in nature and directly related to a person's ability to make something or perform specific skills. Table 9.3 provides a summary of the researcher-completed instruments and the type of data that can be collected using each instrument.

• TABLE 9.3 •

Summary of Researcher-Completed Instruments

Instrument	Use	Advantages	Disadvantages
Focus groups	Used in qualitative studies to gather extensive information about the study topic	Group interview saves time over individual interviews. Comments from one person can trigger thoughts from another person (which does not occur in a one-on-one interview).	Extensive data must be synthesized and analyzed. Experienced facilitator is needed for the discussion. Researcher can introduce a bias in subject selection or data analysis.
Unstructured interviews	Used in qualitative studies and conducted as a face-to-face and one-on-one interview	Researcher gathers rich data in a two-way conversation.	Extensive data must be synthesized and analyzed. Researcher can introduce a bias in subject selection or data analysis.
Observations	Used in qualitative studies when the researcher wants to see what is being studied, instead of just talking to people (e.g., evaluating a swimming instructor)	Documentation is gathered as the experience is occurring (research does not rely on memory). This technique provides field notes on observations.	Observer could introduce a bias into the data. Two observers may be needed for best results in data collection.
Structured interviews	Used in quantitative studies and conducted as a face-to-face interview using an instrument with closed-ended responses	Researcher can clarify any questions from a person through interaction.	Person needs to be trained as an interviewer. Interviewer can influence a response or lead the person to a particular response.
Performance checklists	Used in quantitative studies when the researcher wants to determine what skills a person can perform (e.g., swimming)	Researcher uses observation to document what skills are performed.	Data are limited in scope (only facts or performance).
Product evaluations	Used in quantitative studies to evaluate what a person is making (e.g., pottery class)	The evaluation can help a person identify what needs to be improved.	The evaluation can be the subjective judgment of the instructor or evaluator.
Rating scales	Used in quantitative studies to document the quality of a product or performance (e.g., diving competition)	Evaluator looks at quality, not just the performance of something.	The judges can introduce biases into the rating score; generally two or more judges are needed.
Documents and records	Used in quantitative and qualitative studies to gather information related to the research question	Can assist research in locating data related to the research questions	The information is limited in scope and depth.

■ TEST YOUR SKILLS WITH EXERCISES 9.2 AND 9.3.

Documents and Records The final data collection option available to researchers is also a researcher-completed tool. This option is collecting data by reviewing the documents and records of the agency. Many recreation agencies track customer activities through some type of database program. A researcher can examine program registration numbers, cancellation rates, the number of people on waiting lists, and a variety of customer and program activities. The records and documents within an agency provide a wealth of information about the operations of the agency. These sources of data should not be overlooked in the research and evaluation process. They are used within many research and evaluation projects. The records and documents can provide detailed data on a specific element and valuable background information for a project. The limitation of using documents and records of the agency is the limited scope of the information. This can be overcome by using other sources of information along with the documents and records.

Researchers should closely examine the many options that may be used to collect data for a study. Many professionals immediately jump to the conclusion that a survey or written questionnaire is the best method for collecting the needed data. Instead of immediately deciding on a survey, researchers should select the data collection tool that will enable them to gather the type of data needed to answer the research question. One of the greatest challenges of using researcher-completed tools is controlling biases that can be introduced by the individual collecting the data. Multiple data collectors or multiple data sources are often used to control any biases in the data collection process.

Instrument Selection

After determining what type of data collection tool to use, the researcher must decide whether to use a preexisting instrument or create the instrument himself. This decision can either move the study along or stall the research process (if the researcher does not have the skills to develop the instrument).

The advantage of using a preexisting data collection tool is that these instruments have been tested in the field. In addition, previous researchers have documented the reliability and validity of the instruments. The **reliability** of an instrument is the consistency of the results from the instrument. The **validity** of the instrument refers to the truth of the data and the truth of the conclusions drawn from the data. By using a preexisting instrument, the researcher saves time and effort in developing an instrument, testing the instrument, and analyzing the validity and reliability of the instrument. This work has usually been done for preexisting instruments.

A challenge of using a preexisting instrument is locating an instrument that measures the variables of the study. A wide variety of preexisting instruments are available in the fields of recreation, health, psychology, and sociology. Depending on what is being studied, an instrument may exist that can be used as the data-gathering tool. An evaluation tool available from the National Rec-

1. **Protective surfacing:** The surface should be soft in order to cushion a fall. The mulch should be 12 inches (30.5 cm) deep.

2. **Zone:** There should be a zone around the playground equipment where a child may fall. This zone should be covered with protective surface, and the zone should be a minimum of 6 feet (183 cm) in all directions from the edge of the playground equipment.

3. **Entrapments in openings:** Enclosed openings that may entrap a child's head should be covered. There should be no openings that measure between 3 and 9 inches (7.6 and 22.8 cm).

Figure 9.4 Sample items from the NRPA's playground safety checklist.
Reprinted from NRPA.

reation and Park Association is the playground assessment tool. This is an evaluation form that can be used to evaluate a playground's compliance with national safety standards and to identify hazards to children. Professionals can receive training on how to use this instrument, as well as training to become a playground inspector. This assessment is easy to obtain and easy to use in the field, and it highlights the national standards for playground safety. It does not make sense to create an instrument to evaluate playground safety if one already exists. Figure 9.4 provides a sample of the content of items to check at a playground. The use of preexisting instruments can address challenges far beyond a playground to more conceptual variables or elements within research and evaluation.

A common challenge for park and recreation professionals is evaluating the outcomes of a program for the participants. This is a philosophical shift in program evaluation from how many attended a program to the outcomes for participants in the program. The outcomes evaluation for participants is also a requirement within the CAPRA accreditation process. How does one evaluate outcomes for the participants of fitness classes such as aerobics, yoga, or arthritis water aerobics? Instruments already exist that could be used as an evaluation tool. The instrument selected will depend on the variables that need to be evaluated. Figure 9.5 contains an example of questions from the "Physical Activity Enjoyment Scale." This instrument could be used to evaluate the enjoyment level of participants within a fitness program. Figure 9.6 contains an example of questions from the "Outcome Expectation for Exercise" instrument. These two instruments are contained in the book *Motivating People to Be Physically Active* (Marcus and Forsyth 2003), which has six different instruments that could be used to evaluate the outcomes for participants in fitness programs.

For each feeling, mark the number that best describes you.

1 I enjoyed it.	2	3	4	5	6	7 I hated it.
1 I feel bored.	2	3	4	5	6	7 I feel interested.
1 I disliked it.	2	3	4	5	6	7 I liked it.

Figure 9.5 Sample questions from the "Physical Activity Enjoyment Scale."
Adapted, by permission, from B. Marcus and L. Forsyth, 2003, *Motivating people to be physically active* (Champaign, IL: Human Kinetics), 75.

State the degree in which you agree or disagree with these statements.

Exercise...	Strongly disagree	Disagree	Neither agree nor disagree	Agree	Strongly agree
1. Makes me feel better physically.	1	2	3	4	5
2. Makes my mood better in general	1	2	3	4	5
3. Helps me feel less tired.	1	2	3	4	5

Figure 9.6 Sample questions from the "Outcome Expectation for Exercise" instrument.
Adapted, by permission, from B. Marcus and L. Forsyth, 2003, *Motivating people to be physically active* (Champaign, IL: Human Kinetics), 73.

How does one locate an existing instrument that can be used in a study or evaluation? The best place to look for instruments is the literature, particularly studies that have been conducted in a similar topic area as the researcher's study. If the researcher is studying self-confidence of youth in adventure programs, the researcher should review the literature on this topic. Scholarly studies generally note what instrument was used in the study and how data were analyzed. Even if the instrument noted in a scholarly article would not meet the needs of the researcher, the article may identify other sources of instruments. For every kind of study or evaluation, the researcher should dedicate time to reviewing various instruments and research designs of studies that were conducted concerning similar topics. This information can help the researcher identify a data collection tool to use in the study. The second source for finding existing instruments is through books and reference material from publishers. NRPA, Idyll Arbor, Human Kinetics, and Sage Publishing are some agencies that provide instruments or publications on how to create an instrument.

If the researcher discovers that the instrument needed does not exist, the researcher must create the instrument himself. This generally occurs when interviews or focus groups are selected as the data collection tool. The qualitative data that are needed must be tailored specifically to the research question and the purpose of the study. Locating an existing instrument that meets these needs is highly unlikely, so the researchers are left with no alternative but to create the instrument. Researchers should not "operate blind" when faced with developing an instrument. The literature can provide a wide variety of instruments to review so that the researchers become familiar with techniques used in other qualitative studies. A second category of resources available to the researcher includes experts on the topic of the study. Experts can provide valuable advice, guidance, and instrument examples to review. Finally, the researchers should review books that are specifically written on how to develop instruments. Whether a quantitative or qualitative instrument is needed, numerous publications are available on how to develop the instrument needed for the study. The exact nuts and bolts of how to develop an instrument are beyond the scope of this text. Researchers should review literature, consult with experts, and review books and other resources during the process of selecting or developing an instrument.

Instrument Considerations

Whether using an existing instrument or developing their own, researchers must consider some other factors when making the final decision on which data collection tool to use. These factors include the validity, reliability, objectivity, and usability of the instrument. Reviewing the validity of the instrument is a twofold process. First, the researcher must determine if the instrument measures what it is intended to measure. Second, the researcher must determine if the study results or conclusions provided by the instrument are valid. A researcher would not use a boredom scale to assess the satisfaction of participants with a program. This instrument does not collect information about satisfaction; it collects information about boredom. The conclusions drawn from the data are also invalid in relation to the satisfaction of the customers with their leisure activities. Each instrument must be used in the manner for which it was developed, not to assess something else. There is additional information in this chapter concerning gathering evidence or information to establish the validity of an instrument that the research has developed to collect data for a study.

The second factor to evaluate is the reliability of the instrument. Reliability is the "repeatability" of the results of the study. In other words, if the study was repeated, would it yield the same data and conclusions? If the researcher uses a preexisting instrument, the developers will have likely documented the reliability of the instrument. To determine the reliability of an instrument that is created specifically for a study, the researcher can repeat the study with two or more similar groups and compare the results. The comparison should indicate that the results are consistent, thus establishing the reliability of the instrument. There is additional information in this chapter concerning gathering evidence to establish the reliability of an instrument a researcher has developed to gather data for a study.

The next factor to evaluate is the **objectivity** of the instrument. Objectivity focuses on the instrument having an absence of subjective judgments. This means that the data should be specific enough that they cannot be manipulated or misrepresented to support the beliefs of the researcher. If the researcher believes that the spinning classes are meeting the needs of the customer, the researcher could focus on gathering data to confirm this belief. This researcher could also ask leading questions to encourage participants to respond "yes" regarding whether the class is meeting their needs. For example, the researcher could ask, "Isn't this class meeting your needs?" This question leads the respondent to answer "yes." In comparison, the question "Is this class meeting your needs?" does not lead the respondent to answer "yes." The first question introduces a bias, and the second question is objective.

The final factor to evaluate is the **usability** of the instrument. Usability does not consider the content or intent of the instrument, but rather how user friendly the instrument is for subjects and the researcher to use. This area examines format, directions, amount of time needed to complete the instrument, and how easy it will be to transfer the data for analysis. These are operational issues for the researcher to consider when choosing an instrument. These factors are important to review before selecting or developing an instrument for the study.

Validity of the Instrument

If left with no choice but to develop an instrument, the researcher must determine how to establish the validity of the instrument. Researchers have several options that they may use to establish the validity of an instrument. The three major options are content validity, criterion validity, and construct validity.

Content Validity

Content validity is the first area that the researcher should address to establish the validity of the instrument. This involves examining the format, the type of questions, and the number of questions on the instrument. When evaluating the format, the researcher should determine if the print size is appropriate and readable, if the language is appropriate for the subjects, and if the language is clear to the subjects. If the instrument is designed to collect data from a child, the language must be simpler than language used for an adult. Something as simple as the term *self-confidence* can create confusion for a child. Instead of using *self-confidence,* a phrase is needed to describe how it makes a child feel, such as "I know I can do it." An adult will understand what self-confidence means but may not understand highly specialized or technical terms. The language within the instrument must be understandable for the subjects of the study.

How does a researcher establish content validity? First, the researcher can have individuals from the population review the instrument and provide feedback regarding words, phrases, or sentences that are confusing. These items should be corrected, and the instrument should be reviewed again by the subjects to ensure that the corrections have eliminated the confusion. The second option is to gather proof of content validity by having an expert review the instrument. The expert can also comment on format elements and assist in determining if the instrument will gather the data that are necessary to answer the research question. In other words, does the instrument measure what it was developed to measure? The expert can help answer this critical question, as well as examine the number and type of questions on the instrument. Most instruments will include several questions for each variable or concept that is being evaluated. One boredom assessment related to free time consists of 20 questions across 4 content areas. The content areas are physical involvement, mental involvement, meaningfulness, and time. Several questions are included within the assessment to measure each of these content areas. The combined score then determines the level of boredom. This is more effective than just asking one question: "Are you bored?" Every instrument that is developed for a study should be reviewed for content validity. This allows corrections to be made to the content before the instrument is used for collecting data.

Criterion Validity

After establishing content validity for the instrument, the researcher should then consider if **criterion validity** can be established for the instrument. Criterion validity is the second option that researchers can use to establish the validity of the instrument. This involves comparing the results of an instrument that has been proven valid with the results of the instrument that was developed for the study. Both instruments measure the same variables, but in a different way. Criterion validity can be proven using one of two methods. The first method is to administer both instruments at the same time and then compare results. The second method is to use one instrument to predict the outcome of the second instrument. The researcher will compare the results of the two instruments through a statistical analysis.

An example of gathering proof of criterion validity is when a programmer wants to develop a satisfaction survey to assess the customers' satisfaction level with the fitness classes they participated in during the year. The researcher examines the history of customers' enrollment in fitness classes and wants to use this as the first measurement of the customers' satisfaction score. This historical data indicate a customer's satisfaction level. The number of consecutive sessions that the customer registered for indicates the customer's satisfaction with the fitness classes. A high number of consecutive sessions indicates a high level of customer satisfaction. The programmer then develops a satisfaction survey and gathers data from the customers. If the frequency of enrollment is high and the satisfaction rating is high, this establishes the validity of the instrument. If a researcher wants to establish criterion validity, the challenge is identifying a second source to measure the same variables of the study. This challenge could prove to be insurmountable. If this is the case, the researcher has one final option for establishing the validity of the instrument.

Construct Validity

Construct validity is the final option available to researchers for establishing the validity of the instrument. This technique requires the researcher to gather a variety of data from different sources related to the variables being studied. For example, if the variable that an instrument is measuring is "leisure satisfaction," the researcher must determine what data are needed to measure this variable. The researcher decides to examine the following data: the customer's enrollment records, the customer's satisfaction survey, and observations of the customer during a fitness class. The researcher then uses a technique called **triangulation** to analyze the data. Triangulation uses a minimum of three different sources of data to test a hypothesis. For example, in evaluating the customer satisfaction level, the programmer must use three sources of data during the analysis phase. The first source of data is the customer satisfaction survey, the second source of data is the customer's enrollment records, and the third source is information from observing the customer during class. The programmer forms a hypothesis from the observation data and then tests this hypothesis with the other two sources of data. This allows the researcher to double-check a hypothesis through the three sources of data and to look for evidence that disproves the hypothesis. The researcher continues this process of formulating a hypothesis and testing the hypothesis through the triangulation technique.

Proof of construct validity is gathered by formulating a hypothesis and testing it through mul-

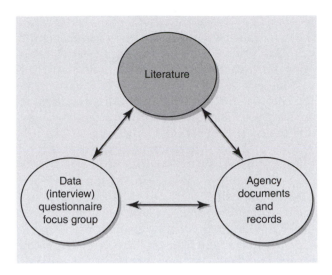

Figure 9.7   Triangulation.

tiple sources of data. This is the only option that permits the researcher to integrate the process of establishing validity into the data analysis phase of the study. Figure 9.7 provides an example of the triangulation process.

The researcher should dedicate time to establishing the validity of a developed instrument. If the researcher does not do this, the results of the study may be invalid and of little use to the organization. The three options presented here (content, criterion, and construct) allow the researcher to determine when to establish the validity of the instrument—either before data collection (content), during data collection (criterion), or during data analysis (construct). The time devoted to this will help ensure that the instrument is measuring what it is intended to measure and that the conclusions from the study are valid.

◼ *TEST YOUR SKILLS WITH EXERCISE 9.4.*

Reliability of the Instrument

Once the researcher has determined how the validity of an instrument will be established, the next task is establishing the reliability of the instrument. Reliability is the consistency or repeatability of the results from an instrument. Researchers have three options for establishing the reliability of an instrument: (1) test-retest method, (2) equivalent-forms method, and (3) split-half method. All three options involve gathering two sets of data for comparison. If the results are similar, this is evidence that the instrument has reliability.

PROFESSIONAL PERSPECTIVES

■ The real world of parks and recreation

Subject-completed instruments are given to subjects involved in the study to complete and return to the researcher. This type of instrument is very valuable to the American Canoe Association (ACA). The ACA puts on an annual meeting where we invite all of our members, staff, and board of directors. The event includes educational sessions, board of directors meetings, a silent auction, the president's reception, and a banquet dinner. The event is a chance for our members to have a voice; they can voice their concerns, what they would like to see in the future, and what is working for them. That is why it is very important to find out how our members enjoyed the event because we want them to come back the next year and bring others with them.

After the event this year, an evaluation was sent out to the attendees. The evaluation was a subject-completed survey that used the Likert scale. The return rate was high for the surveys. These data were analyzed and then sent out to all staff members so the staff could brainstorm for next year's event. We found out that the silent auction needed a lot of improvement, but overall everyone enjoyed themselves. The survey was very helpful to us, and it allowed us to see how we can change the event for the better to attract more members for next year.

Why was research important in this case?

Research is very important in our agency because we are always trying to improve the organization. As I have already stated, the research helps us figure out what we need to change (and what we can keep the same) to bring in more members and to keep the existing members coming back. By using subject-completed instruments, we are involving our members in the process so we can find out what they need from us and what they already find useful. Involving the members is very important to us because we are a member-based organization—and without our members, we would not exist.

Test-Retest Method

The first option for establishing reliability is the **test-retest method.** This requires the researcher to administer the instrument two times with a time lapse between the test and retest. Once the researcher has both scores, he compares the results to determine if they are consistent. If the results are consistent, this is evidence of the reliability of the instrument. In the example of the programmer developing a customer satisfaction survey, the programmer would give the survey to the participants of the fitness class two times— once at the final class and then a second time a week later by mail. The researcher compares the results to determine if they are consistent. If they are consistent, this is proof of the reliability of the instrument. If it is not possible to administer a test two times to the subjects, then the equivalent-forms method is a good option for establishing the reliability of the instrument.

Equivalent-Forms Method

The second option available to researchers is the **equivalent-forms method**. This method requires the researcher to administer two different instruments to the subject at the same time; the two instruments must measure the same variable, such as customer satisfaction. The researcher then compares the results of the two instruments to determine if the results are similar. If the results are similar, this is also proof of the reliability of the instrument. This technique would require the programmer to give both customer satisfaction surveys to the fitness class participants at the final class. This gives the programmer two sets of data to compare from one contact with the customers (instead of two contacts, as in the test-retest method). The results from the two instruments are compared for each customer to determine if they are consistent. The challenge with this method is having two instruments that measure the same variables. This may or may not be an option for the researcher when trying to establish the reliability of the instrument. If this is not possible, then the split-half method may be the best option for the researcher.

Split-Half Method

The **split-half method** is the final option for establishing the reliability of the instrument. This option is appealing to researchers because it creates a comparison within one instrument. The researcher only has to gather data once (not twice as in the test-retest method) and only uses one instrument (instead of two as in the equivalent-forms method). The researcher splits the instrument in half as if there are two instruments. This technique requires the instrument to include at least two questions that ask the same thing but in different ways. These questions provide the data that are examined for the consistency of the responses. If the responses are consistent, this is proof of the reliability of the instrument. The programmer would develop an instrument so that the first half of the instrument is compared to the second half of the instrument. Basically, each half asks the same thing, but in a different way. A researcher must always be concerned with gathering proof related to the validity and reliability of the instrument. Table 9.4 provides a summary of the options for gathering proof to establish validity and reliability of instruments used in research and evaluation projects. This effort helps ensure that the results of the study are true, valid, and accurate.

The use of subject-completed or researcher-completed instruments depends on the type of study the researcher is planning on conducting. Each category includes options that can provide quantitative data or qualitative data. The selection of the instrument is determined by the type of study being conducted and the type of data needed to answer the research questions. As you have probably concluded, the decisions from the beginning of the study to the point of selecting an instrument are all interrelated throughout the research process. As a researcher, you must ensure that the instrument used within a study provides the necessary data to answer the research question.

▪ *TEST YOUR SKILLS WITH EXERCISES 9.5 AND 9.6.*

● TABLE 9.4 ●

Evidence for Validity and Reliability of an Instrument

Validity-related evidence	Element	How
Content validity	Evaluate print size, readability, language level, terms, number of questions, and type of questions.	Have an expert review the instrument. Have subjects review the instrument through a field test.
Criterion validity	Use two instruments or data sources that measure the same variable.	Administer both instruments concurrently (same time). Use one instrument to predict the outcome of the other.
Construct validity	Use at least three sources of data to test each hypothesis.	Each hypothesis that is developed is tested through the different sources of data.
Reliability-related evidence	Element	How
Test-retest method	Administer the same survey two times to the subjects with a time lapse between the first and second time.	Compare the results from the test and retest to determine if they are consistent.
Equivalent-forms method	Administer two different instruments at the same time.	Compare the results from the two instruments for consistency.
Split-half method	Administer one instrument to the subjects once.	Compare the questions that ask the same thing but in a different manner for consistency.

Conclusion

The selection of a data collection tool is a multi-step process. This process requires the researcher to identify what data are needed. The researcher must also determine whether an existing instrument can be used or a new instrument needs to be developed by the researchers. Once these decisions are made, the researcher must evaluate the validity and reliability of the preexisting instrument that may be used. If an instrument is developed specifically for the study, the researcher must establish the validity and reliability of the instrument. These decisions are all interrelated, and they are ultimately guided by the research questions. If the researcher bypasses any of these decisions, the results of the study could be invalid—and the time and resources dedicated to the study could be a wasted expense for the organization.

EXERCISES

■ Exercise 9.1: Subject-Completed Instruments

Identify what type of subject-completed instrument is being used in each of the following statements. Choose from these options:

> Written survey with closed-ended questions
>
> Self-checklist
>
> Written questionnaire or survey with open-ended questions

1. A survey used to find out what camps the parents want in the future
2. Questions asking for suggestions to improve the day camp for next season
3. A five-point Likert scale for rating the customer service element
4. A survey that asks subjects to identify how frequently they used the recreation center and what programs and services they used
5. An evaluation of the class instructor
6. Questions asking what the person likes and dislikes about the facility

■ Exercise 9.2: Researcher-Completed Instruments

Identify which data collection tool could be used for each of the following statements. Choose from these researcher-completed data collection instruments:

> Focus group   Performance checklist
> Unstructured interview   Product evaluation
> Observation   Product evaluation
> Structured interview   Rating scale

1. A survey with closed-ended questions that is read to a subject
2. An interview with seven aerobic participants
3. A camp for soccer skills tracking what skills can be performed
4. Gathering information about social interaction in the fitness center
5. The score of a person's performance of an ice skating routine
6. The judges' reviews of science projects at a science fair
7. An interview with one person concerning her likes and dislikes of arts activities
8. Watching an instructor teach a swimming class

▪ Exercise 9.3: Instrumentation

What data collection tool is being used to collect data for each of the following. Choose from the options listed below.

Survey with closed-ended questions

     Observation   Rating scale   Focus group   Self-checklist

Open-ended questions on a survey

1. Customers' preferences concerning 10 new programs that are proposed
2. Analyzing the layout and traffic flow within the fitness center
3. Average score of divers on the swim team
4. The need among youth sport leaders for new athletic fields in the community
5. Customers' perception (in writing) about the agency's contributions to the quality of life in the community
6. The programs, events, and services that a customer has participated in during the past six months
7. How people interact at the public pool

▪ Exercise 9.4: Instrument Validity

What type of evidence of validity is being used in each of the following statements?

Choose from these options:

     Content   Criterion   Construct

1. Test many different hypotheses with the data.
2. Have an expert review the instrument.
3. Use one source of data that has validity to compare with the data collected.
4. Use field testing of the instrument.
5. Use two instruments; one has validity, and the other is the new instrument that needs evidence for validity.
6. Use a variety of data sources to formulate conclusions.

▪ Exercise 9.5: Instrument Reliability

Which method for establishing reliability is being used in each of the following examples? Choose from these options:

     Test-retest method   Equivalent-forms method   Split-half method

1. Collect data once but use two different instruments.
2. Collect data twice with the same instrument.
3. Several questions within the instrument ask the same thing in different ways.
4. Compare the results of data collected twice using the same instrument.
5. Compare the results of two different instruments.
6. Compare the results within one instrument.

■ Exercise 9.6: Article Analysis

For the following exercise, return to the research articles used in exercise 1.2 and complete the following questions about the instrument or instruments used in each research study.

1. Article:
   a. What type of instrument was used?
   b. Was the instrument's validity addressed in the article? If yes, how?
   c. Was the instrument's reliability addressed in the article? If yes, how?
   d. What are the strengths of the instrument selected?
   e. What are the weaknesses of the instrument selected?
2. Article:
   a. What type of instrument was used?
   b. Was the instrument's validity addressed in the article? If yes, how?
   c. Was the instrument's reliability addressed in the article? If yes, how?
   d. What are the strengths of the instrument selected?
   e. What are the weaknesses of the instrument selected?

CASE STUDY

The American Canoe Association is launching a new Web site. The staff is determining what information should be brought over from the old site, what new information should be included, and what information should be left off. The ACA is thinking about asking its members, instructors, and clubs for their help. What type of subject-completed instrument should the ACA staff put together to send out? Why do you think that particular instrument would be the best?

FOR THE INVESTIGATOR

The Health and Leisure Survey was provided to you for the purpose of framing a study within the time limitations of a semester. In reviewing this chapter, you should have become aware of a number of other data collection options that would yield truthful and meaningful data.

1. What are two other choices of data collection tools that could be used for this study? Why would you select these options?
2. The instrument used in this sample study was a modification of an existing instrument from the Center for Disease Control and Prevention (CDC). The CDC has extensive evidence regarding the validity and reliability of each question on the existing survey. For the two other data collection tools you identified in question 1, how would you establish validity and reliability for each tool?

CHAPTER 70

• OBJECTIVES •

After completing this chapter, you will be able to

- describe the 10 threats to the internal validity of research studies,

- determine which threats to internal validity are threats in specific types of studies,

- identify how to control the 10 threats to internal validity, and

- illustrate how to enhance the internal validity of qualitative studies.

Internal Validity

The program director has approached you and asked you to develop a study about the recreational needs of teenagers at the local high school. You have worked for several weeks on developing the plan for the needs assessment, and you have discovered that planning for the study is a multistep process that requires many decisions. You have determined the focus of the study, identified the sample, and developed the instrumentation plan, which includes using a survey that you developed to gather data. The program director has reviewed your work and informs you that there is still one critical step remaining in the planning process. You must evaluate the entire study design to examine the internal validity of the study.

At this point, you are confused and realize that you must go back and review the three types of validity.

alidity and reliability are a constant point of confusion and concern for many researchers. The concepts of validity and reliability raise concerns or threats that the researcher must address and try to control through the research design or how the research study is being conducted. These threats and corrective options are reviewed within this chapter. The first step that must be accomplished is pulling together the pieces concerning validity and reliability that have been previously covered to show the similarities and differences between the three types of validity and reliability.

Review of Validity

For a research study, the three types of validity are external validity, instrument validity, and internal validity. Each type of validity directs the researcher to review various components of the instrumentation plan and to evaluate how these components will affect the data gathered and the results of the study. If the researchers do not examine the three types of validity for their research, the results of the study may only apply to the group involved in the study or could be invalid. The three types of validity are reviewed in this chapter to clarify what each type addresses as well as the intent of each type. The first type of validity to review is the external validity of a study.

External validity refers to the extent that the results of the study can be generalized beyond the sample used to collect data—in other words, the extent to which the results can be applied to the population that the sample represents. The

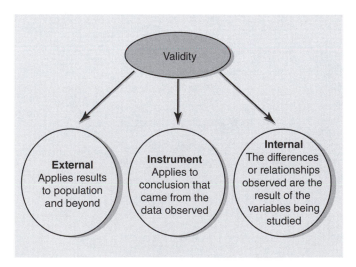

Figure 10.1 Summary of the three types of validity.

sampling process is a critical step in the research or evaluation process because it affects the external validity of the study. If the study results can only be applied to the sample, the study has no external validity. This limitation is due to the study design or the sampling process used to gather data. For example, the results of the study you want to conduct should be able to be generalized to the population as a whole at the high school. The second type of validity is **instrument validity.** Whether the researcher is using an existing instrument or developing a new instrument for the study, the researcher must consider the validity of the instrument. To review, the process of determining the validity of the instrument is twofold. First, the researcher must determine if the instrument measures what it is intended to measure. Second, the researcher must determine if the study results or conclusions provided by the instrument are valid. The final type of validity to review is internal validity, which is the focus of this chapter. Figure 10.1 provides a summary of the three types of validity that must be addressed in every study.

Internal Validity

Internal validity is the third type of validity that a researcher must examine when developing the instrumentation plan. By evaluating the internal validity of the study, the researcher can revise the study plan to ensure that the results of the study are free from the influences of extraneous variables, flaws in the study design, or researcher bias. If a study has internal validity, the differences noted in the data are due to the variables being studied, such as a treatment or a program. If a study lacks internal validity, the observed differences are due to variables outside the scope of the study or to the design of the study itself. A study can also lack internal validity when the data collectors bias the data collection process or the scoring of the data. For example, in the study of recreational interests of the teens at the local high school, the person summarizing the data could bias the results. This person could add numbers to the recreational activities that he likes in order to ensure that these activities are provided to the teens. Some study designs, such as the experimental design, have many more threats to internal validity than other research designs. For example, if a researcher is examining the relationship between exercise and weight loss, the extraneous variable that can influence the results of the study is diet. By examining the internal validity of the study, the researcher can work to identify and control these elements of the study. The items that can negatively affect the internal validity of a study are referred to as threats to the internal validity of the study.

10 Threats to Internal Validity

In research studies, 10 threats to internal validity must be examined and controlled if possible within the instrumentation plan. The researchers must analyze the study design and instrumentation plan to specifically note (1) which threats are threats to the internal validity of the study, (2) why each one is a threat, and (3) how the researchers plan to try to control this threat during the course of the study. Researchers must realize that it is impossible to control all the threats to the internal validity of a study. In other words, there is never a perfect study design that controls all the elements of the study. The goal is to minimize the threats and their impact on the data and conclusions of the study. With that in mind, the review of validity (internal, external, and instrument) and reliability is part of the instrumentation section of a research project. The instrumentation section of every research or evaluation study is the road map for navigating through the study. The goal is to control the threats to internal validity through the instrumentation process so that the results are due to the treatment, program, or service instead of other factors outside the study. Table 10.1

● *TABLE 10.1* ●
Threats to Internal Validity

Threat subject	When	How	Control
1. Subject characteristics	A threat to all studies	Differences among the subjects in a sample (which are unknown to the researcher) can affect the outcomes.	Gather extensive and detailed information about the subjects' characteristics.
2. Mortality	A threat to all studies	Subjects drop out of the study, affecting the results of the study.	Maintain detailed information on subject characteristics in order to replace the subject who dropped out. Use a study design that will decrease the likelihood of subjects dropping out. (This threat is difficult to control.)
3. Location	A threat to all studies	Where data are collected affects the information obtained from subjects.	Keep the location consistent or use the same place for data collection.
4. Instrumentation (threats can occur in three areas: instrument decay, data collector bias, and data collector characteristics)			
4a. Instrument decay	A threat when data must be scored	Data are not scored in the same way (e.g., essay question).	Ensure adequate time to score data consistently.
4b. Data collector bias	A threat when a person gathers data from other people	The data collector biases the data in some way when collecting them.	Ensure that data collectors are properly trained.

(continued)

TABLE 10.1   (continued)

Threat subject	When	How	Control
4c. Data collector characteristics	A threat when a person gathers data from other people	The characteristics of the data collector can influence the information a subject provides.	Standardize the data collectors for the study.
5. Testing	A threat in experimental research and research that uses the test-retest design	When researchers collect data over a period of time using the pretest and posttest process, the subjects know what is coming.	Ensure that the test-retest design is the best research design for the study (this threat is difficult to control when using this design).
6. History	A threat in all studies	Unplanned events occur during the time of the study.	Identify and document the event (this threat is difficult to control).
7. Maturation	A threat for studies that are conducted over a period of time and use the test-retest design	Changes that occur can be due to the passage of time rather than the program or treatment.	Use comparison groups in the study so the results can be checked across groups.
8. Regression	A threat for studies that use test-retest designs when subjects are selected based on extreme scores	Statistical phenomenon occurs that causes extreme scores to move to the mean.	Avoid selecting people based on extreme scores.
9. Implementation	A threat in experimental studies	Groups are treated differently, giving one group an advantage over another group.	Treat all groups the same.
10. Subject attitudes	A threat in experimental studies	One group perceives that they are receiving special attention over others.	Have all groups treated the same.

provides a summary of the 10 threats to internal validity, including when they are a threat and recommendations on how to control the threat. Each of these threats is reviewed in this chapter.

Subject Characteristics

The first threat to internal validity—**subject characteristics**—is a threat in all studies that use human subjects. This threat occurs when subjects have characteristics that can influence the results of the study. For example, if a programmer wants to evaluate the outcomes of the aerobic program for the participants, subject characteristics can affect a subject's response on the evaluation. If the participant has health issues (such as high blood pressure or previous injuries to the knee, shoulder, or back), these characteristics can affect the participant's responses on the evaluation. To control this bias, the evaluator must gather information

from the subjects about any characteristics that can affect their responses on the evaluation. This information can then be included in the analysis stage of the evaluation.

Mortality

The second threat to internal validity—**mortality**—is also related to the subjects of the study and is a threat in all studies that use human subjects. This does not mean that people are dying, but rather that they are dropping out of the study or program. The threat of mortality is higher in studies that occur over an extended period of time. In research studies, mortality presents additional challenges. The researcher cannot simply replace the person who dropped out of the study. The replacement could have very different characteristics from the person who dropped out. With this in mind, the researcher needs to replace the subject who dropped out with a person who is very similar in the key characteristics for the study. This highlights the importance of knowing the characteristics of the subjects in the sample. If the researcher has detailed information about every subject in the sample, this increases the likelihood of replacing a subject who drops out with a person who has similar characteristics. Another option for controlling this threat is to create a study design that will decrease the likelihood of subjects dropping out of the study.

Instrumentation issues such as the duration of the study, the frequency of data collection, and the data collection instrument can influence the mortality rate within the study. If the researcher can limit the time required of subjects to complete the study, the rate of mortality may decrease.

Location

The third threat to internal validity is location, which is a threat in all studies that involve collecting data from human subjects. The place where data are collected can influence the truthfulness and quality of the data. If the programmer wants to administer a survey to the participants of the aerobics program, the location where the data are collected is important. The quality of the data would be compromised if participants were asked to complete the evaluation in the aerobics room with the instructor peering over their shoulders. This is particularly true if the room is noisy and the participants are completing the survey while sitting on the floor. To control the threat of location, the researcher must ensure that the location where the data are collected provides an environment that will not negatively affect the quality of the data. The second consideration is to try to keep the location the same each time data are collected. This keeps the environment consistent through all data collection sessions, which helps control the threat of location. In the case of the aerobics participants, a better place to administer the survey would be in another room in the facility or at their home.

Instrumentation

The fourth threat to internal validity falls within the **instrumentation plan** itself. Three areas within instrumentation can create a threat to the internal validity of a study: (1) instrument decay, (2) data collector bias, and (3) data collector characteristics.

Instrument Decay   The first threat to internal validity within instrumentation is **instrument decay.** This is a threat when data are scored in a way that allows the scorer to subjectively interpret the data. An example of how instrument decay occurs is when an essay exam is graded. Essay answers must be scored based on the instructor's interpretation of the correctness of the response. Instrumentation decay can occur in grading essay questions in several ways. First, the instructor may not grade the essay answers the same way within the class. The instructor may be more lenient with students she likes and more critical with the responses from students she dislikes. The instructor could also try to grade all the essay exams during one sitting. The length of time needed to grade all the essay questions can influence the consistency of the grading process. The instructor could grade the first two exams quite differently than the last two exams. This difference in grading is instrument decay. The best way to control instrument decay is to use an instrument that minimizes the opportunity for differences in scoring. The researcher could also have two scores, which creates a double check process to minimize variances in scoring.

Data Collector Bias   Beyond instrument decay, a bias can also be introduced when a person collects the data from subjects through an interview. The second area of concern within instrumentation is **data collector bias.** This occurs when the person collecting the data from subjects unconsciously favors certain outcomes or responses and therefore introduces a bias within the data. The researcher may also record data from a subject in such a way that the data confirm the researcher's beliefs or hypothesis for the study. The way to control these threats is to first train data collectors specifically on how to collect the data and how to minimize the chances of introducing biases in this step. To control the likelihood of biases being introduced during the scoring phase, the researcher can use more than one person to collect the data. Just as in instrument decay, this creates a double-check process to minimize the likelihood of data collector bias.

Data Collector Characteristics   Within instrumentation, there is one additional threat to internal validity related to the person collecting data from subjects. The third threat to internal validity is the **data collector's characteristics.** This is a threat in studies that use people to collect data from subjects. The characteristics of the person collecting the data can influence the data provided by a subject. As individuals, we tend to be more open and honest with people whom we perceive to be similar to ourselves. A college student would feel more comfortable providing information to another student than to a professor, particularly if the questions are of a personal nature (e.g., questions about drug and alcohol use). The way to control this threat is to standardize the data collectors throughout the data collection phase. The three threats within instrumentation are related to biases in scoring or the influences of the person gathering data on the subject's truthfulness. These threats are controllable within the instrumentation plan if the researcher properly plans for data collection and scoring.

Testing

Research and evaluation studies gather data in a variety of ways, such as surveys, interviews, and observations. One data collection method frequently used in experimental studies is a test-retest design. The use of a test-retest method creates a threat to internal validity called **testing.** And the design itself creates this threat. Anytime subjects are given a pretest, they become aware of what data will be collected, what the correct answers are, and what the researcher is looking for from the subjects. If the professor gives the class a practice exam before the graded exam, the students are then aware of the content of the exam. With this knowledge, the students focus their study efforts on the content of the practice exam. When they take the exam again, they perform much better than on the pretest. This pretesting process affects the posttest results, particularly if the same instrument is used for the pretest and the posttest. The only way to control the testing threat is to not use the pretest and posttest design. The researcher should evaluate other design options that can be used to collect the data necessary to answer the research questions.

History

Some threats to the internal validity of a study are beyond the control of the researcher. **History** is one such threat. This threat is the result of something unexpected happening during the study that the researcher could not control. For example, a professor has scheduled an exam for a particular class. The professor arrives at class to give the exam and discovers that the maintenance staff is jackhammering the sidewalk just outside the classroom. This noise will most likely negatively affect the scores on the exam by disrupting the students' ability to concentrate on the exam. It is very difficult to control these unforeseen events. The best way to control the threat of history is to select a research design that minimizes the chances of unexpected events occurring during the course of the study.

Maturation

An additional threat in studies that occur over an extended amount of time is the threat of **maturation.** This threat is related to the length of time involved in the study. The researcher wants to make sure the differences noted in the study are due to the treatment or program, not the passage of time. A popular program area for parks and recreation agencies is movement classes for preschoolers. These classes combine music, movement, and activities to develop the gross motor skills of children. Skipping is a high-level gross motor skill for all preschoolers to learn. In these classes, preschoolers progress through a series of gross motor skills that consists of walking, running, and hopping—then finally, they learn to skip. An instructor has worked with the same group of four- and five-year-olds each week in a Wiggles and Giggles movement class. At the end of six months, the instructor notes that all of her five-year-old students have learned to skip. Did they learn to skip because of her class content or because of the natural development process of the child? It is impossible to determine how much the class helped the children learn to skip (if any at all). Most children learn to skip between the ages of four and five years because of the development of the neurological system. The best way to control the threat of maturation is to use a comparison group that enables the researcher to evaluate the changes in the study. A **comparison group** is a group that receives a different experience than the first group. In the case of the children's classes, the first group participates in the class, and the second group does not. The researcher can compare the two groups to determine if the movement class participants learned to skip faster than the comparison group.

Regression

The next threat to internal validity is related to how researchers select the subjects to participate in the study. If the researchers select subjects based on extreme scores—either high or low— then **regression** becomes a threat to the internal validity of the study. For example, a youth soccer

Studies that involve children and occur over an extended period of time are susceptible to the threat of maturation.

coach is selecting local soccer players to play on the community travel team, and the coach picks the players based on last year's performances. The best athlete was selected for each position on the team. This included a player who averaged four goals each game. The coach expects this one player to score at least four goals each game during the travel league season. Is this a realistic expectation for the coach to have of this player? No, it is not a realistic expectation because the player will have good days and bad days on the soccer field. Some games the player may score more than four goals, and other games he may score less than four goals. When a researcher selects subjects based on extreme scores, such as the best scores and worst scores, the statistical phenomenon that occurs with both of these groups is called regression. This means that each group's performance will move to the mean or average performance. Figure 10.2 provides a summary of how regression occurs.

The groups with the highest scores can score worse in future tests, and groups that scored the lowest scores can improve their score through repeated testing. The sampling process used to select subjects is the best way to control regression. The researcher should avoid selecting subjects based on extreme scores in order to minimize the threat of regression.

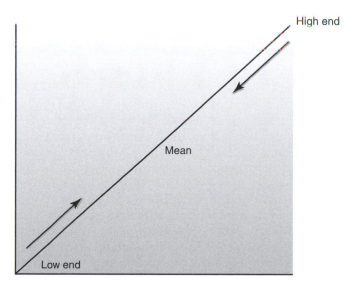

Figure 10.2   Regression.

PROFESSIONAL PERSPECTIVES

■ The real world of parks and recreation

At a local university, a concern about the students' health and welfare stimulated a discussion about upgrading the fitness facility that students, student-athletes, faculty, and staff use on a daily basis. The administration and the Student Government Association (SGA) decided to conduct a study. The study would use a survey to determine if the current student body was in favor of an increase in tuition to fund the construction of a new fitness facility. The problem was that most of the students would probably never have the benefit of using the facility because it would be completed after their graduation. The SGA came up with a four-question survey and administered it during the lunch hour at the student union. The results of this survey indicated that the students were not in favor of the additional charge for the fitness facility. These results were then used to justify keeping the current facility and dropping

any discussion of future improvement. This study lacked internal validity. The research plan was flawed in the development of the instrument, which involved using a convenience sampling technique. In addition, the students conducting the study skipped critical steps in the design of a research project.

Why was research important in this case?

The intent of the research project in this case was important in giving the students a voice in the decision-making process. This example highlights that if you are going to dedicate resources to a study, you need to do the study properly, following the steps of the research process. The outcomes in this case were used as the truth, and an important decision was made based on bad information.

Implementation

This next threat can be created as a result of how people are treated during the course of the study. This threat to internal validity is called **implementation.** The threat occurs when one group is treated differently than another group. This gives the first group an advantage over the second group. This threat can occur if two or more people are used to conduct the "treatment." For example, in a drug and alcohol treatment center, all the patients are required to take the leisure education program. Two staff members conduct this program at the facility. The treatment center wants to determine if the program affects the rate of relapse for the patients. The threat occurs because two different people are conducting this program. Each instructor may conduct the class in different ways, which can alter the results of the study. The best way to control the threat of implementation is (1) to use only one instructor for the program or treatment and (2) to have the instructor teach a standardized course content or treatment. These two steps will assist in controlling the two areas of the threat of implementation.

Subject Attitudes

The final threat to internal validity—**subject attitudes**—is also a threat within experimental designs and centers on how the subjects are treated during the course of the study. The behavior or attitudes of subjects in the experimental group can be influenced by the extra attention they receive from researchers. These subjects may also recognize that they are receiving some type of different experience than others, and this may affect their attitudes or behavior. For example, the staff at a drug and alcohol treatment center wants to conduct an experiment regarding the recreational activities that patients are introduced to during their treatment. The staff wants to determine which types of recreational activities the patients continue after their discharge from the center. A group of patients are selected for an adventure recreation program based on their leisure interests. The patients receive additional recreation time that introduces them to four different adventure activities. The patients recognize that they are receiving different treatment than other patients at the facility. This knowledge can influence their attitudes and behavior during the program. The patients indicate that they have a high level of commitment to continuing the adventure activities after their discharge. In reality, none of the patients continue the activities after they are discharged from the center. The best way to control this threat is to give both groups special treatment instead of just giving it to the experimental group. This should minimize the perception that one group is being treated differently than the other group.

The 10 threats to internal validity must be reviewed to determine if each one is a threat within a study. If any of them are identified as a threat, steps should be incorporated into the research plan to minimize or eliminate the threat.

Validity in Qualitative Designs

The threats to validity are not just a concern in quantitative studies but also within qualitative studies. The previous information about threats to internal validity primarily addressed quantitative studies. If you recall, the purpose and process within qualitative studies are different from quantitative studies. Qualitative studies generally use a smaller sample, and the data gathered are generally words, descriptions, observations, or information from documents. Within the various qualitative research designs, the researcher must review the instrumentation plan and identify the threats to the internal validity of the study. The researcher must then identify steps that can be taken to control these threats.

The 10 threats to internal validity covered within this chapter are most often connected to quantitative research and evaluation designs, such as experimental, correlation, and survey studies. This does not mean that the threats should not be addressed in qualitative studies, such as case studies, historical studies, and ethnographic studies. The threats of testing and regression are not threats in qualitative studies because these studies do not use a test-retest design. The threats of implementation and subject attitudes are not threats in qualitative studies because the experimental design is not used as the study design. Instrument decay is not a threat to qualitative studies because data are not scored. The threats of subject characteristics, mortality, location, data collector bias, data collector characteristics, and maturation can be threats to the internal validity of qualitative studies. The steps that were previously reviewed to control these threats apply to both quantitative and qualitative studies. Table 10.2 provides a summary of which of the 10 threats to internal validity are and are not threats in qualitative studies.

In qualitative designs, the internal validity has an additional concern that centers on the credibility of how the data are collected. In qualitative studies, the researcher is the primary data collection instrument. This creates a situation where the researcher must establish procedures to control any biases during the data collection process. To control the biases, the researcher must ensure that the questions, observations, and notes focus on the phenomenon or situation being studied. The increased time a researcher spends in the field collecting data for qualitative studies allows the researcher to confirm or dispute previous discoveries in the data. The greatest challenge to overcome in qualitative studies is the effect of the researcher being present as the data are collected. This reactive or instrumentation threat to internal validity is a challenge to qualitative researchers. Researchers must ensure that the data they have collected are valid and credible.

To improve the credibility or internal validity of a qualitative study, the researcher can do several things. First, the researcher must fully understand what is being studied and the general areas in which data are needed to answer the research questions. The researcher will develop hypotheses through the data collection process, but he must realize that these may need to be changed as additional data are collected. In addition, during the data analysis phase, direct quotes from the data should be used to support the conclusions.

• TABLE 10.2 •

Threats to Internal Validity for Qualitative Studies

Threats that do not apply to qualitative studies (because of the study design)	Threats that do apply to qualitative studies
Testing	Subject characteristics
Regression	Mortality
Subject attitudes	Location
Implementation	Data collector bias
Instrument decay	Maturation

The researcher should also use a technique called **member check** during data summary. The member check process requires the researcher to go back to the subjects and have them review the information collected from them for accuracy. This allows the subjects to catch errors in the data or conclusions. The member check process enhances the internal validity of the study results. Another technique that can enhance the validity of the study is triangulation. This requires the researchers to use different sources of data to verify or dispute a hypothesis or conclusion. The researcher should use at least three different data sources to formulate and test hypotheses. The triangulation technique requires the researcher to look for data that confirm and dispute the hypothesis of the study.*

To better understand these concepts related to the internal validity of qualitative studies, let's examine how they would be used in a study. The League for Disabled People, Inc. provides a year-round program for people with disabilities. This agency runs a summer residential camp program. The researcher wants to discover what the benefits are to the individuals who participate in the camp and to the caregivers of these individuals. The researcher decides to do the following: (1) review the literature concerning the benefits to both parties, (2) work as a staff member of the camp for a summer, (3) interview staff at the camp, (4) interview campers, and (5) interview the caregivers of the campers. This plan provides a variety of data sources for triangulation, such as literature, interviews, and observations.

The researcher works during the summer as a staff member and documents what he observes, including the program components and visual observations about the campers' level of participation and enjoyment. During the summer, the researcher interviews the staff and participants when possible (not all participants are capable of participating in an interview). After each session, the researcher conducts a phone interview with the caregivers at home about the benefits of attending the camp to the participant and the caregiver. The researcher conducts member checks with the staff, campers, and caregivers to ensure that the data collected are accurate. As the researcher develops hypotheses, he goes back to the data and performs repeated testing using triangulation to determine if each hypothesis is true or not. The researcher continues this process each week with the various groups that attend the residential camp. He further collects data, interprets data, and develops hypotheses and conclusions through member checks and triangulation. He also documents the data collection process, all data collected, the analysis process, and the interpretation process that led to the conclusions of the study.

As you can tell, the data collection and analysis process for qualitative studies requires much more time than for quantitative studies. This extensive process is necessary to fully understand the entire experience (for the campers, staff, and caregivers) and the benefits to the campers and caregivers. This type of study could not be conducted through quantitative techniques because the variables related to "benefits" are not known; therefore, these benefits must be discovered through a qualitative study.

Reliability

The second major area of concern for researchers is reliability, which goes hand in hand with validity. In simple terms, reliability is the "repeatability" of the data. In other words, if the researcher conducts the study multiple times, the results will be similar or consistent. Researchers must be concerned about external reliability, instrument reliability, and internal reliability. Each area looks at the consistency or similarities of the results of the study. Figure 10.3 is the same as figure 10.1 except the word *validity* is replaced by the word *reliability*. External reliability addresses the consistency of the results from a study. This helps ensure that the results of the study apply to the population, not just the sample. As with internal validity, this is linked

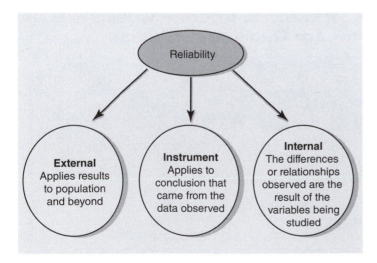

Figure 10.3 Three types of reliability.

*Adapted, by permission, from K. Henderson, 1991, *Dimensions of choice: A qualitative approach to recreation, parks, and leisure research* (State College, PA: Venture Publishing), 135.

with the sampling process used in the study. Instrument reliability, which was reviewed in detail in chapter 9, also focuses on the consistency of the data collected during the study. To enhance instrument reliability, the researcher can use a test-retest method, an equivalent-forms method, or a split-half method. Reliability does not focus on the truthfulness of the data, but rather on the consistency of the results. Finally, internal reliability focuses on how the study was conducted (as with internal validity). If the study is not conducted in a manner that has good internal validity, then the internal reliability is negatively affected as well. The threats to internal validity can affect the consistency of the results, or the internal reliability.

Reliability is also a concern in qualitative studies; in these studies, reliability is referred to as **dependability.** This examines what the researcher reports and what was actually happening in the area being studied. In other words, if a second researcher decided to replicate or repeat the study, would the researcher see, experience, and discover the same data? The best way to improve reliability in qualitative studies is to document what was done during the study. This serves as the instrumentation plan for future researchers who want to replicate the study. The challenge at the beginning of the study is that the researcher does not know every step of the process at that point. Therefore, the researcher should document every step of the process as the study is performed, including data collection, interpretation or analysis, and how conclusions were formulated. By documenting the entire research process from beginning to end, the researcher enables other researchers to replicate the study, thus enhancing the reliability of the study. Now that all three areas of validity and reliability have been reviewed in this chapter, let's look at the relationship between validity and reliability.*

Relationship Between Validity and Reliability

Researchers should view validity as being more important to establish than reliability. This does not mean that reliability should be overlooked, but validity must be established first, then reliability. Why is validity so important? To answer this question, let's examine the possible combinations of validity and reliability. The three combinations are as follows: (1) low validity and low reliability, (2) low validity and high reliability, (3) high

validity and high reliability. To better understand the four combinations, consider the example of chipping on to a green in golf. Figure 10.4a is an example of low validity and low reliability. The golf balls are on the green, but they are in a

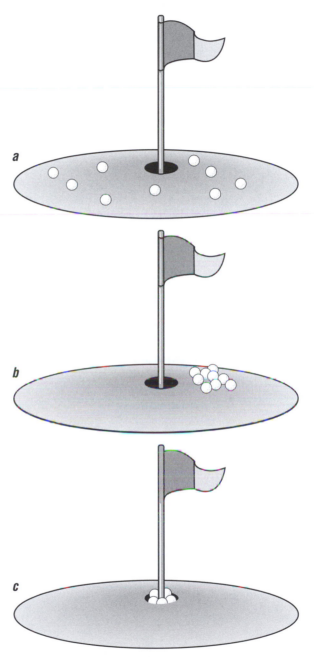

Figure 10.4 In the first figure (a), the balls are all over the green; this illustrates low validity and low reliability. In the second figure (b), the balls are placed consistently, but consistently off target; this illustrates low validity and high reliability. In the third figure (c), the balls are consistently in the hole; this illustrates high validity and high reliability.

*Adapted, by permission, from K. Henderson, 1991, *Dimensions of choice: A qualitative approach to recreation, parks, and leisure research* (State College, PA: Venture Publishing), 137.

random pattern all over the green area. The golfers are trying to sink the balls in the hole and have consistently missed. The golfers lack validity and reliability, which means their putting lacks accuracy and consistency. Figure 10.4*b* represents a study with low validity and high reliability. The golfers still cannot sink the ball, but their putting is consistent, as shown by the tight cluster of balls. The problem is that the golfers are consistently off the mark. In research, this would mean you are consistently wrong. If a study has high reliability and lacks validity, the results will likely be consistently wrong and invalid. This is not the type of research you want to be conducting in the field of recreation.

In figure 10.4*c,* the golfers have achieved high validity and high reliability—every ball hit has landed in the hole. The golfers are accurate and consistent with every shot. This is the combination that researchers should strive for, knowing that ultimately it may not be achieved. The relationship between validity and reliability is an important one that must be reviewed in research studies. As a researcher, you want to conduct a study in the same manner as a golfer sinking every ball while putting on to the green.

■ *TEST YOUR SKILL WITH EXERCISES 10.1, 10.2, 10.3, AND 10.4.*

Conclusion

The broad-based concerns related to validity and reliability, particularly internal validity, can appear to be an overwhelming task. The threats to internal validity must be examined and addressed in the instrumentation plan of every research project. If these threats are not examined, the results of the study could be based on error or extraneous variables, causing the results to be invalid. The time and effort dedicated to this step will identify the strengths and weaknesses of the study before it begins. This allows the researcher to make the necessary revisions to the instrumentation plan to ensure that the results of the study are valid. The final considerations addressed in this chapter are the three areas of validity and reliability and their relationship. This information can be confusing, but it is important to review when preparing to conduct a study. Doing so will help ensure that the results are valid and that the time invested in the study is used efficiently and effectively.

EXERCISES

■ Exercise 10.1: Threats Created by the Study Design

When are the following a threat to internal validity? Use table 10.1 in the chapter to assist you with this exercise. Multiple answers may apply for each item. Choose from these options:

   a. A threat to all studies that use human subjects

   b. A threat in experimental studies

   c. A threat when people gather data

   d. A threat when a test-retest design is used

1. Subject characteristics

2. Mortality

3. Location

4. Data collector bias

5. Data collector characteristics

6. Testing

7. History

8. Maturation

9. Regression

10. Implementation

11. Subject attitudes

■ Exercise 10.2: Identifying Threats to Internal Validity

What threat to internal validity exists in each of the following? Use the table 10.1 in the chapter to assist you with this exercise.

1. Groups in an experimental study are treated differently.
2. The study is conducted over a six-month period with children who are five years old.
3. The person scoring the test adds points to his favorite subjects' scores.
4. The researcher gives a test two times with an interval of two weeks between each testing session.
5. The data are collected at several different sites.
6. The researcher selects the best athletes from the group.
7. Three people have dropped out of the study.
8. Different people are used to collect the data.
9. Different people administer the "treatment," and one group is given a heads-up about the content of the final test.

■ Exercise 10.3: Controlling Threats to Internal Validity

Identify the threat or threats for each statement and specify how each threat can be controlled.

1. The programmer decides to mail a customer satisfaction survey to the participants in the aerobics program.
   a. What is the threat?
   b. How can the threat be controlled?
2. The programmer wants to evaluate all the swimming instructors. She decides to have a peer evaluation where each instructor will evaluate two other instructors.
   a. What are the threats?
   b. How can each be controlled?
3. The programmer has decided to try two new methods of behavior management during the therapeutic recreation day camp. He trains the 12 staff members of the camp on the two methods. Then he collects data on the number of incidents for which each method was used and the effectiveness of each method.
   a. What are the threats?
   b. How can each be controlled?
4. The programmer decides to select the best swimmer from each age group for the A team. He projects the points for each meet that should be won based on each swimmer's best performance.
   a. What is the threat?
   b. How can it be controlled?

■ Exercise 10.4: Article Analysis

What are the possible threats to internal validity for each research article used in exercise 1.2? Specify whether each listed threat is a threat in the study for the article. Also note how each threat to the study could be controlled (if controlling it is a possibility).

• TABLE 10.3 •

Analysis of Article 1

Return to the articles used in exercise 1.2 and complete the following charts concerning threats to internal validity or the study.

Threat to internal validity	Is it a threat in the study (yes or no)? If yes, how is it a threat?	Can it be controlled (yes or no)? If yes, how can it be controlled?
Subject characteristics		
Mortality		
Location		
Data collector bias		
Data collector characteristics		
Testing		
History		
Maturation		
Regression		
Implementation		
Subject attitudes		

• TABLE 10.4 •

Analysis of Article 2

Threat to internal validity	Is it a threat in the study (yes or no)? If yes, how is it a threat?	Can it be controlled (yes or no)? If yes, how can it be controlled?
Subject characteristics		
Mortality		
Location		
Data collector bias		
Data collector characteristics		
Testing		
History		
Maturation		
Regression		
Implementation		
Subject attitudes		

CASE STUDY

How would you have conducted the study discussed on page 136? Consider using things such as literature, usage figures, comparisons to other institutions, data gathered from students, information about options in funding, and user groups (students, student-athletes, coaches, faculty, staff).

FOR THE INVESTIGATOR

In every study, the researchers are always concerned about the internal validity and reliability of the study. The sample study is no exception. Review table 10.1 of the text and identify the following:

1. Which of the threats to internal validity are not a threat to this study? Explain why it is not a threat.
2. Which of the threats to internal validity are threats to this study? Explain why they are a threat within the study.
3. What can be done (if anything) to control the threats to internal validity that were identified in question 2?

• OBJECTIVES •

After completing this chapter, you will be able to

- show how to develop a histogram and polygon,
- calculate the mean, median, and mode for a set of data,
- apply the use of range and the normal curve for the purpose of data analysis,

- analyze scores using standard deviation and the normal curve, and
- describe how to analyze qualitative data.

Data Analysis

The program director has approved your study plan for the evaluation of the Wiggles and Giggles classes, except you have forgotten the last critical component of the instrumentation plan. The instrumentation plan has progressed through the process of specifying the population, the sample, the instrument to use to gather data, validity and reliability, and the data collection process. The final piece of the instrumentation plan is data analysis. The program director asks you, "What should be done with the data once you have collected them?" Many researchers and evaluators skip this step of the overall instrumentation process, which creates problems in developing conclusions for the study. You are reminded that there is a thought process that must be completed to ensure that the collected data can be analyzed in a manner that enables you to answer the research questions.

*M*ost studies have a series of research questions related to the primary question. For each question, you must show what data are being collected to answer the question, how the data will be analyzed, and how the data will be reported. These elements are the same for quantitative studies, qualitative studies, and evaluation. This process ensures that there are common threads that link all research efforts to the research questions. If this step is omitted in the planning process, the researcher is more likely to have data that do not answer the research questions or cannot be analyzed in a manner that answers the research questions. If the researcher intends to conduct a correlation study but only gathers data on one of the necessary variables, the research questions cannot be answered. As discussed earlier, correlation studies examine the strength of the relationship between two variables. Therefore, by conducting a study that does not gather data on at least two variables to analyze, the researcher has wasted time, effort, and other resources. To ensure that research and evaluation projects are conducted in the most efficient and effective manner possible, the plan must be comprehensive and must be completed before conducting the study. If changes occur during the planning process, you can ensure that all pieces of the study are in line with the changes.

Figure 11.1 provides an example of three types of research questions—one qualitative, one quantitative, and one evaluation. For each research question, information is provided about how data will be collected (e.g., through surveys or interviews) and whether the data are quantitative or qualitative data. The final two pieces of information for each research question identify how data will be analyzed and reported. Researchers who gather quantitative data generally begin with descriptive statistics as the first step in data analysis.

Quantitative Study

Research question: What is the relationship between cleanliness of the facility and customer satisfaction?

Data: Quantitative data from closed-ended questions on a survey

Data analysis: Descriptive statistical analysis for each question, frequency of each response, and percentages

Data reported: Frequency histogram and narration of table with a written summary

Qualitative Study

Research question: How does working with a personal trainer influence the person's commitment to regular physical activity?

Data: Qualitative data from interviews, customer evaluation with open-ended response, review of fitness plans

Data analysis: Code by themes of data

Data reported: Narration of data analysis and hypotheses from each question

Evaluation Study

Research question: Have the outcomes or objectives for the Wiggles and Giggles class been obtained?

Data: Instructor and parent evaluation of outcomes using written closed-ended questions

Data analysis: Descriptive statistics for each question; frequency and percentages for each response; category for each question; mean, median, and mode for each question

Data reported: Table and narrative of data collected

Figure 11.1 Three types of research questions.

he greatest challenge at this step of the research project is planning how to manage and organize the data. For most projects, you will have a pile of information from the literature review, a pile of information from the planning and implementation process, and a pile of information that contains the data you have collected. People use different systems, such as folders or notebooks, to organize their literature and planning documents. You should organize the information in a way that best meets your needs. For example, you could keep like items together—journal articles together, trade magazine articles together, and agency documents together. Or you could organize the information by topic area instead of the type of source. Some researchers choose to organize the information by time frame, starting from the most current information and having the later information follow in sequential order (or the opposite order could be used). No matter which way the information is organized, storing the documents in file folders or notebooks will save you time because you will not have to search each pile for a particular piece of information.

Your data can be organized and sorted in the same way as the other information, such as like items together (surveys, interviews, or observation sheets). This helps ensure that all the data are used and that the confidentiality of the subjects is maintained. It will also help you move quickly into data input, analysis, and writing the report. Now that you've decided how to organize the information, you must also decide how to manage the material in electronic files that are used for the data analysis. For quantitative data, such as surveys or questionnaires, the data are usually entered into an Excel spreadsheet or some other type of computer statistical package. You need to determine how these files will be set up. You should make multiple copies of the electronic files in case the computer crashes or is attacked by a virus. With qualitative data, you should also make multiple copies of the electronic files, such as those containing the data or the analysis information. This ensures that you have backup copies of this critical information.

Descriptive Statistics

Descriptive statistics provide the most foundational and simplistic analysis of data. These statistics describe frequencies, percentages, and the distribution of the responses from the subjects. To use descriptive statistical techniques, researchers must have quantitative data to summarize. For example, a researcher is conducting an evaluation of the Wiggles and Giggles program to determine if the objectives of the class were achieved. The agency currently offers 10 sections of the same class taught by two different instructors. The instructors worked collaboratively to develop the class content, which resulted in standardized class content across all 10 sections of the class. At the final class meeting for each section, a written evaluation survey is distributed to the parents of the children. The survey asks questions concerning demographic variables, the objectives of the class, and the number of times the person has participated in the class before this program session. An evaluation is also given to the instructor to note specifically how each class objective was achieved during the 10-week class. In addition, if the instructor or parent perceived that one of the class objectives was not achieved, space is available to note why it was not met and what the parents would suggest for the future.

The instrument that was used to gather data was a survey consisting of primarily closed-ended questions. Figure 11.2 lists the research questions for the evaluation study, along with the objectives from the Wiggles and Giggles class and the additional variables that the programmer is interested in including in the evaluation. The programmer determined that the demographic information, the history of classes, and the suggestions were also important variables for gathering data relevant to the evaluation process.

The survey will include at least one question for each objective, each demographic characteristic, and the person's history with the class. The survey will also have a question for soliciting comments and suggestions. The programmer wants the survey to be completed by 100 parents who have attended the Wiggles and Giggles class with their preschooler during the current program session. The programmer hopes that this number of subjects will provide the data needed to evaluate the classes. Figure 11.3 provides the survey questions that will be used. Note how each research variable identified in figure 11.2 has at least one question on the survey so that data can be collected on that variable.

Once the data are collected, the programmer must begin analyzing the information. Several types of descriptive statistics may be used, and each type provides information that describes the data. The researcher can use frequency tables, histograms, and polygons to provide a summary of

1. Class objectives:

   a. The participants will complete two music activities each class (marching, band drill, scarves).

   b. The participants will complete three gross motor activities each class (run, hop, arm circles, rolling, throwing, catching).

   c. The participants will complete two partner activities each class (interaction with one other toddler in class).

   d. The participants will complete one aerobic activity each class (toddler aerobics, minitrampoline).

   Did the instructor meet the class objectives?

2. Demographic information to be gathered:

   a. Age of parent (What is the age of the parent?)

   b. Age of child (What is the age of the child?)

   c. Ethnicity (What is the parent's ethnicity?)

   d. Socioeconomic status (What is the socioeconomic status of the household?)

3. History with agency:

   a. First timer

   b. Number of programs previously participated in during the past 12 months

   How many programs has the parent participated in during the past 12 months?

4. Suggestions or comments (open-ended responses)

Figure 11.2 Research questions for the Wiggles and Giggles evaluation.

the results for each question. The researcher can also use the measurements of central tendencies—that is, the mean, median, and mode—for more detailed information about the data. The range and standard deviations can be used to examine how dispersed or spread out the results are along a continuum. This provides the researcher with more information about the scores than central tendencies provide. If the researcher wants to examine the scores as they apply to a normal curve, the standard deviation is the number that is needed. These options for descriptive statistical analysis are covered in the following sections, along with examples of how these techniques can be used when analyzing the data collected to evaluate the Wiggles and Giggles classes.

Frequency Tables, Histograms, and Polygons

When analyzing data, the first step that many researchers perform is using some type of descrip-

tive statistical analysis. As previously mentioned, researchers use descriptive statistics to describe the data in relation to the questions asked on the data collection tool. The use of frequency tables, histograms, and polygons provides the researchers with summary information and visual representations of the data for each question. The researcher will usually take all the data collected and begin to summarize them by putting the information in a form that is easier to work with and understand.

Frequency tables allow the researcher to summarize a large amount of data or responses that have been collected by presenting the data in a table. This table enables the researcher to determine how many people selected each response option for the question. The **histogram** and **polygon** take the information in the frequency table and present it in a visual manner for the researcher. Many times it is difficult to understand what a frequency table is telling you as the researcher, so

Wiggles and Giggles Survey

a. Did the class complete two music activities each class?

    (1) Yes

    (2) No

b. Did the class complete three gross motor activities in each class (such as hopping, arm movements, throwing, catching, or dance)?

    (1) Yes

    (2) No

c. Did the class complete two partner activities in each class?

    (1) Yes

    (2) No

d. Did the class complete one aerobic activity in each class (such as trampoline, skipping, or hopping)?

    (1) Yes

    (2) No

e. What is your age?

    (1) 18-22

    (2) 23-27

    (3) 28-32

    (4) 33-37

    (5) 38-42

    (6) 43 or older

f. What is your ethnic origin?

    (1) Caucasian

    (2) African American

    (3) Asian American

    (4) Pacific Islander

    (5) Native American

    (6) Latino or Hispanic

g. What is the annual household income at the home where the child lives?

    (1) 25,000

    (2) 26,000-29,000

    (3) 30,000-35,000

    (4) 36,000-40,000

    (5) 41,000-45,000

    (6) 46,000 or above

h. How many times has your child completed a Wiggles and Giggles class?

    (1) First class completed

    (2) One other class

    (3) Two other classes

    (4) Three other classes

    (5) Four other classes

i. How many other programs have you or others in your household participated in at this recreation center in the past year?

    (1) None

    (2) 1-3

    (3) 4-6

    (4) 7-9

    (5) Over 10

j. What suggestions would you make to improve the Wiggles and Giggles classes?

Figure 11.3 Sample survey questions.

the visual presentation of the data within a histogram or polygon provides a "picture" of the data. In a histogram, the height of the bar indicates the frequency of that response or response category. In a polygon, the height of the point also represents the frequency of the response. These two visual aids can be used to display the response to one question in a survey or to summarize a set of data in a visual format.

To further explore these options within descriptive statistics, let's apply the frequency tables, histogram, and polygon to one question from the sample survey. In table 11.1, the question used in the example of a frequency table is the age of the parents. This demographic variable is one of the important variables that the researcher must understand in order to develop a customer profile based on the characteristics of the participants. By understanding the key demographic variables of the customer, the agency can more specifically market the Wiggles and Giggles classes to families that meet the profile characteristics.

The first descriptive statistic that is used with this type of data is a frequency table for each question. To present data in a frequency table, the researcher lists the response category and the number of responses for each response category. In the example in table 11.1, you can see that 5 parents were between the ages of 18 and 22, 19 parents were between the ages of 23 and 27, 40 parents were between the ages of 28 and 32, 21 parents were between the ages of 33 and 37, and 15 parents were between the ages of 38 and 42. This gives the researcher a first glance at the data in a fundamental manner. This same information can be presented in a visual manner with a frequency histogram and a frequency polygon. In a frequency histogram and frequency polygon, the vertical axis represents the frequency, and the horizontal axis represents the response categories or scores.

Figure 11.4 is a histogram of the responses from the age question on the survey for the adults attending the Wiggles and Giggles class with their child. This diagram provides a different visual display of the numeric data collected from the survey. In the frequency histogram, the frequency of each response category is represented by a column. Histograms are often used to summarize data in a visual manner for the reviewer. This same information can also be displayed in a frequency polygon, which is an additional way to summarize the information. In the frequency polygon, the frequency of each category is represented by a point, and the points are then connected with a line. Figure 11.5 presents the information from the age question as a frequency polygon. With these techniques, the information communicated is very limited but provides an overview of the data set. These are not the only descriptive statistics used to analyze data. The next step is to determine the central tendencies of the data for each question.

Central Tendencies: Mean, Median, and Mode

Descriptive statistics are also used by researchers to measure **central tendencies.** The three measurements of central tendencies are (1) mean, (2) median, and (3) mode. These measurements represent the data set with one number. The most familiar measurement of central tendencies is the **mean,** or the **average.** This is calculated by adding up the responses and dividing them by the total number of scores. For example, if students scored 7, 6, 5, 4, 3, 2, and 1 on a 7-point quiz, the teacher first adds all the scores to determine the sum, which is 28; then the teacher divides the sum by the total number of scores, which is 7. So this is 28 ÷ 7 = 4. The average score—or mean score—on the 7-point quiz is 4. This mean score represents the average score on the quiz, and the teacher knows that some students scored above the mean and others below the mean. This process of calculating a mean on the quiz is summarized in table 11.2.

Mean

In the example of the Wiggles and Giggles class, the age of the parents has been collected based on an interval, not an individual score. The response numbers for each category (1, 2, 3, 4, and 5) serve as the "score" used to calculate the mean, which is the average score of a data set. If

• TABLE 11.1 •

Frequency Table

Question: What is your age? (parent)

Response category	Number of responses for category
(1) 18-22	5
(2) 23-27	19
(3) 28-32	40
(4) 33-37	21
(5) 38-42	15
	Total: 100

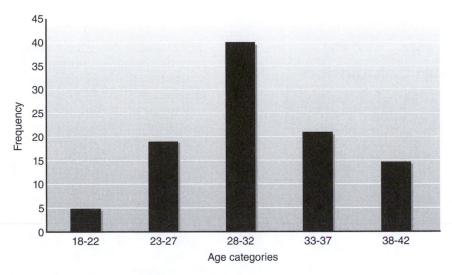

Figure 11.4 Frequency histogram for age of parents.

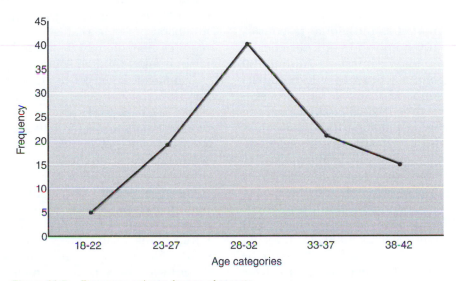

Figure 11.5 Frequency polygon for age of parents.

● TABLE 11.2 ●

Mean Score on a Seven-Point Quiz

Student	Score	Sum = 28
1	7	28 ÷ 7 = 4
2	6	Mean = 4
3	5	
4	4	
5	3	
6	2	
7	1	
	Sum = 28	

• TABLE 11.3 •
Mean Calculation

Response category		Frequency	
5 (ages 38-42)	×	15	= 75
4 (ages 33-37)	×	21	= 84
3 (ages 28-32)	×	40	= 120
2 (ages 23-27)	×	19	= 38
1 (ages 18-22)	×	5	= 5
	Sum	100	322

the data were reported as individual responses, there would be 100 numbers to add together to calculate the mean for this question. Adding 100 individual responses would be very cumbersome, and the likelihood of an addition error also increases. The mean is best calculated from the frequency table because it simplifies the calculation process with this type of data. To calculate the mean from the frequency table, the researcher multiplies each response category number by its frequency to determine the total for that response category. Table 11.3 provides this calculation. For example, the response category of ages 38 to 42 is represented by a 5. This number represents a category or categorical variable, not a score or quantitative variable. To calculate the total for

this response category, the researcher takes the response category number (5) and multiplies it by the frequency for that category (15). This is a total number of 75. This multiplication process is done for each response category.

Then the researcher adds the total of all the response categories to determine the sum, which is 322. The researcher knows that 100 people completed the survey and divides the sum of 322 by 100 to determine the mean. The number is 322 ÷ 100 = 3.2. Because there is not a response category of 3.2 and this number is below 3.6, the number is rounded down to 3. (If the number was 3.6 or higher, the number would be rounded up to 4.) This number represents the mean age of the parents, indicating that the mean is between the ages for response number 3, which is 28 to 32 years old. The process of translating response categories where the number represents a category or category interval requires more thought than simply calculating the mean from individual scores.

The mean is one of the most frequently used descriptive statistics for describing the central tendency of a data set. However, researchers need to be aware that the mean can be affected by extreme scores. If a data set has an extremely large or small score, this one score can alter the mean. Table 11.4 provides an example of this problem. The scores represent a set of exam scores from a program planning class. As the table demonstrates, one extreme score in class A made a difference of 3 points in the mean. The impact of extreme scores on the mean is one reason that researchers use other measures of central tendencies to describe

• TABLE 11.4 •
Mean and Extreme Scores

CLASS A			CLASS B		
Score	Frequency	Mean calculation	Score	Frequency	Mean calculation
99	1	99	76	1	76
75	2	150	75	2	150
74	2	148	74	2	148
73	2	146	73	2	146
71	2	142	71	2	142
	Sum	685		Sum	662
	Mean	76		Mean	73

the data set. The median is another measure that is often used along with the mean for analyzing data.

Median The second measure of central tendencies is the **median.** This is the point where half the scores fall above the median and half the scores fall below the median. This concept seems relatively simple, but it becomes a bit more complicated depending on whether the data set has an odd number of responses or an even number of responses. If a data set for a 7-point quiz is 6, 5, 4, 3, 2, and 1, the central two scores are the scores of 4 and 3. The median is the point halfway between 4 and 3, which is 3.5. The median for this data set is 3.5. Let's assume that the scores on a 7-point quiz are 7, 6, 5, 4, 3, 2, and 1. The score where half the scores fall above the point and half the scores fall below is 4. The median is 4 because this data set has an odd number of scores. The general rule to remember is that if the data set contains an even number of scores, then the median is a point between two points. Second, if the data set contains an odd number of scores, then the median is a point of the data set.

In the case of the Wiggles and Giggles class, calculating the median is different because the numbers used to record responses represent an interval of age. Because the data set includes 100 responses, which is an even number of responses, the median will fall between two responses— between the 50th and 51st responses. To identify the median age category, the frequencies of responses are added for the categories, beginning with response category 5. This category has 15 responses, and this number is added to the total number of responses for category 4, which has 21 responses. The calculation is 15 + 21 = 36. This total is not yet to the median point of the 50th and 51st responses. If 14 of the responses from response category 3 are added to the total, the amount has reached 50 responses (36 + 14 = 50). Response category 3 has a total of 40 responses, so the 50th and 51st responses of the data set are both within category 3. Therefore, the median is 3 (the median is not between two points because the 50th and 51st response are both in category 3). Table 11.5 provides an example of calculating the median for the Wiggles and Giggles class survey.

In these examples, the mean and median both fall within response category 3. Many researchers also use a third measure of central tendencies— the mode.

Mode The **mode** is the most frequent response or score. If the scores for a 7-point quiz were 7, 6,

5, 5, 5, and 2, the most frequent score was 5. This score occurred three times, while all other scores occurred only once.

In the case of the Wiggles and Giggles class and the ages of the parents, the most frequent response was 3, which represents the age group of 28 to 32. This category had 40 responses. No other response category exceeded this total. Table 11.6 provides an example of identifying the mode. The frequency table assists the researcher in identifying the mean, median, and mode.

Range

The calculations of central tendencies are useful in describing responses or scores, but these

• *TABLE 11.5* •

Median Calculation for the Wiggles and Giggles Class

Response categories	Frequency	Median calculation
5 (ages 38-42)	15	15
4 (ages 33-37)	21	15 + 21 = 36
3 (ages 28-32)	40	36 + 14 = 50
2 (ages 23-27)	19	
1 (ages 18-22)	5	
	100	

• *TABLE 11.6* •

Mode for the Age of Parents in the Wiggles and Giggles Class

Response categories	Frequency	Mode
5 (ages 38-42)	15	
4 (ages 33-37)	21	
3 (ages 28-32)	40	Mode with 40 responses
2 (ages 23-27)	19	
1 (ages 18-22)	5	
	100	

measures do not describe anything about the distribution of the scores. Are the scores closely clustered or spread out along a continuum? The **range** can describe how the scores are dispersed. To calculate the range, the researcher simply takes the highest score and deducts the lowest score. For example, when examining the results for a test, if the highest score on the test is 97 and the lowest score is 63, the range is 97 − 63 = 34. The scores are dispersed among a range of 34 points, or all scores fall within a 34-point range. The results for a second exam have a range of 15. Which exam has scores more closely clustered? The second exam has the smaller range, indicating less variance or a tighter cluster of scores. Figure 11.6 provides a graph of the range for each exam.

In figure 11.6, the range for each exam is represented by a curve. The larger the range, the flatter the curve appears. The smaller the range, the higher the peak of the curve appears. Exam 1 has a flatter curve, while the curve for exam 2 has a higher peak because the same number of scores must be fit within a smaller range. The range helps the researcher visualize how dispersed the scores are on a continuum. The range provides additional information to the researcher beyond the mean, median, and mode. For example, table 11.7 contains information for two sets of scores that have the same mean, median, and mode. But the curves would look very different because of the differences in the range. This provides the researcher with better information than just a particular point or score from the central tendencies.

• TABLE 11.7 •
Test Score Analysis

Exam 1 = 100 points	Exam 2 = 100 points
Mean = 75	Mean = 75
Median = 75	Median = 75
Mode = 75	Mode = 75
30 students	30 students
Range = 25	Range = 10

The range of scores is a good description of the dispersion or variability of the scores or responses, but there is still one remaining descriptive statistic that provides better information in relation to a set of scores or responses.

Standard Deviation

A better indicator of the variability of scores, responses, or data is the **standard deviation.** The standard deviation indicates how dispersed scores are around the mean. The larger the standard deviation, the more dispersed the scores are. The easiest way to understand standard deviation is to see its application to the **normal curve** (more commonly known as the **bell curve**). The normal curve serves as the foundation for many types of statistical interpretations. This is why under-

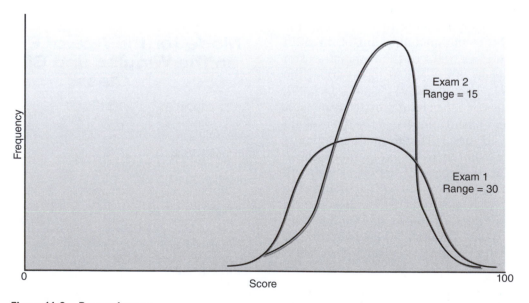

Figure 11.6   Range of scores.

standing the foundational concepts will assist researchers in understanding more advanced statistical analysis. The normal curve has the mean, median, and mode all positioned at the center of the curve. If you fold the curve in half around that point, you discover that each half is a mirror image of the other half. The percentages listed for each interval represent the percentage of scores that will fall within that particular interval. Each half of the curve also represents 50 percent of all scores. The + and − sign indicates which side of the mean the score falls on, either above (+) or below (−) the mean. The numbers 1, 2, and 3 indicate the distance from the mean. If a score falls 1 standard deviation (SD) above the mean, it is noted as +1SD. If a score falls 2 standard deviations below the mean, it is noted as −2SD. Figure 11.7 provides the normal curve with percentages and standard deviations.

The standard deviation assists the researcher in determining how the scores are dispersed along the normal curve. This information is also helpful in determining the percentage of subjects' scores that fall on each interval. The percentages noted for each interval are always the same for the normal curve. The percentages for each interval noted in figure 11.7 are as follows:

1. 34 percent of the scores fall between the mean and +1SD.

2. 34 percent of the scores fall between the mean and −1SD.

3. 13.5 percent of the scores fall between +1SD and +2SD.

4. 13.5 percent of the scores fall between −1SD and −2SD.

5. 2.15 percent of the scores fall between +2SD and +3SD.

6. 2.15 percent of the scores fall between −2SD and −3SD.

7. 0.13 percent of the scores fall above +3SD.

8. 0.13 percent of the scores fall below −3SD.

What does the standard deviation number really mean? If the mean on an exam is 80 and the standard deviation is 2, what does the distribution look like? The first step is to place the number for the mean (80) at the center of the curve. The standard deviation represents the numeric value of each interval. In this case, the interval for the distribution is always 2. To move from the mean to 1 standard deviation above the mean, you need to add the standard deviation to the mean—in this case, add the standard deviation of 2 to the mean of 80, which is 82. The exam score that is 1 standard deviation above the mean is 82 (80 + 2 = 82). What is the exam score at 2 standard deviations above the mean? To calculate this score, take the score at 1 standard deviation above the mean (which is 82) and add the standard deviation (which is 2) to determine the score at +2SD. The calculation is 82 + 2 = 84. What is the exam score for +3SD? The calculation is 84 + 2 = 86. The

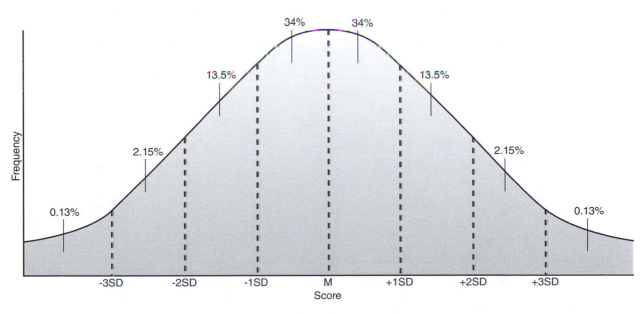

Figure 11.7 Normal curve.

Adapted, by permission, from J. Thomas and J. Nelson, 2001, *Research methods in physical activity* (Champaign, IL: Human Kinetics), 101.

exam score for 3SD above the mean is 86. What is the exam score for –1SD, meaning 1 standard deviation below the mean? To determine this, take the mean (80) and subtract the standard deviation (2) from the mean, which is 80 – 2 = 78. The exam score at 1 standard deviation below the mean is 78. What are the exam scores at –2SD and –3SD? The score at –2SD is 78 – 2 = 76; the score at –3SD is 76 – 2 = 74. Figure 11.8 provides the normal curve for the exam.

To examine what percentage of scores fall within a specific interval, let's revisit figure 11.7 and try to answer the following questions. What percentage of scores fall between the score of 80 (the mean) and 82 (+1SD)? The curve shows that 34 percent of the scores fall between 80 and 82. What percentage of scores fall between 78 (–1SD) and 82 (+1SD)? The graph shows that 34 percent of the scores fall between 80 and 78, and that 34 percent of the scores fall between 80 and 82. To calculate the total, add the percentages for each interval: 34% + 34% = 68%. This determines that 68 percent of the scores fall between 78 and 82. What percentage of scores fall between 76 (–2SD) and 82 (+1SD)? To calculate this, add the percentages for each interval in the range, which is 13.5% + 34% + 34%. This determines that 81.5 percent of the scores fall between –2SD and +1SD. The total percentage for any question asked in this manner is determined by adding the percentages of intervals within the range specified in the question.

The normal curve is also useful because it allows researchers to determine where on the curve a score falls. Figure 11.9 provides an example of how the normal curve can be used in this manner. Where does the exam score of 74 fall on

the normal curve? This score is –3SD, which is 3 standard deviations below the mean. Where does the exam score of 84 fall on the curve? This score is +2SD, which is 2 standard deviations above the mean. Researchers also use the normal curve and standard deviation to determine where a score falls in relation to the mean. Standard deviation is the final descriptive statistic that is used to describe the data and how diverse the scores are in the data set. This can be used along with the frequency or measures of central tendencies. These are not the only types of statistical analysis used to analyze data. Many times researchers want to do more than describe the data. Other statistical options that can be used for analyzing data are listed in table 11.8.

Pearson Product-Moment Coefficient

The correlation coefficient is a commonly used statistical analysis in correlation studies. The **Pearson product-moment coefficient** is used when the researcher is examining the strength of the relationship between two variables. If you recall, the correlation coefficient is a number that falls between –1.0 and +1.0. The closer the number is to either +1.0 or –1.0, the stronger the relationship. The closer the correlation coefficient is to 0, the weaker the relationship (0 indicates no relationship). If the coefficient is a negative number, then as one variable increases, the other variable decreases. If the coefficient is a positive number, then as one variable increases, so does the other variable. Figure 11.10 (page 158) provides scatter

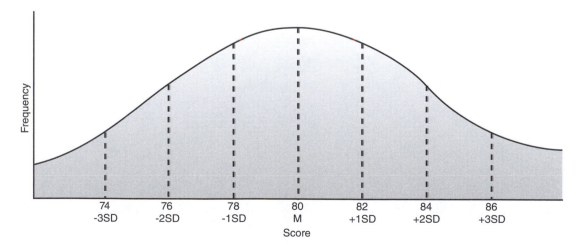

Figure 11.8 Normal curve for exam.

Adapted, by permission, from J. Thomas and J. Nelson, 2001, *Research methods in physical activity* (Champaign, IL: Human Kinetics), 101.

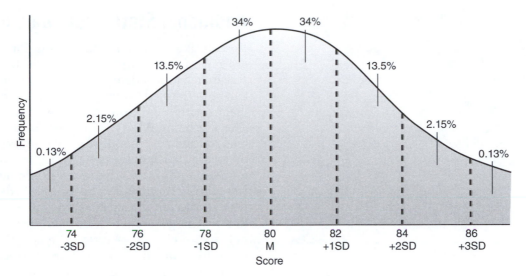

Figure 11.9 Options for statistical analysis.

Adapted, by permission, from J. Thomas and J. Nelson, 2001, *Research methods in physical activity* (Champaign, IL: Human Kinetics), 101.

plot graphs that visually display the relationship between variables with a positive correlation coefficient (11.10*a*), a negative correlation coefficient (11.10*b*), and no relationship (11.10*c*).

To create a scatter plot, the first step is to create a frequency table that lists the scores or data for each person for variable A and variable B. Each axis of the graph represents a variable; one axis represents variable A, and the other represents variable B. Now plot each person's data for both variables. Each dot represents the score of data for variable A and variable B for each subject. This scatter plot gives you a visual representation of the data on two variables and also provides a visual representation of the strength of the relationship. The closer the dots fall on a line or are clustered along a line, the stronger the relationship. If the dots are scattered all around the scatter plot, a relationship between the two variables is less likely. To fully understand if there is a statistically significant relationship, you should complete a calculation of the correlation coefficient to determine the strength of the relationship between the variables. The calculation for a correlation coefficient is a multiple-step process when performed by hand, but this is one of the statistical functions within spreadsheet computer packages. If you have the data on a spreadsheet with the data listed in columns for variable A and B, the help function within the spreadsheet program can guide you through the specific steps to calculate the correlation coefficient.

• *TABLE 11.8* •

Statistical Analysis

Statistical analysis	Use	Type of data
Correlation product-moment coefficient	Used to examine the relationship between two variables that are not manipulated in the study	Two variables (any combination of categorical or quantitative)
T test	Used to examine differences in the means between two groups to determine if the difference is statistically significant. This can be used with variables that are manipulated or variables that are not manipulated in the study.	Two means
ANOVA (analysis of variance)	Used to examine differences in the means between three or more groups (as in an experimental study)	Three or more means

a

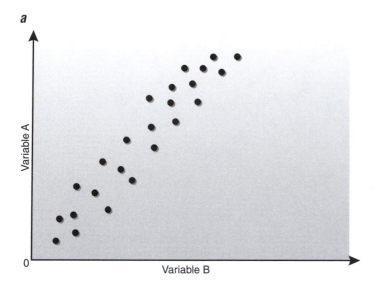

b

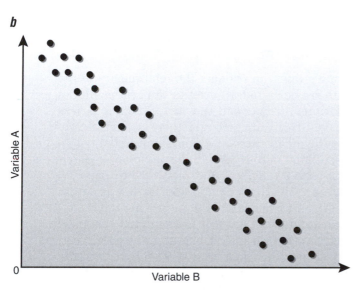

c

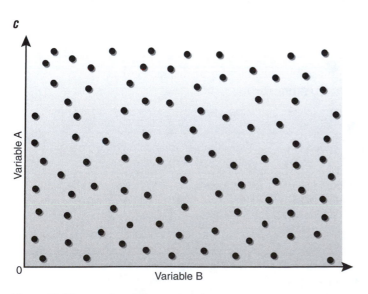

Figure 11.10*a-c* Correlation scatter plots.

Additional Statistical Analysis

Descriptive statistics and correlation analysis are not the only options available to you as a researcher. More advanced statistical calculations can be performed to analyze the differences in the means within the group and between the groups. The **T test** and **ANOVA** are used for this type of analysis and are generally used within experimental studies. Both of these statistical tests are used to determine if the differences in the means are statistically significant. This is done to determine if the treatment in the study created a difference that was large enough to be significant and was not due to chance or error. The calculations of these two statistical options are also an option within the statistical package of most computer spreadsheet programs. If you have difficulty in setting up the spreadsheet to use these analyses or interpreting the results of the analyses, you should work with a person who is skilled at interpreting the results of statistical calculations. This will ensure that you fully understand the results of the analysis and what the results mean in relation to the research questions. Many professionals gain assistance in these analyses from local universities and colleges. Every university or college has a math department that will have faculty, graduate students, or undergraduate students who can assist you with the calculations and interpretation of the results. The calculations and interpretation of these statistical options are beyond the scope of this text, but the researcher should be familiar with the most frequently used statistical calculations and how each is used. The content of this chapter has provided this functional knowledge. The items covered to this point are all appropriate for quantitative data analysis, but what can be done with qualitative data?

Qualitative Data Analysis

Qualitative data analysis requires the researcher to work with statements, words, and written responses. Some of the techniques that are commonly used to analyze qualitative data include enumeration, chronologies, various types of data displays, and coding. These techniques require much more time and effort than simply inputting numbers into a spreadsheet. To analyze data using enumeration, the researcher reviews the data and counts how many times a certain phrase or statement occurs. In the case of the evaluation of the Wiggles and Giggles class, the individual

PROFESSIONAL PERSPECTIVES

■ The real world of parks and recreation

As a staff member at South Run Recreation Center, I was given the task of coordinating the tot program and instructors at the facility. During any given program cycle (3 to 4 months), I had approximately 35 tot classes for which I needed to coordinate instructors, arrange facility usage, evaluate classes, and help with future planning. The recreation center had a database program that tracked enrollment, customer characteristics, and other variables. I decided to use the data that were available within this program to analyze the enrollment trends in the tot classes over the previous 2 years. Through this simple analysis, I identified classes that were consistently cancelled over the 2-year period, including specific times of the day and days of the week that they were cancelled. This information was used to revise the next 12-month schedule for the tot classes. Without this analysis, the programmer would have used the same program schedule that she had used in the past.

Why was research important in this case?

The agency's database was important in helping the programmer schedule classes to meet the needs of the population. In addition, by not scheduling the classes that were always cancelled, the recreation center had valuable facility space available to offer additional programs to adults and seniors.

responses have all been put into an electronic document to simplify the analysis process. The researcher reviews the comments and begins to see common statements. The frequency of these statements is noted and recorded to be included in the final report. This information will also be used with another data analysis technique.

Another common technique used for data analysis is chronologies. This technique is best used in historical studies, studies of a particular phenomenon, or studies that occur over an extended period of time. With this technique, the researcher takes the data and puts them in sequential order based on time—what happened first, second, third, and so on. Now the researcher can examine this information to identify relationships, actions, events, and responses. Researchers will often use a table, matrix, or flowchart to create a visual representation of the event or phenomenon in order to examine key elements.

The coding process requires the researcher to break the data down by theme or category. Categories could be place, time, process, responses, or relationships. This allows the researcher to analyze the data in parts within categories, rather than as a whole. Coding by themes moves from concrete statements to more abstract concepts in order to subdivide the data. In the case of the Wiggles and Giggles class evaluation, the researcher must first gather all the data or open-ended responses and review them several times to become familiar with the content. In the evaluation of the class, one qualitative question was asked: "What suggestions do you have to improve the class?" This question provides the subject with an opportunity to freely respond and write anything that comes to mind. These responses are all compiled into one document for the programmer to review. Once the researcher reviews the comments, he then goes back and begins to reorganize the information based on themes. Themes can be phrases or concepts that are repeated through the data, such as musical instruments. Figure 11.11 provides a sample of responses to the question. In reviewing the responses, the topic of musical instruments emerges as a theme. Three comments are related to this theme (comment number 1, 2, and 4). The researcher puts these comments together under the theme musical instruments. The next theme that comes from the data is music. Five comments are related to the music played during the class (comments 5, 6, 7, 8, and 9). These comments are all combined under the music theme. This reorganizing of the data by themes assists the researcher in coming to conclusions based on the themes.

1. Need shaker eggs for instruments

2. Need a complete set of instruments for all participants

3. Have scarves for slower music activities

4. Have one large drum that all the children can play

5. Have more varieties of music during the class

6. Have more movement variety during classes with music

7. Have some jazz music

8. Have classic rock music for some classes

9. Have classical music at some point in class

Theme 1: Instruments (comments 1, 2, and 4)

Theme 2: Music (comments 5, 6, 7, 8, and 9)

Figure 11.11 Sample responses to one survey question, demonstrating possible themes.

The researcher then works within each theme area to formulate conclusions based on the information within the theme. If a large amount of data falls within one theme, the researcher can review this information and break down the larger theme into smaller, more specific themes. This provides more focused theme areas to help the researcher formulate conclusions.

The process of analyzing qualitative data is much more time consuming than analyzing quantitative data. With that in mind, the results from qualitative data tend to be richer in content beyond a single number that describes something. Qualitative data analysis can provide results that are impossible to achieve with quantitative data analysis. The purpose of data analysis goes beyond calculating numbers or rearranging words—the purpose is to find meaning in the data. Some researchers will calculate a mean but forget to review what that number actually tells them. These meanings are the results of the study and provide the answers to the research question.

The answers are what a researcher is striving for in research and evaluation projects.

■ *TEST YOUR SKILLS WITH EXERCISES 11.1 AND 11.2.*

Conclusion

Both quantitative and qualitative data analyses provide the information necessary to ensure that research and evaluation studies are useful. The researcher determines the type of data analysis necessary for the study by reviewing the research question, the study design, the data collection instrument, and the type of data provided from the instrument. There is a logical thread that pulls all the pieces of the study together from beginning to end. This thread must connect all the pieces in order to provide meaningful results. Without this common thread, the results can be meaningless to the organization.

EXERCISES

■ Exercise 11.1: Statistical Calculations

This exercise allows you to practice using basic statistical calculations.

1. The following is a set of scores for a 10-point quiz in the research methods class.

Student	Score
1	9
2	5
3	6
4	8
5	7
6	7
7	3
8	4

   a. Develop a frequency table for the data set.
   b. What is the mean?
   c. What is the median?
   d. What is the mode?
   e. Draw a histogram for the data set.

   f. Draw a frequency polygon for the data set.

2. The following is another data set for a 10-point quiz from the research methods class.

Student	Score
1	9
2	7
3	6
4	8
5	7
6	7
7	3
8	4
9	9
10	8
11	6

12	5
13	1

a. Develop a frequency table for the data set.

b. What is the mean?

c. What is the median?

d. What is the mode?

e. Draw a histogram for the data set.

f. Draw a frequency polygon for the data set.

3. The following is a set of data from a customer satisfaction survey that uses a five-point Likert scale to identify whether customers agree with this statement: "The facility staff were very helpful."

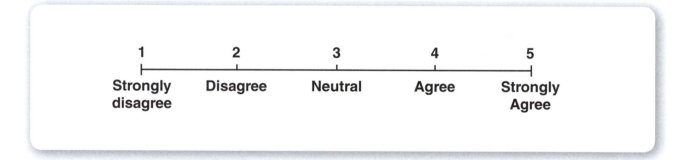

Frequency of responses for each category

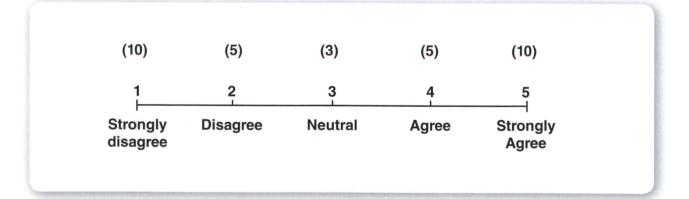

a Develop a frequency table for the data set.

b. What is the mean? What does the mean tell you about the customer satisfaction level?

    c. What is the median? What does this mean?

    d. What is the mode? What does this mean?

    e. Draw a frequency polygon for the data set.

    f. As the manager, would you be concerned about this rating? Why?

4. The following is a set of data from a customer satisfaction survey that uses a five-point Likert scale to identify whether customers agree with this statement: "The instructor was well prepared for each class."

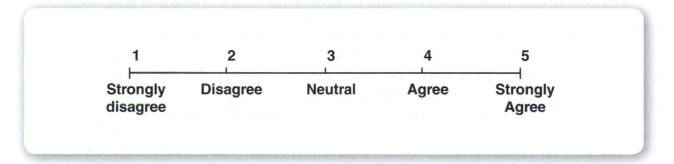

Frequency of responses for each category

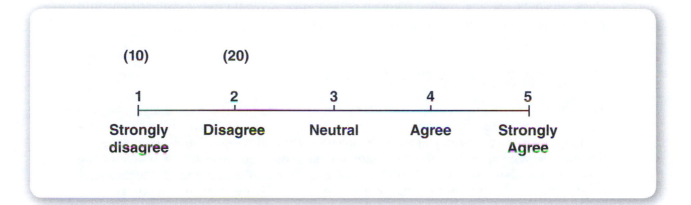

    a. Develop a frequency table for the data set.

    b. What is the mean? What does the number mean?

    c. What is the median? What does this mean?

    d. What is the mode? What does this mean?

    e. Draw a frequency polygon for the data set.

    f. As the manager, would you be concerned about this rating? Why?

■ Exercise 11.2 The Normal Curve

The following questions are based on the normal curve.

1. The boredom assessment was taken by Tom, who scored a 20 on the assessment. The mean score on the assessment is 10, and the standard deviation is 5.
   a. Identify the scores at –1SD, –2SD, –3SD, +1SD, +2SD, and +3SD for the boredom assessment.
   b. Where does Tom's score fall on the normal curve?
   c. What percentage of scores fall above Tom's score?
   d. What percentage of scores fall below Tom's score?
   e. What percentage of scores fall between the mean and Tom's score?

2. The leisure skills assessment was taken by Tom, who scored a 55 on the assessment. The mean score on the assessment is 25, and the standard deviation is 10.
   a. Identify the scores at –1SD, –2SD, –3SD, +1SD, +2SD, and +3SD for the assessment.
   b. Where does Tom's score fall on the normal curve?
   c. What percentage of scores fall above Tom's score?
   d. What percentage of scores fall below Tom's score?
   e. What percentage of scores fall between the mean and Tom's score?

CASE STUDY

You are the programmer at a recreation center. This recreation center has a database that tracks classes, enrollment, cancellation, revenues, and expenses for each program or class. The database also tracks customer demographics. What type of evaluation would you conduct on an annual basis using the available data?

FOR THE INVESTIGATOR

The data for the Health and Leisure Survey can be used to practice data analysis and the use of the spreadsheet program. The first step in the analysis of the data is to determine the frequency of each response for each question. This calculation can be completed by the spreadsheet program using the frequency function. The next step in analyzing the data is to calculate the central tendencies of mean, median, and mode. These measurements are also functions within the spreadsheet program. These measurements of central tendencies are not appropriate for all the questions on the survey. This information is not appropriate for the individual questions that represent a categorical variable, such as the demographic variables. You cannot calculate the average ethnic origin or sex of the sample. Remember, with categorical variables, the subject is one or the other, not a mixture of the response categories. The measures of central tendencies should only be calculated for the questions that represent quantitative variables.

Now it is time to complete the calculations to answer the research questions. If you recall, a number of correlation analyses can be calculated for pairs of variables. The variables can be both categorical, both quantitative, or one quantitative and one categorical. The correlation analysis is done to determine if the relationship is statistically significant and to answer the research questions.

1. Determine the frequency of each response category for each question using the function within the spreadsheet program.

2. Calculate the mean, median, and mode for all the quantitative questions on the survey using the specific function within the spreadsheet program.

3. Finally, calculate the correlation coefficient for the pairs of variables that are noted in the research questions provided by your instructor.

CHAPTER 72

• OBJECTIVES •

After completing this chapter, you will be able to

- explain the value of creating the research report,
- identify the components that need to be included in the research report,
- recommend how to present the information in a concise manner, and
- evaluate the importance of information for each section of the report.

The Research Report

You have been working diligently for weeks preparing to conduct a study that evaluates the programs provided by the recreation agency where you are employed. You have identified the problem, and you have conducted background research to learn more about the evaluation process and the issues related to evaluating programs. You have also developed the instrumentation plan, collected data, and analyzed the data. You now have all the information needed, but you are unclear about how to put it all together in a report for your supervisor and the recreation commission. You begin to feel overwhelmed again with the volume of information you currently have and the thought of completing this final step in the research process. Once again, you gather your information related to the study and review the guidelines for preparing a research report in the literature. You discover that there are two primary ways to prepare the report. One is a formal research document that is used within higher education for a thesis and dissertation. The reviewers are all educators at the university, and the research document is a requirement for graduation. This is not your current situation. The second way that research documents are prepared is for presenting information to supervisors, recreation commissioners, city councils, and other leaders and decision makers who make important decisions related to an agency's operations. This is the format that will meet your needs in preparing a research report.

Writing the research report is a critical step in the communication process with decision makers. The report will serve as a reference for decisions and should be reviewed before and during the decision-making process. Every agency, business, and nonprofit in the field has a preferred format for these types of reports. The federal government has a format for research reports that is different from a nonprofit format. The first thing you need to review is the guidelines or the template for the agency's required format. The components reviewed in this chapter provide a template for a research report that can be switched around to meet an agency's specific requirements.

Each section of a research report has a specific purpose and pulls in information that has been gathered during the course of the study. The purpose of the research report is to efficiently and effectively communicate what was done during the course of the study as well as the results of the study. The report synthesizes and summarizes information so the reader understands the purpose, process, procedures, and results of the study. The thread that links all the sections together is the problem of the study. The challenge in creating this type of report is to provide enough information so the readers understand what was done, but not so much information that it becomes burdensome to read, to understand, and to review. This balancing act between content and comprehension requires the author of the report to focus carefully on what is communicated and how it is communicated. In this case, large amounts of information (or filler information) are not better, and the length of the document does not equal quality. The reverse is actually true—less is more, as long as the author is clearly communicating the pieces of each section of the report. Each section of the report has a specific purpose in communicating information related to the research study. The research report is generally composed of six sections:

- Executive summary
- Purpose of the study
- Background information and justification
- Methods
- Results
- Summary, conclusions, and recommendations

Executive Summary

The **executive summary** is the first section of the research report that the readers review, but it is the last section that the author writes. The purpose of the executive summary is to provide an overview of the content of the report. This summary may highlight some specific information that will be explained in more detail within the content of the research report. This section states the purpose of the study, why the study was necessary, how the study was conducted, and the highlights of the results and recommendations.

For example, in the study that evaluates the recreation programs at the recreation center, the executive summary explains the purpose of the study, which is to evaluate the outcomes for the participants of the recreation programs and classes. The summary would also highlight how evaluations are one of the requirements of the CAPRA accreditation process and how evaluations help determine if the objectives of the programs were achieved for the participants. (The CAPRA information and the benefits of research and evaluation are reviewed in chapter 1 of this text.) The justification for the study is also presented within this section of the report. It highlights how the outcomes of the study can be used to assist in revising programs for the next year and can serve as an educational tool for the public. The justification should also indicate that the study will document how the agency is meeting specific needs in the community and contributing to the quality of life within the community. In addition, the executive summary contains the research questions and describes how they relate to documenting the performance of the agency. Finally, a summary is also provided about how data were collected and analyzed. The executive summary pulls together information about the overall focus of the study and highlights the information that is covered in more detail in the following sections.

In the example, a customer survey was used to provide the necessary data to answer the research questions. A brief description is provided related to how the data were analyzed to answer the research questions. This section also includes a brief description of the recommendations that the report contains. The executive summary also refers readers to specific sections in the report where they can find additional information about the content described in this section. For example, the information provided in the executive summary regarding the instrumentation for the study will refer readers to the section that contains more explicit information.

Selected text based on B. van der Smissen, M. Moiseichik, and V.J. Hartenburg, 2005, *Management of parks and recreation agencies* (Asburn, VA: National Recreation and Park Association), 663.

Purpose of the Study

The second section of the report provides information related to the problem that the study addresses, the purpose of the study, and why the study was needed. This section states each element so the reader fully understands the focus and intent of the study. (Information related to the research problem, the purpose of the study, and the research question were reviewed in chapter 3 of this text and are part of the research planning process.) This section is usually short, but it is very important because it provides the foundational information that the reader needs in order to understand the remaining sections of the report. The researcher may also want to briefly review the type of study conducted—such as evaluation, correlation, or case study—and how the study design relates directly to the purpose of the study.

For the example of evaluating the recreation programs, table 12.1 lists the problem of the study, the purpose of the study, the research questions, and the study design. Each piece of information is necessary but needs to be presented concisely and briefly. The information contained in table 12.1 serves as the guide for developing the content of this section of the report.

Background

The background section provides more information about the problem of the study. This section generally begins with a broad focus; then the focus is narrowed down to address the problem of the study. The information in this section provides a broader base of knowledge about the scope of the problem, presenting in-depth information that was not provided in the section covering the purpose of the study. The review of literature provides the information needed for this section of the research document (the literature review was discussed in chapter 4 of this text). This section then provides the justification for the study and relates the justification to the background information about the problem.

For example, in the study evaluating the programs and services of the agency, the background information presented may begin with a national focus reviewing the CAPRA accreditation process and the need to evaluate programs and services. Next, the researcher could provide a review of the information noted generally through the literature regarding the benefits of evaluating programs and services. The next step is to more narrowly focus on the agency that will be conducting the study. This includes providing background information on the agency and its missions. An overview of the agency's programs and services should also be provided. Then the information about CAPRA and the benefits of evaluating the programs are reviewed specifically for the agency. This narrowing process from a national focus to a local focus allows the reader to understand that this is a national concern within the park and recreation

• TABLE 12.1 •

Information for the Purpose of the Study Section

Information piece to cover	Information
Problem	The XYZ Recreation Center has not evaluated the programs and services provided by the center.
Purpose	The purpose of this study is to develop and implement an evaluation plan for all the programs and services provided by XYZ Recreation Center.
Research questions	1. Are the objectives being met for the programs and services at the recreation center? 2. What is the evidence that is collected to determine if the objectives are being met or not? 3. What is the customer satisfaction level with the programs and services at the recreation center? 4. What suggestions do customers have to improve the programs and services at the recreation center?
Study design	An evaluation design was selected to be used within this study. Within this design, both quantitative and qualitative data will be gathered through a survey for the customers who participated in the programs and services.

industry. At the same time, the reader learns the importance of conducting the study at the local agency. The final subsection of the background information covers the justification for the study. The justification states why the study is important and the future implications to the agency related to the results. This pulls together the information about the purpose of the study (from the previous section) and the background information so the reader fully understands the importance of the study to the agency and its future operations. This information prepares the reader to move on to the next section of the document, which is the methods section.

Methods

The methods section of the research report summarizes the instrumentation plan. The instrumentation plan involves a huge amount of information that could be included in this section; however, the author needs to determine the major areas that should be communicated to the reader. This could include variables and hypotheses, ethics in research, sampling, instrumentation, validity and reliability (internal, external, and instrument), or data collection tools. The challenge in creating this section is to provide enough information for the reader to understand what was done and why without covering areas that the reader may not fully understand, such as validity and reliability. Generally, this section summarizes how the study was conducted, including who was involved (subjects), how data were collected, when and where the data were collected, and who collected the data.

In the example of evaluating the programs and services of the recreation center, the methods section would summarize information about who was involved in the study, how data were collected (instrument), whom the data were collected from (sampling), when and where the data were collected, and who collected the data. Figure 12.1 provides an example of this information as it relates to the research questions of the study. The information in figure 12.1 addresses the data collection process, which includes course data sheets and customer surveys. This limited amount of information provides the reader with a good understanding of what data are being collected; whom the data are being collected from; and how, when, and why these data are being collected. Most reviewers like to see the instruments that were used in the study; a good way to include

the instruments in the report is to provide them as attachments within an appendix at the end of the report. This allows the reader to understand the process and not be overwhelmed with a series of surveys and class tracking sheets embedded within the report itself. The other feature to notice is how the method of collecting data is directly linked to each research question. This allows the reader to see the direct link between the purpose of the study and the method in which the study is being conducted. This overview information regarding the method of the study is all that is necessary. The researcher does not want to bog down the reader with an overwhelming amount of details from the instrumentation plan. Obviously, in a research report or document, more information is provided than is contained in figure 12.1, but the major topic areas would remain the same. The author would provide additional information that the reader needs to know to understand the method in which the study was conducted.

Now that the reader understands what was done to collect data, the next section of the report provides an explanation of how the data were analyzed and the results of the analysis.

Results

The results section provides a brief description of how the data were analyzed. This description is generally necessary so that the reader understands how the results were formulated. This section also presents the results of the data analysis along with a description of what the results tell the researcher. The information for the results is usually presented in tables or charts; an explanation of what the numbers mean is also included. There is nothing more frustrating than looking at a table of numbers and not understanding what the numbers indicate in relation to the study. When creating this section, an important thing for researchers to remember is that they need to report just the facts as indicated from the data analysis (along with an explanation), not the researcher's interpretation.

For example, one of the questions on the customer survey was related to the participant's rating of the instructor. The question asked the participant to rate the instructor's performance in conducting the class or program. Table 12.2 provides the question and the percentages of responses for each category.

The information in table 12.2 provides a summary of the data for a specific question and a nar-

1. **Are the objectives being met for the programs and services at the recreation center?**

   Data will be collected from class records, instructors, and participants in the program with a written survey that highlights the objectives of the program, instructor performance, and satisfaction level of their experiences. The data will be collected from all the participants at the last class or program meeting by the instructor. The data from all the instructors and records will be collected after the conclusion of the program or class by the programmer.

2. **What evidence is collected to determine whether or not the objectives are being met?**

   Each program and class has objectives to achieve during the course of the class or program. The instructors keep track of progress through program and class data sheets and turn them in at the conclusion of the program.

3. **What is the customer satisfaction level with the programs and services at the recreation center?**

   The customer satisfaction level components are included in the survey given to participants at the conclusion of the class or program.

4. **What suggestions do customers have to improve the programs and services at the recreation center?**

   An open-ended question asking for suggestions of improvements to the programs and services at the recreation center is the last question on the survey given to the participants at the conclusion of the class.

Figure 12.1 Sample of information that might be included in the methods section of a research report.

• TABLE 12.2 •
Survey Question Summary

	Strongly disagree		Agree		Strongly agree
The instructor was well prepared for each class.	1	2	3	4	5
	75%	15%	10%	0%	0%

The participants of the class rated the instructors as well prepared for each class; 90 percent of the ratings were above average, and 75 percent of participants rated the instructors at the highest level possible on the evaluation.

ration summarizing what the percentages mean in relation to the question. The researcher must decide which way to present the data and narration based on the data analysis. Some researchers prefer to present this information question by question. Others prefer to provide a summary of each section or a summary by instructor or class.

Many options are available to the researcher for presenting the results of the study. The challenge is selecting the option that helps the researcher clearly present the results of the data analysis.

This section must also contain the research questions, the data for each research question, and narration for each research question. The

PROFESSIONAL PERSPECTIVES

■ The real world of parks and recreation

Every evaluation and research project concludes with a report. Why bother conducting a project if you do not summarize the information, share the information, and use the information for future decisions? The park and recreation commissioners of Frostburg were asked to conduct a comprehensive evaluation of all the park and recreation facilities of the city. As a commissioner, I assumed the role of pulling together all the information from the evaluation sheets of the playground, ball field, pool, gym, walking trails, bathrooms, concession stands, and open space. The report began with an executive summary and sections for each facility category, specifically noting deficiencies and making recommendations for a repair and maintenance plan. At the time of this evaluation project, the city did not have a repair, maintenance, or replacement plan. The report provided the foundation to develop such a plan.

Why was research important in this case?

First of all, the report was used as a tool to educate the mayor and city council about the dangers that exist in the community and the need for a repair, maintenance, and replacement plan for the park and recreation facilities. The second benefit was that some very dangerous playground equipment at two sites was removed and replaced with equipment that met the current playground safety guidelines. A third benefit is that this report has served as the document that guides annual decisions concerning repair, maintenance, and future construction within the parks and recreation department. Without this report, dangerous situations would continue to exist, and routine maintenance (such as fixing or replacing the bleachers at the fields) would be overlooked.

information can begin with individual data for questions and then conclude with the results for the research question. This permits the reader to understand how the individual pieces of data were summarized to answer each research question. The important consideration in this section is to present enough information without overwhelming the reader. The information should provide a smooth and logical transition to the recommendations section of the report. The recommendations section is the final section of a research report.

Recommendations

The recommendations section is the only section that allows the researchers to introduce their perceptions in relation to the results of the study. All the other sections of the research document only report factual information without interpretation. This section is critically important for educating the reader and influencing the future decisions of the organization. It takes the data provided in the

results and presents concrete recommendations for the future of the agency. These recommendations are related to the research questions stated in the second section of the report, which is the purpose of the study. The information links the purpose of the study with the data and recommendations.

The researcher usually begins this section by summarizing the results information in order to frame the recommendations that will follow in relation to the research questions. This serves as the foundation for the recommendations that will be made within this section. This information varies from research report to research report depending on the research questions, the results, and the recommendations. For example, in evaluating the programs and classes, the research questions are as follows:

1. Are the objectives being met for the programs and services at the recreation center?

2. What is the evidence that is collected to determine if the objectives are being met or not?

3. What is the customer satisfaction level with the programs and services at the recreation center?

4. What suggestions do customers have to improve the programs and services at the recreation center?

The recommendations in this section should be related to the research questions, and they should be focused on improving the operations of the agency. The recommendations are usually listed in numeric order (such as 1, 2, and 3) and are not in a narration within a paragraph. This allows the reader to easily understand what is recommended for the future. Beyond the recommendation, the researcher must explain why each recommendation is made in relation to what the data or results of the study indicate. This pulls together all the pieces within the report into a logical process from beginning to end. Within this section, many researchers also include recommendations for future studies.

Conclusion

The process of preparing the research report is as challenging as planning the study. This step in the overall research process is very important in documenting the process, the results of the research, and the recommendations for the future. The document can serve as a guide for future priorities, decisions, and operational changes. The information gained through the research process is invaluable in assisting with future decisions and invaluable in documenting the agency's performance. This type of information also meets specific standards within the CAPRA accreditation process and assists in developing long-term plans and short-term priorities. Without these types of planning tools, the agency may not be operating as efficiently and effectively as possible. The agency may also lack the necessary information to compete for future funding. The reality of today's recreation industry is that it is considered a business—not a social service—in many places within the United States. Understanding this fact, professionals in the field must begin to use research and evaluation to justify operations, document the agency's contributions to the quality of life in the community, and compete for limited financial resources. Research and evaluation studies provide invaluable information, and they are now an expectation within the recreation and leisure industry.

CASE STUDY

You are the programmer at a community park and recreation center. Each year you are required to provide a year-end report summarizing program registration, revenues, expenses, needs, and recommendations for the coming year. What are some examples of the components you would include in the year-end report? How would this information be used in the planning process for the next year?

FOR THE INVESTIGATOR

The report pulls together all the information about the study and presents the results and recommendations based on the analysis of the data. The challenge in pulling all the pieces together is synthesizing the information. This means putting the pieces together by topic area while weaving together concepts related to the focus, purpose, and process of the study. This information concisely communicates the purpose and process of the study to the reader in terms that the reader can understand. The difficulty in preparing the report is to present the proper amount of information—that is, enough information so that the reader understands what was done in the study and understands the results, but not so much information that the reader is overwhelmed. Try your hand at developing the report that synthesizes the information from chapter 3 to chapter 11. The report should include the following information:

1. Background information related to the topic of the study (this comes from the review of literature). This begins broadly and then narrows down to the agency conducting the study.

2. The problem, purpose, and research questions for the study, as well as the justification for the study.

3. The instrumentation plan that pulls the information from the sampling chapter, instrumentation chapter, and data collection chapter.

4. The results of the data analysis completed in the exercise for chapter 11.

5. Finally, the recommendations based on the data analysis and recommendations.

action research—A research design that is used in situations that are internal concerns within the agency. Action research can be either a quantitative or qualitative study design, but the study focuses on answering a research question that is unique to the agency and has limited application to other agencies.

ANOVA—A statistical calculation that is used to determine if the differences in the means for different data sets are statistically significant.

average—A measure of central tendencies that is calculated by adding up the responses and dividing them by the total number of scores; also referred to as the mean.

bell curve—A curve used for statistical analysis; commonly known as the normal curve.

CAPRA (Commission for Accreditation of Park and Recreation Agencies) accreditation—A comprehensive evaluation and review process used to accredit park and recreation agencies that meet the standards within the review process. The program is conducted through the National Recreation and Park Association.

case study—A qualitative study design that focuses on gathering very comprehensive data about an individual or a small group of individuals.

categorical variable—A variable that does not vary in degree, amount, or quantity. The number does not represent more or less of something but rather a category that can be used to sort data for analysis.

central tendencies—Descriptive statistics that represent a data set with one number. The three measurements of central tendencies are mean, median, and mode.

certified park and recreational professional—A certification awarded from the National Recreation and Park Association to individuals who meet the eligibility requirements and pass the certification exam. The certification serves as evidence of meeting industry standards for a professional and to maintain the certification the one must complete a specified number of continuing education units within a two-year cycle.

closed-ended questions—Questions on a survey or questionnaire for which the subjects must select from a limited number of response options.

cluster random sampling—A random sampling technique that is used when the researcher cannot easily identify all the individuals in a population but *can* easily identify groups or organizations within the population. This technique focuses on using preexisting groups or organizations and randomly selecting entire groups to include in the sample (instead of individuals).

comparison group—A group that receives a different experience than the first group in the study. In experimental studies, a comparison group is often called the control group. The control group does not receive the "treatment" that the experimental group receives.

constant variable—A variable that remains the same for all subjects in the study, such as sex or age.

construct validity—A method for establishing the validity of a data collection instrument. Proof of construct validity is gathered by formulating a hypothesis and testing it through multiple sources of data.

content—The environment that the study is conducted within either in the real world or in a controlled environment.

content validity—A method for establishing the validity of a data collection instrument. This method involves examining the format, the type of questions, and the number of questions on the instrument.

control group—A comparison group in an experimental study that does not receive the treatment.

convenience sampling—A nonrandom sampling technique in which the researcher selects subjects from whoever is available at a given place at a given time. This type of sampling creates a bias in the results and does not represent the population as a whole.

correlation coefficient—A number between −1.0 and +1.0 that indicates the strength of a relationship in a correlation study. The closer the correlation coefficient is to either −1.0 or +1.0, the stronger the relationship. The plus (+) or minus (−) sign indicates whether the relationship is a positive correlation or a negative correlation.

correlation research design—A research design used to study the strength of a relationship between two variables as they occur in a natural setting. In the correlation design, there is no manipulation of the variables, and the study is conducted in the natural environment.

criterion validity—A method for establishing the validity of a data collection instrument. This method involves comparing the results of an instrument that has been proven valid with the results of the instrument that was developed for the study.

data—The information that is gathered to answer the research question.

data collector bias—A threat to the internal validity of the study that occurs when the person collecting the data from subjects unconsciously favors certain outcomes or responses.

data collector's characteristics—A threat to the internal validity of a study that may occur when people are used to collect data from subjects. The characteristics of the person collecting the data can influence the data provided by a subject.

dependability—A term used to describe reliability in qualitative studies. Dependability examines what the researcher reports and what was actually happening in the area being studied. In other words, if the study was repeated, would the researcher see, experience, and discover the same data?

dependent variable—The variable that is measured to determine the effect of the treatment in experimental studies. The dependent variable is "dependent" on the independent variable. The dependent variable is also called the outcome variable.

directional hypothesis—A hypothesis that predicts a specific change in a variable.

discipline—A single focus within the scientific method of inquiry, such as leisure, psychology, sociology, outdoor resources management, and health.

equivalent-forms method—A method used for establishing the reliability of a data collection instrument. In this method, the researcher administers two different instruments to the subject at the same time. The researcher then compares the results of the two instruments to determine if the results are similar.

ethnographic research design—A qualitative study design that involves studying and recording the everyday life practices and daily occurrences of an individual, group, or culture.

evaluation—A type of research that uses the research process to focus on a particular element of an agency's operation. The study is narrowly focused, involves studying many variables, and is conducted in the real world.

executive summary—The first section of the research report. The purpose of the executive summary is to provide an overview of the content of the report. This should be the last section that the researcher writes.

experimental design—A study design that is used to study cause-and-effect relationships; that is, if A is done, then B will occur (A and B represent variables that are the focus of the study).

external validity—This refers to the extent to which the results of the study can be applied to the population that the sample represents.

extraneous variable—A variable that is not being studied but may influence the results of the study. These variables can be present in all research projects, and the researcher needs to identify and control them; otherwise, the changes noted in the study may be due to the extraneous variables, not the variables being studied.

focus—The intent of the research or evaluation study that is provided either by testing a theory or researching a problem or question concerning the agency.

focus group—A group interview on a specific topic.

forced-choice questions—Questions on a survey or questionnaire for which the subjects must select from a limited number of response options.

frequency table—A tool used by researchers to summarize a large amount of data. The table lists the responses and identifies how many people selected each response.

general references—The indexes or databases that researchers use to search for books, articles, and research studies related to the topic of the study.

heterogeneous—Refers to a group that varies widely on the characteristics being studied.

histogram—A visual presentation of the data with the score or response on the horizontal axis and the frequency of that score or response on the vertical axis. The height of the bar indicates the frequency of that score or response.

historical research design—A qualitative research design in which the researcher investigates and records the development of a particular activity, attitude, or idea through time.

history—A threat to the internal validity of a study that occurs when something unexpected happens during the study that the researcher could not control.

homogeneous—Refers to a group when the group members are very similar. For a study of a homogeneous group, the number needed in the sample is smaller than if the group varies widely on the characteristics being studied.

hypothesis—A prediction about the relationship of the variables or the outcome of the study. Using a hypothesis is not appropriate in all studies (e.g., a hypothesis is not used for a survey or a qualitative study).

implementation—A threat to the internal validity of a study that occurs when one group is treated differently than another group. This gives the first group an advantage over the second group. This threat can occur if two or more people are used to conduct the treatment.

independent variable—The variable that is manipulated to determine the effect on the dependent variable, or outcome variable. The independent variable can be either a quantitative variable or a categorical variable, and it is used as the treatment variable in experimental research designs.

instrumentation—The process used to conduct the study that includes a step-by-step guide of how the study is to be conducted. This includes the population, what data is needed, where to collect the data, how to collect the data, who will collecte the data, when to collect the data, and how the data will be analyzed and reported.

instrumentation plan—The plan that serves as the road map for sampling, data collection, data analysis, and the sharing of information for the study.

instrument decay—A threat to the internal validity of a study that occurs when data are scored in a way that allows the scorer to subjectively interpret the data.

instrument validity—The validity of the data collection instrument. The process of determining instrument validity is twofold. First, the researcher must determine if the instrument measures what it is intended to measure. Second, the researcher must determine if the study results or conclusions provided by the instrument are valid.

internal validity—To check for internal validity, the researcher must examine the instrumentation plan to ensure that the results of the study will be true and valid.

interval measurement scale—A measurement scale where the intervals between 0 and 1, 1 and 2, and 2 and 3 are the same unit of measurement. The second feature is the use of a zero. The twist is that it is not a true zero, meaning a total absence of something. A thermometer for measuring the outside temperature uses an interval scale.

Likert scale—A numeric scale used to measure an individual's attitudes or beliefs about a variable. The number indicates the person's attitude or belief.

maturation—A threat to the internal validity of a study that occurs over an extended amount of time. The researcher wants to make sure the differences noted in the study are due to the treatment or program, not the passage of time.

mean—A statistical calculation that provides the average score of a data set.

measurement scale—The four measurement scales for variables (nominal, ordinal, interval, and ratio) are used to assist in determining what type of statistical calculation can be performed with the data.

median—The point where half the scores fall above and half the scores fall below.

member check—A technique used in qualitative studies to enhance the validity and reliability of the study. The process requires the researcher to go back to the subjects and have them review the information collected from them for accuracy. This allows the subjects to catch errors in the data or conclusions.

method—The method used in a study is selected from options that produce accurate data and are acceptable methods in the research community and is used to determine the effects of a program on the variables of interest.

mode—The most frequent response or score in the data set.

mortality—A threat to the internal validity of a study that occurs when subjects drop out of the study.

negative correlation—A relationship between variables where as one variable increases, the other variable decreases.

nominal measurement scale—A scale applied to categorical variables. The numbers serve the purpose of assisting the researcher in breaking down data by categories only, such as sex, age, ethnicity, or any type of program.

nondirectional hypothesis—A hypothesis that predicts there will be a difference but does not predict the direction of the difference.

nonrandom sampling techniques—In nonrandom sampling techniques, the probability of being selected is not the same for each individual, group, or organization of the population. These techniques include purposive sampling, convenience sampling, volunteer sampling, and snowball sampling.

normal curve—A curve used for statistical analysis (also known as the bell curve). The normal curve has the mean, median, and mode all positioned at the center of the curve. If the curve is folded in half around that point, each half is a mirror image of the other half. Percentages are listed for each interval to represent the percentage of scores that will fall within that particular interval.

objectivity—The objectivity of a data collection instrument refers to the instrument having an absence of subjective judgments.

observations—The data from observations document what occurs within the natural environment as it happens. The researcher records what is observed through her own perceptions over an extended amount of time.

open-ended questions—An open-ended question allows the subjects to write a response in their own words, instead of forcing subjects to choose a response from a limited number of options. This type of question can be used to collect qualitative data.

ordinal measurement scale—A scale used with data that are ranked in order (first, second, third, and so on) based on some attribute. The intervals between first, second, and third vary; they are not a standard interval.

outcome variable—The variable that is measured to determine the effect of the treatment (i.e., the independent variable) in experimental studies. The outcome variable is also called the dependent variable. The dependent variable is "dependent" on the independent variable.

Pearson product-moment coefficient—A correlation coefficient calculation used when the researcher is examining the strength of the relationship between two variables. The correlation coefficient is a number that falls between −1.0 and +1.0. The closer the number is to either +1.0 or −1.0, the stronger the relationship.

performance checklist—A tool used to document what a person can and cannot perform. For example, a swim instructor uses a performance checklist to determine if the swimmer is ready for the next level of swimming classes.

polygon—A visual presentation of the data with the score or response on the horizontal axis and the frequency of that score or response on the vertical axis. The height of the point indicates the frequency of that score or response.

population—The group of all individuals, organizations, or artifacts that could be involved in the study. The population is also the group that the researcher wants the results of the study to apply to at the conclusion of the study.

positive correlation—A relationship between variables where as one variable increases, so does the other variable.

primary source—Research articles published in a professional journal that are identified through the review of literature. The person who conducted the research is the author of the journal article.

product evaluation form—A tool used to evaluate a product. For example, to evaluate bowls created on a potter's wheel, an art instructor may use a checklist that includes the particular evaluation criteria, such as roundness, height, thickness of the sides, and thickness of the base.

purpose—This guides the research projects efforts and focus and states the intent of the study.

purpose statement—The purpose statement of the study is one sentence that states what the study is investigating.

purposive sampling—A nonrandom sampling technique that is most frequently used for a qualitative study, such as a case study or historical study. This technique allows the researcher to identify the specific individuals who have the information the researcher needs related to the research question.

qualitative design—The focus of a qualitative study is to understand the entire experience, not just a limited number of variables. Qualitative studies can examine one person, historical documents, or the development of a societal trend. The data are gathered in the form of words, observations, or artifacts.

quantitative design—The focus of a quantitative study is to measure the defined variables of the study. The data are gathered in the form of numbers.

quantitative variable—This type of variable is used within experimental studies, correlation studies, and evaluation studies. This is a variable that exists in varying degrees or is represented by an amount on a scale indicating more or less of something. The numbers indicate how much of that variable is present.

random sampling techniques—A group of sampling options where the probability of being selected to be part of the sample is the same for each individual, group, or organization.

range—The number that describes how dispersed the scores are in a data set. To calculate the range, the researcher simply takes the highest score and deducts the lowest score.

rating scale—A rating scale allows the researcher to document the quality of a product or performance. Rating scales are frequently used in sport events, such as ice skating competitions and gymnastics competition, to evaluate each athlete's performance.

ratio measurement scale—A scale that has equal intervals between points (such as 1, 2, and 3) and uses a zero in the measurement scale. The difference between interval and ratio scales is that the zero in the ratio scale means the absence of something.

regression—A threat to the internal validity of the study that may occur if the researcher selects subjects based on extreme scores, either high or low.

reliability—A term that means "repeatability" of the data. In other words, if the researcher conducts the study multiple times, the results will be similar or consistent.

replicating—This is repeating a study again in the same manner in which it was done before by the researcher or another researcher.

research—A general term that is used to refer to any type of scholarly research. This includes the scientific method of inquiry, evaluation, and action research.

researcher-completed instruments—Data collection instruments that are completed by the researcher. With these instruments, the researcher serves as the primary data collector.

research problem—The problem that is being examined in the research study. The research problem is usually generated out of a need within an agency or some issue or concern within the community.

research questions—Questions that clearly define the scope and focus of the study and also indicate whether a quantitative or qualitative study is being conducted. Many studies will have a series of questions that the research study will address, and conclusions will be formulated to specifically answer each individual question.

review of literature—A comprehensive examination of information that exists related to the research topic. The researcher will look for this information in literature sources such as scholarly journals, trade publications, books, and other mass media sources.

sample—The subset of individuals, groups, or organizations selected through the sampling process to participate in the study.

sample size—The size of the sample is directly related to sampling error and sampling bias. A number of issues will guide the decision about sample size, including the research question, the purpose of the study, the type of study being conducted, and the characteristics of the population.

sampling—The process used to identify the individuals, groups, or organizations from the population that will participate in the study.

sampling bias—This occurs when one type of individual, group, or organization is overrepresented in the sample, resulting in a sample that does not represent the population as a whole. Sampling bias can occur in random and nonrandom sampling techniques.

sampling error—A statistical calculation of the sampling bias that occurred in the sampling process for the study. The larger the sample, the smaller the sample error will be; this is because a larger sample is a better representation of the population.

scholarly literature—This may be original research from a professional journal, information from textbooks and other books related to the research topic, or relevant information from professional trade journals. These are sources that can provide information to help in your research project.

scientific method of inquiry—A type of research that focuses on testing a theory in a controlled setting. The research is conducted over an extended amount of time and examines a limited number of variables.

secondary sources—Textbooks and books identified through the review of literature. The information contained in books is not new knowledge; rather, it is current and existing knowledge that is presented in a different manner.

self-checklist—A subject-completed data collection instrument that can be used to gather factual information about behaviors, attitudes, and preferences from the subject.

simple random sampling—A random sampling technique where the researcher must be able to identify every individual in the population. In addition, every person in the population has the same chance of being selected.

snowball sampling—This nonrandom sampling technique begins with the researcher identifying one person for the sample. The first person selected is asked to make recommendations of other people to gather data from for the study. This technique is based on recommendations from the subjects.

split-half method—A method for establishing the reliability of a data collection instrument. The researcher splits the instrument in half as if there are two instruments. This technique requires the instrument to include at least two questions that ask the same thing but in different ways.

standard deviation—A statistical calculation that indicates the variability of the scores around the mean. The larger the standard deviation, the more dispersed the scores are.

stratified random sampling—A random sampling technique that requires the researcher to first divide the population by a stratum (such as sex) and then select a certain number of subjects randomly from each stratum for the sample.

stratum—A concept or characteristic that is used to subdivide the population into smaller groups, such as sex (male and female).

subject attitudes—A threat to the internal validity of the study that occurs when the behavior or attitudes of the subjects in the study are influenced by the extra attention they receive from researchers. These subjects may also recognize that they are receiving some type of different experience than others, and this may affect their attitudes or behavior.

Subject characteristics—A threat to internal validity that occurs when subjects have characteristics that can influence the results of the study.

subject-completed instruments—Data collection instruments that are given to the subjects involved in the study to complete and return to the researcher.

subjects—The individuals included in the study. The subjects are selected from a larger group that they are a member of.

survey—A study design used to gather data that will describe the group being examined in order to better understand their characteristics, attitudes, preferences, or beliefs.

systematic random sampling—A random sampling technique where each person in the population has an equal chance of being selected for the study. All individuals within the population are identified, and after a random selection from a list, every "nth" person (e.g., every 40th person) is selected for the sample.

testing—A threat to the internal validity of a study that occurs when the researcher uses the test-retest method.

test-retest method—A method for establishing the reliability of a data collection instrument. This method requires the researcher to administer the instrument two times with a time lapse between the test and retest.

theory—A statement that explains an event or an occurrence of something.

time frame—The period of time over which the study will be conducted.

T test—A statistical calculation that is used to determine if the differences in the means for two data sets are statistically significant.

treatment variable—The variable that is manipulated in a study that uses the experimental research design. In this type of study, one variable (the treatment variable) is manipulated, and the effect of the treatment on the other variable (the outcome variable) is then measured.

triangulation—A data analysis technique in which the researcher uses a minimum of three sources of data to test a hypothesis.

two-stage random sampling—A sampling technique that combines cluster random sampling and individual random sampling. The first step is to identify preexisting groups (or clusters). The researcher then randomly selects individuals from each group for the sample.

unstructured interviews—A face-to-face interview with one person where the researcher asks open-ended questions.

usability—Indicates how user friendly a data collection instrument is for subjects and the researcher to use.

validity—The validity of a data collection instrument refers to the truth of the data and the truth of the conclusions drawn from the data.

variables—The specific elements or items that are measured or identified in a study. The variables serve as the focus of data collection and analysis.

volunteer sampling—In this type of nonrandom sampling, the researcher asks people to volunteer to participate in the study. With this type of sampling, there are no mechanisms used to ensure that the sample represents the population of the study.

BIBLIOGRAPHY

Frankel, J.R., and N.E. Wallen. 2003. *How to design and evaluate research in education.* 5th ed. New York: McGraw-Hill Higher Education.

Henderson, K. 1991. *Dimensions of choice: A qualitative approach to recreation, parks, and leisure.* State College, PA: Venture.

Hurd, A., R. Barcelona, and J. Meldrum. 2008. *Leisure service management.* Champaign, IL: Human Kinetics.

Lussier, R., and D. Kimball. 2009. *Applied sport management skills.* Champaign, IL: Human Kinetics.

Marcus, B., and L.A. Forsyth. 2003. *Motivating people to be physically active.* Champaign, IL: Human Kinetics.

NRPA (National Recreation and Park Association). 2008. *The dirty dozen* [brochure].

Patten, M. 2000. *Understanding research methods.* 2nd ed. Los Angeles: Pyrczak.

Pfister, R., and P. Tierney. 2009. *Recreation, event, and tourism business.* Champaign, IL: Human Kinetics.

Riddick, C., and R. Russell. 1999. *Evaluative research in recreation, parks, and sport setting.* Champaign, IL: Sagamore.

Strass, A., and J. Corbin. 1990. *Basics of qualitative research: Grounded theory procedures and techniques.* Newbury Park, CA: Sage.

Thomas, J., and J. Nelson. 2001. *Research methods in physical activity.* 4th ed. Champaign, IL: Human Kinetics.

Trochim, W. 2001. *The research methods knowledge base.* 2nd ed. Cincinnati: Atomic Dog.

van der Smissen, B., M. Moiseichik, and V. Hartenburg (Eds.). 2005. *Management of park and recreation agencies.* 2nd ed. Ashburn, VA: National Recreation and Park Association.

INDEX

NOTE: An italicized *f* or *t* following page numbers indicates a figure(s) or table(s) will be found on those pages, respectively.